TRENCH WARFARE

1850–1950

TRENCH WARFARE 1850–1950

BY

ANTHONY SAUNDERS

Pen & Sword
MILITARY

First published in Great Britain by
Pen & Sword Military
An imprint of
Pen & Sword Books Ltd
47 Church Street
Barnsley
South Yorkshire
S70 2AS

ISBN-13: 9781848841901

Pen & Sword Books Ltd incorporates the Imprints of Pen & Sword Aviation,
Pen & Sword Family History, Pen & Sword Maritime, Pen & Sword Military,
Wharncliffe Local History, Pen & Sword Select, Pen & Sword Military Classics,
Leo Cooper, Remember When, Seaforth Publishing and Frontline Publishing

Contents

Acknowledgements

The research and writing of this book has, inevitably, involved the assistance of a number of people without whose help everything would have been considerably more difficult. Firstly, I would like to thank Mike Hibberd, formerly of the Firearms and Exhibits Department, Imperial War Museum, without whose help many years ago this book would not have been written.

Norman Bonney is always tirelessly helpful. Norman is a former lieutenant colonel in the Royal Army Ordnance Corps, Territorial Army, in which capacity he became an acknowledged authority in the field of First World War munitions, especially grenades. His expertise has led to him assisting the Belgian Army, for example, in identifying unexploded ordnance from 1914–18. He has an unrivalled collection of grenades and fuzes and an impressive document archive, all of which has been acquired over three decades. H.A.B. Newton, the son of the late Henry Newton, was happy to talk to me about his father who was the first commanding officer of the Second Army Workshops during the First World War. I was put in touch with him via his sister, a friend of whom told her about a letter I had written to the *Derby Gazette* about Henry Newton and his family; the Newton family came from Derbyshire and had an engineering business in the town at the time of the First World War. The Newton family gave me access to some of Henry's wartime papers. Alas, many had been lost in a house fire in the late 1970s.

Professor Ian Beckett, Professor of History at the University of Northampton, very kindly read early drafts of some of the material for this book and offered advice, while Professor Jeremy Black in the Department of History in the School of Humanities and Social Sciences at the University of Exeter has also offered guidance. His enthusiasm, insight and knowledge of all things historical have been expressed with a friendly forthrightness.

I would also like to thank Phillip Powell, Stock Control Manager in the Department of Printed Books of the Imperial War Museum, London, for photocopying a large number of Stationary Service documents for me.

Finally, I would like to thank Liz Tipping, graphics expert, for giving me advice on the best way to clean up some rather messy images so that they were presentable and printable.

Any mistakes are, of course, mine.

CHAPTER 1

Genesis of Trench Warfare

The construction of temporary earthworks by an army laying siege has a long history. While the use of such earthworks predates the introduction of gunpowder to European battlefields in the fourteenth century, earthworks were of particular significance to artillery. With the widespread use of gunpowder from the sixteenth century onwards, their sophistication increased and by the eighteenth century had become complex, covering vast areas. Earthworks and trenches allowed the guns to be brought up close enough to batter down fortifications because they protected the guns and the gunners from hostile fire. The practice of using temporary earthworks for artillery in open battle was well established by the time of the English Civil War (1642–52). While artillery had considerable destructive power, its disadvantage was the short range of the guns, a problem that persisted well into the nineteenth century. Thus, the guns had to be brought up close to the target, which inevitably brought them within range of enemy guns and musketeers. Protective earthworks were essential. The tactic of building earthworks and trenches to allow artillery to be brought to bear on a besieged town probably reached its apotheosis in Europe between the 1680s and 1740s. During this period, sieges were more common than battles, while artillery became more powerful and more reliable than hitherto. At the same time, the musket and bayonet finally ousted the musket and pike as the principal infantry weapons.

During the eighteenth century, European wars were more about seizing strategic advantage than they were about destroying an enemy or about taking land and holding it. The destructiveness of massed musket fire and short-range artillery meant that battles were often bloody, yet indecisive. The Battle of Malplaquet, fought in 1709 during the War of the Spanish Succession (1701–14), cost the Allies 24,000 casualties compared to French losses of 12,000. While the battle was an Allied victory, the French Army was able to leave the field in good order. Earthworks and entrenchments constructed by the French contributed to the high casualties suffered by the Allies when they attacked. Significantly, indecisiveness by the Dutch contingent of the Allied army had given the French time to prepare defensive positions. Herein lay two crucial factors of positional warfare: the preparation of earthworks by the defenders needed time, and well-made positions presented major obstacles to the attackers. Malplaquet demonstrated that attacking a defensive position was a costly business. The significance of this was not made apparent until the American Civil War (1861–5) in which more powerful artillery and small arms contributed to the need for entrenchments. Even so, the cost of frontal assaults on strong positions was not fully brought home to the major European powers until the Russo-Japanese War (1904–05).

Malplaquet demonstrated the importance of field defences in battle long before the notion of trench warfare evolved. Although field defences became more important by the end of the eighteenth century, siege was still a feature of warfare into the nineteenth century. They always involved the construction of entrenchments. By the time of the War of the Spanish Succession, siege work had become highly formalized. Typical of such operations was the siege of Lille in 1708 during which several miles of trenches were dug by the engineers of the besieging army. The siege lasted four months, somewhat longer than was customary at the time. Sieges have continued into the present era. They occurred at Sebastopol (1854) during the Crimean War, at Vicksburg (1863) in the American Civil War, at Paris, Metz and Belfort during the Franco-Prussian War (1870–1), at Plevna (1877) during the Russo-Turkish War, at Ladysmith and Mafeking during the Boer War (1899–1900), at Port Arthur during the Russo-Japanese War (1904–05), at Liege in 1914 and at Verdun in 1916 during the First World War, at Leningrad (1941), Sebastopol (1943) and St Malo (1944) during the Second World War, at Pusan (1950) during the Korean War, and at Khe Sanh (1968) in the Vietnam War. There have been many others besides these. Indeed, the most significant siege in the history of warfare occurred on the Western Front in 1914–18; this was mutual siege along a vast expanse of Flanders and France, from the North Sea to Switzerland.

By the end of the eighteenth century, a new concept of warfare emerged, that of annihilation, whereby the object was not merely to defeat an enemy on the battlefield but to destroy him. Napoleon's victories at Austerlitz (1805) and Jena (1806), for example, were battles of annihilation and thus very different from Blenheim (1704) and Fontenoy (1745), when defeat did not mean destruction. By the time of the American Civil War, annihilation was being extended to include the destruction of the state waging war, rather than seeking strategic victory in which both sides emerged economically and politically unscathed. Indeed, the American Civil War was a turning point in warfare in that it established a new type of warfare: industrialized war. The economy of the state was now turned over to waging war and mass production of munitions became necessary to supply large armies, which required ever greater quantities in order to continue fighting effectively. This process was aided by the regulation of manufacture, whereby each copy of a munition's component was identical to all the other copies so that they were interchangeable and not specific to a given weapon, which had been the case in the eighteenth century. The industrialization of warfare and the concept of total war which emerged from the American Civil War mirrored the growing industrialization of the economic capability of America and the European nations.

2

The industrialized war of the American Civil War did not find immediate parallels in Europe or Asia, however. While the major European powers sent observers to America, the conclusions that were drawn showed that the Europeans did not regard the American Civil War as prescient of European wars to come. Indeed, the European wars of 1866 and 1870 showed no similarity with the American Civil War. Nevertheless, trench warfare began to become a feature of wars outside Europe. While it did not occur during the Franco-Prussian War of 1870, it was a feature of the Russo-Turkish War fought only seven years later. Trench warfare had also been a feature of the Crimean War. Indeed, the trenches around Sebastopol may be regarded as the birthplace of what was to become known as trench warfare. And it was a major feature in Manchuria during the Russo-Japanese War. Thus, there was a tendency to regard Europe as the theatre of traditional open warfare, whereas less sophisticated modes of fighting developed elsewhere. Europeans assumed a superiority of strategic skill from their success in concluding wars speedily through decisive battle, such as the Austro-Prussian War of 1866 which lasted seven weeks, and the Franco-Prussian War of 1870 which lasted seven months. This was attributed to tactical skill. However, siege was still an important element in war-making.

That siege operations still occurred during the European wars of the second half of the nineteenth century was seen as part of the traditional way of making war. The outcomes of these sieges were not, however, attributable to superior tactical doctrines of the besieging armies. Indeed, firepower was a defining feature, although its significance was perhaps obscured during the Franco-Prussian War by French ineptitude. Infantry tactics employed by both sides were those of the assault. Both Union and Confederate armies used French tactical doctrines in the American Civil War, but had been forced to change them because overwhelming firepower devastated assaulting infantry, which contributed to the increasing importance of entrenchments to attacking infantry, as well to defenders. Such tactics were derived from the same source: the experience of the Napoleonic Wars. They paid no heed to technological differences in armaments between 1815 and the 1860s and 1870. Such developments were not merely a matter of degree but were of a quite different order. This was evident in the lethality of rifles, artillery and other new armaments that were introduced to the battlefield during the nineteenth century.

Warfare has always been a brutal business, of course. The idea that trench warfare and industrialized warfare made warfare more savage is a disingenuous view of military history. The bloodshed of the First World War for what, in the popular imagination, appears to have been for very little purpose on the Western Front gave rise to the notion that war is futile. This was epitomized by the pointlessness of the trench warfare of the Western Front. However, for shear brutality, it would hard to find a battle that surpassed Towton fought in 1461 during the Wars of the Roses. For numbers of casualties inflicted on an enemy during a single day of battle, Cannae in 216 BC was perhaps one of the costliest ever fought

– or lost; four times as many Romans died at Cannae as British died on the first day of the Battle of the Somme on 1 July 1916, which is usually cited as the epitome of carnage. Neither Cannae nor Towton involved high-explosive munitions, neither took place in trenches, yet they were as brutal as any battle could be. Of course, the difference between the Somme, and Towton and Cannae, is the fact that the former was not fought and concluded in one day but continued for several months, although the British suffered high casualties on the first day, most occurring within minutes of the troops going over the top. Indeed, it can be argued that the outcome of the Somme campaign as a whole, which included many major battles, was even more inconclusive than Malplaquet had been. However, it is unwise to stretch this comparison too far since this is not comparing like with like. Cannae, Towton and Malplaquet, for all their casualties, were unlike the Somme in one important respect: the size and depth of the battlefield and, hence, the size and depth of the lethal zone. Moreover, the outcome of any one of the battles fought during the Somme campaign could never be as clear cut as Cannae, Towton or Malplaquet because the battlefields of the Somme were more complex places than the others.

There is also the issue of intention, that is, the purpose of battle. The object of battle has not remained constant throughout history. The battles of the eighteenth century had different outcomes from battles in the second half of the nineteenth century because they had different objects. In other words, the definitions of victory and defeat have changed with changing tactical doctrines. The battles of annihilation on the Eastern Front during the Second World War, for example, whereby an enemy was encircled and utterly destroyed, was an approach to battle that would have been alien only a century earlier. Clearly, there were not only tactical and strategic considerations, but ideological and racial factors in such battles. Complete annihilation of that sort was not the purpose of battle in the nineteenth century. Indeed, although annihilation was not an object during the Gulf Wars of 1991–2 and 2002, nevertheless, it could still occur because of a combination of tactical and technological factors combining in such a way that it was inevitable rather than intended. This highlights a crucial element in trench warfare in particular: the combination of technology with tactics, so that a synergistic effect results. In other words, the whole is greater than the sum of the parts.

The beginning of trench warfare is usually put at the siege of Sebastopol in the Crimean War. This raises the question of why it should have occurred then, rather than earlier; which also raises the question of what constitutes trench warfare. For trench warfare to develop there has to be stalemate and for this to occur two things have to happen: the defending troops have to construct secure cover from enemy fire in order to sustain their positions and to repel the attackers; while the attackers have to be unable to overcome the defenders and be forced to take shelter themselves from the defenders' fire. However, satisfying these criteria alone does not constitute trench warfare since almost any siege of the eighteenth century could be said to fulfil these requirements. The missing factor is the impact of technology on the ability of both defenders and attackers to break the stalemate; or, rather, it is their inability to break it that gives rise to positional warfare. On the face of it, the suggestion that increased firepower encouraged deadlock rather than prevented it, or broke it, seems perverse and contradictory.

There is no doubt that the technical revolutions of the nineteenth century transformed the battlefield by increasing the size and depth of the lethal zone which the infantry had to cross in order to engage the enemy. The increase in the accurate lethal range of rifle fire during the nineteenth century was a major factor in the rise in importance of the temporary shelter in the form of entrenchments. This was not due to a single innovation alone, but to a series of innovations that occurred over a sixty-year period which, together, completely altered the nature of the lethal zone. Equally, the increase in range and accuracy of artillery, together with the introduction of high-explosives for shell fillings, had a significant impact on the conduct of warfare. Irrespective of the desire of tacticians to dictate the nature of infantry assaults, derived from experience of Napoleonic warfare, as well from an idealized view of the role of infantry, the huge increase in firepower during the nineteenth century meant that tactical theory and practical considerations of lethality were in direct conflict. In essence, the problem came down to whether firepower or élan would carry the day. There was both an unwillingness to accept that the spirit of the assault could not overcome firepower, and a consequent blindness to just how destructive munitions were becoming. The impact of munitions changed during the nineteenth century. The breechloading rifle was not merely a modernized version of a muzzle-loading, smooth-bored musket; it was a force magnifier because its range, its rate of fire and its lethality all increased exponentially.

The answer to this conflict of principals was obvious to the tactical thinkers of the nineteenth century. As far as they were concerned, élan would always overcome mere firepower. While with the benefit of hindsight this now seems naive in the extreme, the issue was less clear cut at the time, however, largely because of a mindset derived from the experience of the past. Until the American Civil War, no army anywhere in the world had faced having to address the practical issues of how to deal with defensive firepower on the scale that was now available. And while the Americans were forced to find solutions, these were not heeded by European powers such as Britain, France and Germany, none of whom considered that they would ever have to fight the kind of war that the American Civil War became. Part of the trouble for European observers in America was that it was a civil war on a continent with no military tradition. The American forces on both sides were influenced by French tactical theories. However, the lessons of the war in America did not make themselves felt on the Europeans. Britain, for example, was really only concerned with small wars in its growing empire. Britain's army was trained and equipped accordingly. The French and the Germans viewed each other as their main threats and anticipated wars of manoeuvre with set-piece battles. Indeed, the

European wars of the second half of the nineteenth century conformed to this model and did not reflect the warfare that had occurred in America.

While Prussia defeated France in Napoleonic style in 1870 without recourse to trench warfare, both sides had to the confront the conflict of firepower versus élan. The latter won but assaults by massed infantry were very costly. Nevertheless, the success of the infantry assault only served to reinforce the idea that élan would always win over mere firepower. When firepower did prevail so that the assault either faltered or failed, it was attributed to insufficient élan being displayed by the attackers. The idea that firepower could dominate a battlefield was viewed as nonsense because tactical thinking could not conceive of such an event. Even as late as the 1890s, when the Germans performed their annual military exercise, the effects of firepower were underplayed, or dismissed entirely as unfair, attributing the success of firepower to officers failing to execute their orders correctly.

The war in Manchuria between the Japanese and the Russians led the European powers and the Americans sending military observers to both sides to gain insights into how these two nations, the old corrupt giant and the smaller emergent Asian power with pretensions to Europeanization, went about the business of war. Many reports were produced on every aspect of the war, from sanitation to tactics, from new weapons to discipline. When the siege of Port Arthur turned into a slugging match of trench warfare, the observers tended to claim moral and tactical superiority, suggesting that this was only to be expected from such protagonists. Here, again, the conflict between firepower and élan made itself evident, but this time the outcome was less clear. The evidence did not support the idea that firepower could be overcome by determined assault alone, yet this was certainly the conclusion which the European observers tended to prefer. When what they saw did not accord with this view, they tended to excuse the contrary evidence by explaining that European armies were different from both the Russian and the Japanese armies. In other words, the armies of the major European powers would conduct themselves differently in battle from the hash of things made by these less tactically wise nations.

At least one British officer noted that the Japanese used trenches in the assault to enable their infantry to get within charging distance of Russian positions, rather than attempting assaults entirely over open ground. Thus, the infantry rushed forward some distance then dug in before repeating the exercise up to three or four times. This was, of course, a variation on an old theme, but it went against the European doctrine of open assault, the infantry attack, and, hence, contradicted the notion of élan being superior to firepower that dominated European tactical thinking. The British and the Germans also noted the use of hand grenades in the trench fighting around Port Arthur. And the Germans paid particular attention to the introduction by the Japanese of an improvised mortar, although it was a feeble weapon and militarily useless.

The grenade and the mortar had a long association with siege warfare, of course, going back to the fifteenth century. For reasons which are far from clear, the grenades of the Russo-Japanese War, all of them improvised from locally available materials, especially captured the imaginations of observers, despite the fact that grenades had continued to figure in many siege-like operations throughout the nineteenth century. The idea that grenades were 'revived' in Manchuria is curious and there seems to have been no rational basis for such a conclusion. This idea of a revival was to have profound consequences. Ironically, neither the grenade nor the mortar was significant to the fighting in Manchuria. The British had a muted enthusiasm for this 'revival' of an obsolete weapon and set about devising a new grenade for British service despite the fact the traditional grenade had only been declared obsolete in 1902. The Germans also began to devise their own grenades and a weapon that was subsequently to become known as the trench mortar.

Despite the emergence of trench warfare in Manchuria, during a war in which both sides used guns which were less modern than those in most European armies, France and Germany, in particular, still expected to fight a war of manoeuvre in which open battle would decide the outcome. Indeed, everyone anticipated that the next war would be quickly concluded, lasting no more than a few months. Perversely, this view was based on the unwavering faith in the spirit of the attack as well as more than a nod to the increasing power of artillery. The Schlieffen Plan, by which the Germans eventually attacked France in 1914, was devised after the Russo-Japanese War and, although various meddling changes were made to it after its inception in 1905, none were made on the basis of the sort of warfare that occurred during the Russo-Japanese War.

The First World War saw a revolutionary change in warfare brought about largely because of the stalemate on the Western Front or, rather, the need to break the deadlock. On the Western Front especially, the issue of firepower versus mobility was forced to a resolution and by so doing an entirely new form of warfare emerged, from which new doctrines were developed. Many subsequent wars have been fought according to these new principals. What emerged at the end of the First World War was so-called deep battle, or three-dimensional warfare. Curiously, rather than remove the necessity for trenches, this increased their necessity. Indeed, trench warfare became an inescapable feature of battle, although its duration has never again approached the protracted agony of the Western Front. Periods of trench warfare occurred on most fronts during the Second World War, especially when the momentum of an attack diminished. Trench warfare was especially savage on the Eastern Front when offensives paused or were halted, but it also occurred in North-West Europe during the Normandy campaign in 1944, and subsequently in the battles in the Hürtgen Forest, the Ardennes and during the final stages of the war in Germany. The US forces in the Pacific engaged in trench warfare against the Japanese, although this was of a different sort compared to that of European warfare. In the Pacific, it was every bit as savage as the trench battles on the Western Front in 1916 and 1917. Savage trench fighting also occurred on the Imjin in 1951 during the Korean War. The Iran-Iraq War of 1980 and the two Gulf wars in 1991–2 and 2002 all involved trench fighting.

The emergence of trench warfare was not an aberration, as is sometimes thought, but part of a wider change in modes of warfare that took place over a period of about sixty years, in which technological, ideological, tactical and strategic issues all played their parts. Trench warfare has been blamed on stupid army commanders, on technological advances and on technological failures, but the target of such criticism is usually aimed solely at the First World War rather than at trench warfare in a wider context. The most common misconception about trench warfare on the Western Front is that it was somehow avoidable and that the prolonged stalemate between 1914 and 1918 was the result of general incompetence. Had that been the case, all commanders in all armies engaged in the fighting would have suffered the same malaise for four years until, miraculously, a cure was suddenly plucked from the ether for the disease of trench warfare, then quickly administered to the warring armies so that movement was immediately restored to the stagnated soldiery. This is not what happened.

Part of the problem lies in understanding the nature of trench warfare. After all, trenches and earthworks were essential features of both battle and siege for centuries, yet so-called trench warfare did not occur until the mid-nineteenth century, and did not become a dominant factor in warfare until the beginning of the twentieth. The question is: what differentiates traditional siege work, in which trenches figured prominently, and fighting that may be described as 'trench warfare'? In other words, what is trench warfare?

Trench warfare is usually described as military operations between two entrenched armies. It is a form of stalemate in which neither side can breach or outflank the defences of the other so that breakthrough cannot be achieved, irrespective of the size or type of operation carried out to achieve that aim. In other words, it is mutual siege. The manner in which the fighting is conducted, and the nature of the weapons used and their numbers, all factor into the equation since these contribute to the stalemate and its intractability. If this were not the case, 'trench warfare' would have occurred in the eighteenth century. Clearly, there is a complex relationship between the various factors which, in the right balance, produce stalemate and, hence, trench warfare. In other words, there has to be a fluid balance between the opposing armies to prevent breakthrough in order for trench warfare to occur.

While artillery was a major factor in the development of stalemate during the First World War, the development of trench warfare in the American Civil War was attributable to the greater firepower of small arms. In both instances, however, there was a conflict between firepower and tactics which resulted in the inability of tactical theories to overcome the practicalities of firepower. The relative proportions of such weapons and the amount of ammunition available to the guns all contributed to the formation and continuation of the stalemate. Thus, forward movement by the infantry could not be achieved nor the defences broken because defensive firepower broke up attacks, while the firepower of the attackers was insufficient to break the defenders. There was a dynamic relationship between guns, trenches and tactics. It is the relationship between these, more than anything else, which determines whether stalemate and trench warfare will occur. While the invention of barbed wire in 1873 was not originally devised for military use, its potential was quickly appreciated by governments and it added a new dimension to the battlefield. It was to become a defining feature of trench warfare.

With the establishment of entrenched positions from which opposing armies faced each other came a defining motif of trench warfare: no-man's-land. This is the region between the opposing armies which belongs to neither, but dominance of which may be hotly contested because therein lies one of the keys to successful trench warfare. This is not merely a question of ownership but it pertains to the very nature of the fighting which now develops. In order to engage the enemy, no-man's-land has to be crossed. Hence, obstacles are put there to prevent incursions, while guns are sighted on it to deny free passage by the enemy. The increasing level of sophistication shown in the defence of no-man's-land during the First World War helped to define the nature of trench warfare in a way that had not occurred previously. Two of the major problems in the First World War was the issue of how to cross no-man's-land without being annihilated in the process, and the question of how to prevent this from happening. In no other war had the battle for no-man's-land evolved into a tactical challenge. At the same time, the question of what actually constituted no-man's-land became less easy to answer. While in 1914, no-man's-land was precisely the region between the entrenched armies, by the end of 1915, this definition was no longer valid. By the end of 1916, the concept of no-man's-land was quite different from the notion of contested real estate between the front lines of the entrenched enemies. The whole notion of which army 'owned' what land changed because the concept of defence changed. By the middle of the war, the complexity of the defensive lines was such that their depth – that is, the distance between the forward and rearmost edges of the defence zone – could be measured in miles, with up to three lines of defences. Moreover, the first line ceased to be a trench line but was transformed into a series of strongpoints with all-round defensive capabilities. Thus, the idea that no-man's-land lay to your front ceased to be valid; it was all round you.

The nature of the fighting that followed the establishment of stalemate was determined by the fact that these positions now had to be breached or outflanked. At the very least, the status quo had to be maintained which meant preventing the enemy from making incursions. There is also the issue of patrols in no-man's-land. Crudely, trench warfare is a mixture of close combat and long-range bombardment. On the small scale, it is a fight from one trench traverse to the next, while on the large scale, it is a battle to take a strongpoint or an area of ground bounded by arbitrary lines defined according to the nature of the objective. Rarely is it concerned with taking a village or a town, or with destroying the enemy. However, attrition is an aspect of trench warfare whereby an enemy is worn down in his positions physically and psychologically by relentless shelling and mortaring, although not necessarily on a regular basis. And rather than being merely a question of brute force, trench warfare requires a wide range of skills. Clearly, the relationship between firepower and tactics determines its conduct, tempered by the psychological make-up of the troops and commanders on each side. Trench warfare is complex and requires a scientific approach to its management.

In trench fighting and assaults on enemy trenches, whether as part of an offensive that is intended to break through the enemy lines, or as part of a smaller operation with a less ambitious objective, the infantry always bear the brunt of it. To describe the role of the infantry merely as trench fighting disguises the complexity of their task. While in the American Civil War and in the Russo-Japanese War, infantry assaults on enemy trenches were essentially similar in character, by the time of the First World War, trench fighting was about to change radically. By 1916, a whole new way of fighting was being developed and, by 1917, this new system had evolved still further, so that by 1918, it was a sophisticated tactical system. Part of the reason for these developments was the introduction of novel weapons which had not been available in previous wars. But a crucial reason for the evolution of tactics was a greater understanding of the need for a fluid approach to battle.

Paradoxically, the factors which created stalemate also provided the answer to its resolution. By 1918, tacticians had come to understand the relationship between mobility and firepower. Firepower, instead of being the alternative to mobility, now became its partner in a new tactical doctrine which had been developed from the experiences of 1915, 1916 and 1917. Indeed, it is a common misconception that the tactics of the Western Front were unchanging; quite the reverse, in fact. A better appreciation of the strengths and weaknesses of modern weapon systems, especially artillery, and the development of a cooperative all-weapons approach to tactics, which incorporated innovative new weapons such as the Stokes mortar, and the development of technical skills in the fields of map-making and meteorology, all came together to turn warfare into a twentieth-century science. Hitherto, it had been a variation on Napoleonic warfare.

The new tactics tried in the battles of 1917 were shown to be highly effective and were subsequently refined to become decisive in the battles of 1918. Now, aircraft, artillery, cavalry, tanks and armoured cars were used cooperatively to disrupt the enemy's ability to fight. Instead of simply targeting front-line positions so that the infantry could attack in waves, the second-line positions, artillery batteries, communications centres and headquarters were all bombarded. Areas in which reinforcements might form up for counter-attacks were interdicted. More importantly, all this was done simultaneously and without warning. The infantry no longer advanced in linear waves but infiltrated forwards in small groups. The technique, known as three-dimensional warfare, or deep battle, resolved the stalemate of trench warfare and thereby transformed warfare. It has been the basis of battle tactics ever since, from Kursk (1943) and Normandy (1944) to the Gulf Wars of 1991–2 and 2002.

CHAPTER 2

Evolution of Weapons and Warfare

The development of the rifle and its ammunition throughout the nineteenth century was a major factor in the evolution of infantry warfare. While it is misleading to suggest that the rifle was the sole cause of tactical change, nevertheless, innovations in the field of small arms contributed to an ever-increasing lethal zone on the battlefield, and this had an effect on tactics. The change was not progressive, however. Indeed, change was resisted, especially change driven by developing technologies. The notion that new technology brings about advantageous change has never been a universally accepted idea. A reluctance to adopt new weapons to replace those currently in service has often been the normal response of armies and governments. Indeed, evaluators of new weapons tend to reject them rather than accept them, especially if they are conceptually different from what is regarded as the standard. Between around 1900 and 1918, Major Todhunter of the Experimental Section at the School of Musketry tested most if not all of the automatic rifles of the time. While many were seriously flawed and needed refinement, he rejected them all because he could see no advantage over manually operated rifles. He saw automatic rifles as devices in which loading was automated, not as weapons capable of delivering a high volume of fire. He saw musketry as aimed shots; automatic rifles moved away from this form of shooting. Yet volume of fire had become an issue of considerable significance which affected tactics from about the 1850s onwards.

From about the middle of the nineteenth century, there was a surge in invention in all fields of engineering across Europe and America, and this was especially true in the field of armaments. One of the most potent incentives for inventing was reward, brought about by modern patenting systems which protected innovation from theft. While the USA had its first modern patent law in 1790, Britain did not get similar legislation until 1852. In Britain, the new legislation simplified the patenting process and laid the foundations for commercial exploitation of what was to become known as intellectual property. Hitherto, British inventors had tended to conceal their inventions, rather than show them off, to prevent the unscrupulous from stealing their ideas. Now that inventing had become a commercial activity, there was money to be made from exploiting innovation. Invention became its own driver. Not only were rivals able to find out what each was doing because of the publication of patent specifications, but they then had to find ways to do it better or differently if they were not to lose out commercially. This was a great incentive to innovate.

During the same period, developments in artillery increased the lethal zone in depth and in density. In the early 1800s, smooth-bored, muzzle-loaded cannon fired roundshot, canister and shrapnel. By the 1850s, longitudinal shells were beginning to replace solid roundshot, while rifling and breech-loading were becoming more common. Breech-loading rifled artillery showed its superiority over muzzle-loaded smoothbores in range and rate of fire during the American Civil War; although muzzle-loaders were more widely used. It was not until the 1870s that the greatest innovations occurred in artillery and ammunition. Over the next thirty years, artillery was transformed into the dominant force on the battlefield, a fact that was either denied, ignored or misinterpreted by contemporaries. Rather than infantry deciding the outcome of battles, artillery became the decisive instrument. It was changed from an ancillary which aided the infantry in its assault to one which infantry ignored at their peril.

Armaments went through a revolution during the nineteenth century, resulting in an exponential increase in firepower which outpaced tactical developments. At about the time of Waterloo, a musket had a killing range of about 200 metres, but was only accurate to about 100 metres. With a rifle firing a Minié bullet, the accurate killing range had increased to about 500 metres by the time of the American Civil War and, by 1900, a rifle firing a conical bullet had a lethal range in excess of 1,000 metres. In Manchuria, during the Russo-Japanese War, it was noted that 'few Japanese dead were ever observed at distances much beyond 700 yards from the Russian positions', most of whom had been killed by small-arms fire. While the lethal range of small arms was increasing during the century, artillery range also increased, from about 1,000 metres (9-pounder roundshot) in 1815, to 3,000 metres during the American Civil War and to 6,500 metres by 1900. Roundshot was replaced by high-explosive shell during this time. And yet, for the two hundred years before about the second decade of the 1800s, few changes to guns and small arms had resulted in a significant increase in lethal range or, indeed, lethality.

By the 1870s, the pace of change in weapons technology had accelerated to such an extent that innovative new weapons were beginning to appear in quick succession. Obsolescence became a feature of these munitions; what was innovative in 1860 was obsolescent by 1880. This process was repeated several times between about 1870 and 1914. Hitherto, obsolescence had been a process measured in centuries. The invention of such munitions as ogival shells (1850s), centrefire metallic fixed small-arms ammunition (1866), recoil and recuperator systems for artillery (1872), smokeless propellants (1884), high explosives (1885), quick-locking breech mechanisms for both artillery (1880s) and rifles (1839) all fuelled this revolution.

These developments were aided by innovations in manufacturing techniques which allowed the cheap and reliable rifling of gun barrels and the reliable mass production of weapon components. This meant that any given part of a weapon system could be manufactured to a consistent standard, thereby allowing the parts to be interchangeable rather than specific to a given weapon which had been the case up to about the 1800s. There were more developments in weapons technology in the second half of the nineteenth century than in the previous two hundred years. This process of change was encouraged by the rising importance of intellectual property, patents in particular, as a business asset.

It has been suggested that the Crimean War inspired British inventors to invent weapons and munitions. There is no question that the British public learned what was happening in the Crimea very much faster than in previous wars thanks to *The Times* and its correspondent, William Russell, but there is nothing to suggest that this inspired the general public to invent new weapons. While it is true that there was an increase in the number of patents granted for firearms, ammunition and ordnance in Britain during the 1850s, all granted to armaments firms, this had little to do with the war in the Crimea. It came about largely because of the Patents Law Amendments Act 1852, Britain's first modern patents legislation which made patenting simpler and patents more defensible. After its introduction, the number of applications increased from 400 to 2,000 a year. By 1863, the number of applications had increased to 3,000. However, there was not one patent for a hand grenade in the 1850s. Only one inventor submitted a novel hand grenade to the Ordnance Board during the Crimean War, yet there is nothing to suggest that he was inspired by the war despite the fact that hand grenades were used by the British, French and Russians during the siege of Sebastopol in 1854–5.

An improved patenting system meant that commercial interests became an ever-increasing factor in the development of new munitions. Not only commercial interests affected armies, of course, but also adherence to tactical doctrines which failed to take into account their rapidly increasing firepower. Armaments firms encouraged armies to buy advanced armaments by playing on the fear that their enemies would get the better of them if they failed to stay up to date. There was a growing sense that firepower was important yet tacticians remained convinced that courage and élan would carry the infantry to victory. Tacticians were not prepared to concede that firepower could ever overcome pure spirit.

This conflict of élan versus firepower remained unresolved throughout the nineteenth century, despite increasing evidence that élan alone could not overcome the firepower of rifled breech-loading artillery and breech-loading rifles. There was an ambivalence about innovative technology. This was exemplified by the Austrians who adopted the Dreyse needle gun in 1841 but, although it was used to help quell the Dresden uprising of 1849, it did not see battlefield use until 1864 and the Second Schleswig War. In 1866, the French adopted the more advanced Chassepot rifle (devised in 1857) which employed a similar bolt action. The Austrians not only lost the advantage of a technologically advanced rifle through a paranoid fear that their enemies, both internal and external, would take the weapon and use it against the Empire, but in so doing they reinforced the paradoxical notion that new technology was irrelevant to the battlefield. By the time it was used in battle, it was approaching obsolescence. Rather than ushering in a revolution, the bolt-action, breech-loading rifle took about sixty years to be adopted by the armies of all the European powers. There were thus three opposing elements in the modernization of European armies: new technology, attitudes to the technology, and tactics. While armies continued to adopt ever more technologically advanced weapons, no effort was made to integrate these with tactical developments that maximized the advantages these weapons conferred on the armies which employed them, while minimizing the disadvantageous consequences of doing so.

Of course, the rifle was not a new weapon in 1800. Indeed, the process of rifling was well known in the sixteenth century but it was expensive, so few weapons had rifled barrels. Hence, armies were equipped with the smooth-bored musket which was easier to make and hence cheaper. Moreover, rifles had the disadvantage that they were slow to load and fire compared to their smooth-bored cousins and offered no advantage on the battlefield. Neither their better accuracy not their longer range was considered to be beneficial from a military standpoint. The flintlock smooth-bore musket was the dominant infantry weapon from the second decade of the eighteenth century, but it had taken sixty years for this to happen because it had been introduced in the mid-seventeenth century. Again, this was a matter of complexity and cost compared to matchlocks.

Smooth-bore muskets, irrespective of their ignition system, had two serious drawbacks: they were very inaccurate and had only a short range. They were therefore used en masse against a big target such as a large body of men. Thus, the disadvantage was converted into an advantage since, for the most part, infantry actions involved ranks of musketeers firing on the ranks of enemy musketeers at short range, about 100–200 yards. Although, by the beginning of the nineteenth century, rifles were beginning to be issued to skirmisher regiments, they were not used in the same way as muskets and hence played only a subsidiary role in battles. This situation could not change until the disadvantages of the rifle were addressed by gunsmiths, but until the middle of the nineteenth century there was no reason to adopt rifles. Indeed, not only was there no impetus for change, there was no desire for change. However, change was brought about by the engine of technology.

Several significant innovations in firearms occurred during the first three decades of the nineteenth century, although none had any impact on weapon design until much later. The percussion cap (1805), the bolt-action breech-closure system (1824), and the expanding conoidal bullet (1832) were all invented. None of these early incarnations of such important improvements to the rifle received official support when first presented. Indeed, all were turned down. Yet, without these inventions, smooth-bore muskets would have remained in service until the twentieth century. The most important development for the emergence of the rifle was in combining new approaches to three different aspects of firearms: the method of igniting a cartridge; the nature of the bullet fired; and the manner in which barrels were rifled. Inventions in these areas laid the foundations for a revolution in small arms that was to occur in the last quarter of the century with the invention of smokeless propellants, which were more powerful than black powder, and the adoption of reliable magazine feeds.

The process of change was not the inevitable march of progress, however. Inventors worked independently of each other; there was no sense of collaboration or even of working additively since awareness of what others were doing in related fields was largely absent until much later in the century. The reason for this was simple: secrecy. In order to protect an invention, especially while it was being developed into a workable prototype, the best policy was to keep it secret. There was no way to protect a novel idea as anyone could copy it with impunity. The patent legislation that existed before the 1850s was unhelpful when it came to preventing infringement. Thus, there was a strong disincentive to reveal an idea to a potential competitor, which patenting certainly did. For this reason, most developments in small arms prior to about the 1850s were created by engineers working without regard to what anyone else might be doing.

Running counter to these technological advances was tactical change. Indeed, throughout much of the nineteenth century, tactics paid little heed to technological advances in small arms. There was an almost unshakable belief that spirit would always overcome firepower. It would be unwise, however, to view this from the perspective of the early twenty-first century and condemn the tacticians for foolhardiness. The manoeuvre of military formations on the battlefield took precedence over firepower. It was not until the 1870s that the subject of mechanization of war began to be discussed. The experience of the Napoleonic Wars became a focus for tacticians who encapsulated the ethos of the assault in the tactical doctrines they developed. Thus, at the time of the Crimean War and the American Civil War, the idea persisted that the assault, if undertaken with the right spirit, and with enough determination and courage, would always prevail over a defender. This presupposed that the defender was out in the open facing the attacker. However, the ethos was applied to all forms of assault, including those on fortified positions.

While the latter had always been costly enterprises, they became even more so when the lethal zone grew in size and density following the adoption of rifles and the Minié bullet in the middle of the nineteenth century. The problem was that the attacking infantry had to cross this zone before it could engage the enemy, the object of any assault being to cross blades with the enemy in a bayonet charge. It was all very well inculcating spirit and élan but if the infantry could not cross this zone, the ethos was not only useless but deadly. Moreover, mass close-ranked formations of the sort employed on Napoleonic battlefields could not survive intact and were liable to be cut to pieces, a fate that occurred to such attacks in the American Civil War.

Herein lay a major obstacle, but one which was not readily apparent to European armies even after the American experience of civil war in the 1860s. While the European powers sent observers to America, what they saw was considered irrelevant to European wars. Indeed, the Franco-Prussian War of 1870–1 seemed to contradict all the object lessons thrown up by the Civil War and reinforced the idea that élan would always overcome firepower. Thus, technology was not seen as significant to the conduct of wars. And yet it was becoming increasingly evident that technology was changing the nature of warfare. Two schools of thought developed: one believed that the spirit of the infantryman was paramount and the bayonet charge was the epitome of the offensive; while the other school emphasized the importance of firepower over mere manpower. The unwillingness to consider the possibility of the two working cooperatively rather than competitively prevented the realities of increasingly mechanized armies being considered.

To a large degree this was due to the way in which technology and engineering was viewed by military men. While the industrialization of the civilian world was seen as positive and beneficial to the welfare of the state, if it was considered at all in relation to warfare, it was seen as detrimental and harmful to the art of war. Armaments firms were beginning to find that research costs were rising at a considerable rate due to the rising level of sophistication of innovation in the armaments field. Such costs could only be recouped by selling more armaments to established customers and by seeking out new customers further afield. While governments bought these increasingly more expensive and more sophisticated armaments, neither they nor their armies considered how these might be employed on the battlefield. That is to say, they viewed them as no more than better engineered versions of what they already had. This was especially true when it came to artillery and, often, armies were unaware of the capabilities of the new munitions.

Artillery became the dominant force on the battlefield during the nineteenth century, although this was not fully appreciated until the First World War. Indeed, up to about 1915, artillery was intended purely to support the infantry in its assault, in which capacity the guns were positioned amongst the infantry at the start of a battle so that the gunners could fire over open sights at targets they could see. Direct fire was considered to be the only viable means of engaging enemy infantry and enemy batteries were rarely targeted, although the range of the Minié bullet meant that gunners became vulnerable to small-arms fire. From about the 1850s, the guns were moved back to just behind the infantry and theoretically out of range of enemy rifle fire at the start of a battle. A rifle firing a Minié bullet could outrange a smooth-bored muzzle-loaded canon, while breech-loaded rifles could shoot faster than canon because, unlike cannon, breech-loaders used fixed ammunition, that is, the bullet was fixed inside the mouth of a metal cartridge. There was therefore a growing conflict between technology and tactics which contributed to the rise in the use of entrenchments in what was otherwise conventional battle.

Although the techniques of gun-making improved considerably between 1600 and 1800, the guns themselves and the shot they fired remained essentially the same. Between 1800 and 1850, a number of significant advances occurred, not only to the technology of guns but also to their ammunition. By the late 1850s, rifled breech-loading guns, although unreliable, were beginning to replace smooth-bored muzzle-loaders in some armies; rifled artillery was already replacing smooth-bored cannon. At the same time, the explosive shell was starting to replace the solid roundshot and canister that smooth-bore cannon customarily fired. This was not motivated by a military demand for 'better' guns but by commercial interests on the part of the armaments firms such as Armstrong and Whitworth in Britain and Krupp in Prussia. By the middle of the nineteenth century, the cost of developing new guns and new manufacturing techniques, as well as new materials from which to make the guns by these techniques, was huge and the only way to recoup them was to sell more guns. Thus, new technology found its way into armies which had little idea of the capabilities of these technologically advanced guns. This situation was made worse by the acceleration of change during the second half of the nineteenth century. Whereas obsolescence had been measured in half centuries up to about 1800, by the 1880s it was being measured in half decades.

The key technological advance for artillery was the development of cheaper, faster techniques to rifle a gun barrel during the 1850s by Whitworth and Armstrong in England and by Krupp in Prussia. The Armstrong breech-loader was a direct consequence of experience in the Crimean War. With the advent of an improved method of rifling, breech-loading became more desirable since it was not easy to ram a tight-fitting projectile down a rifled barrel. The projectile had to fit tightly otherwise the propellant gases escaped past it when the gun was fired, which effected range inconsistently. In the 1850s and 1860s, muzzle-loaded rifled guns were still much more common than breech-loaders, but smooth-bored cannon remained the principal form of artillery. There was considerable resistance by governments to adopt rifled artillery, not the least reason being the cost of replacing all their smooth-bored muzzle-loaders with rifled breech-loaders. Government reluctance was reinforced by the fact the early rifled breech-loaders were more expensive than muzzle-loaders, and the technology of making the breech mechanism easy to open, gastight when it was closed and sufficiently robust to withstand repeated operation was underdeveloped. Nevertheless, the rifled breech-loader was the future of artillery, especially when married with the ogival shell which was also under development during this period. The first breech-loaders firing ogival shells, Armstrong guns, were adopted by the British Army in 1860.

The American Civil War was the first opportunity for armaments manufacturers and artillerists to compare rifled breech-loaders with smooth-bored muzzle-loaders and rifled muzzle-loaders under combat conditions. Union and Confederate armies fielded few rifled breech-loading artillery pieces, however. By

1865, this situation had changed in favour of the Union armies, whose artillery now had a high proportion of rifled breech-loaders. These were 12-pounders made by the British firms of Whitworth and Armstrong. Unfortunately, the rifled guns, whether breech-loaders or muzzle-loaders, were not as reliable as smooth-bore cannon. During the American Civil War, and again during the Austro-Prussian War of 1866, barrels burst far too often, which dissuaded some governments from equipping their armies with rifled breech-loaders. An inevitable consequence of rifling and close-fitting projectiles was higher barrel pressures, a situation made worse by the fact that the new methods of fabricating rifled barrels had not been perfected.

The rifled breech-loader had a far greater range and was far more accurate than smooth-bored muzzle-loaders, but until at least the 1870s was much less robust than the rifled muzzle-loader. A smooth-bore cannon had a range in the region of 1,200–1,600 metres, while a rifled gun could shoot a projectile to 3,200 metres. Moreover, a Parrot gun of the Civil War period could hit a target at 1,500 metres with its fourth shot, something which no smooth-bore cannon could achieve. Unfortunately, long-range capability was mitigated by human deficiency: a gunner could not see a target at such distances. At that time, gunnery was almost entirely dependent upon gunners being able to see their targets so that shooting was by direct line of sight. Indirect shooting with field artillery was rarely attempted. The increase in range and accuracy of rifled breech-loaders highlighted a quite different problem: that of fusing. It was all very well being able to hit a target at a greater range than had been possible with muzzle-loaded cannon, but these rifled guns fired shells not roundshot and the shell had to explode at the target if it was to be effective. Hence, there was a need for a reliable time fuse. Although some percussion fuses had been used in the American Civil War, none was very satisfactory.

Rifled artillery did not supersede smooth-bore cannon until the 1870s. Indeed, the Prussian Army which defeated the French Army in 1870–1 was the first to be equipped entirely with rifled guns. Revolutionary innovations in guns, ammunition, propellants and fusing which solved many of the deficiencies of the early breech-loading guns did not occur until the 1870s and 1880s. The combination of inventions and developments in these areas brought about the realistic possibility of transforming artillery tactical doctrines in the last decades of the nineteenth century. Now, it was entirely feasible for gunners to engage the enemy by indirect fire, that is, firing on a distant target that they themselves could not see but which was identified by means other than direct line of sight. However, tactics still centred on the infantry assault and on infantry firepower, so that artillery which could outrange and outshoot the infantry with ease was still being used much as Napoleonic cannon had been used seventy or eighty years earlier. Despite the huge increase in artillery firepower during the second half of the nineteenth century, its advantages were not exploited, despite the growing evidence that guns now dominated the battlefield, not the infantry.

Breech-loaders made by Krupp in the late 1870s and early 1880s were the first to be properly gas-tight, which substantially increased the range of these guns. While the breech-loaders of the early 1860s had a range of about 4,000 metres, Krupp guns had doubled this to 8,000 metres. By the 1890s, the armies of all the major powers had finally abandoned all their smooth-bore muzzle-loaders and were equipped exclusively with rifled breech-loaders. This process of change had taken forty years.

The innovation that was eventually to have the most profound effect on artillery tactics was the recoil and recuperator system, which enabled the barrel to recoil then return to its original position on the carriage, thereby ensuring that the whole piece did not move from its position. Hence, the gun did not have to be relayed each time a shot was fired. Recoil could make a gun run back 2 metres on firing. Relaying a gun was time-consuming and severely limited the rate of fire. A gun fitted with a recoil and recuperator system was much more stable than a gun without such a system. This opened the way to the development of bigger and more powerful guns with ever greater ranges. Recoil and recuperator systems meant that the rate of fire could be increased from a round every few minutes with guns in fixed carriages, to several rounds a minute. This was a very significant increase in firepower since a battery of four or five guns could now deliver a weight of fire equivalent to several batteries of fixed-carriage guns.

The first artillery pieces to be fitted with a recoil system were a Prussian gun in 1867 and a Russian gun in 1872, although numerous inventions relating to the management of gun recoil predated these pieces. That recoil was a matter that had to be addressed by the armaments firms became clear in the 1850s; greater range and power inevitably increased the recoil which was a limiting factor in gun design. There was a limit beyond which the force of unabsorbed recoil would render the gun impractical. Measures for dealing with recoil included pneumatic pistons, springs, rubber bands and even a muzzle break in the form of holes bored through the upper surface of the barrel. None of these was entirely reliable or effective. The best of the new recoil-recuperator systems was a hydropneumatic, long-recoil mechanism invented by Capitaines Deport and Sainte-Claire Deville in the 1890s. Their system was fitted to the French *Soixante-Quinze* (Materiel de 75mm Mle 1897).

The gun barrel was mounted so that it could slide along the carriage. When the gun was fired, the recoil forced the barrel back along the carriage without causing the carriage to move back with it. The hydropneumatic system incorporated two interconnected cylinders containing pistons whereby the recoil energy of the gun was absorbed, stored, then released to push the barrel back to its original position on the carriage without the carriage being moved significantly by the recoil. The process was aided by a splayed trail, the ends of which were provided with spades to prevent the gun from moving backwards with successive firings. The speed with which the barrel was restored to its original position on the carriage meant that the Seventy-Five was capable of fifteen rounds a minute, a rate of fire that was also made possible by a quick-locking breech mechanism. Subsequent recoil systems also used hydromechanical means which used strong metal springs instead of air to restore the barrel to its original position after firing. The Seventy-Five entered French service in 1899, but its revolutionary recoil system was kept secret even after the Boxing Rebellion in 1900 when the quick-firing capability of the Seventy-Five was well demonstrated.

The quick-firing gun did not come into its own until the early 1900s. After the French adopted the Seventy-Five, the Germans improved their new 77mm piece, which they had adopted in 1896, with a similar system in 1905, while the British introduced a 13-pounder and an 18-pounder in 1904. Such guns could fire up to 8,000 metres at a rate of about twenty rounds a minute. Rates of fire of this order could only be achieved with fixed ammunition, whereby the shell was combined with a brass case of propellant. This innovation was introduced in the 1880s at around the same time that smokeless propellants based on cellulose nitrate were introduced. These propellants were much more powerful than black powder and produced much less fouling. Fixed ammunition not only allowed faster loading of ammunition into the breech than was possible with separate propellant bags and shell, it also had the advantage of better obturation in the breech than could be achieved with bagged propellants. The brass case expanded outwards against the chamber walls when the propellant was fired, making a gas-tight seal. The disadvantage of quick-firing artillery was logistical: much more ammunition was expended than had been possible with the early breech-loaders and a ready supply therefore had to be available to the guns. This required the industrial might of mass production combined with precision engineering if the guns were to be fed to their capacity.

These field guns fired at higher muzzle velocities than earlier guns and the trajectories of the shells were therefore flatter. The guns were not designed to be fired at the high angles required for plunging fire. This was perfectly good while gunners were using direct line of sight to engage targets that were out in the open on relatively flat terrain. However, troops on reverse slopes or who were entrenched were less easily engaged by these guns because the trajectory could not be altered to allow the shells to plunge on to the target at a high angle. This problem was not new but was a feature of rifled guns. Indeed, it was highlighted in the Russo-Turkish War of 1877 when entrenched Turkish troops at Plevna remained relatively well protected from Russian shellfire because the guns could not properly engage them. In the past, siege mortars would have been brought up to the front line for this purpose, but new technologies had rendered them obsolescent. The old-style siege mortar had a relatively short range and had to be closer to the enemy trenches than was prudent when the defenders were armed with rifles which could outrange the mortars. The solution to this problem was the howitzer, which combined the plunging fire of the mortar with the power of the new types of gun.

The howitzer was not a new weapon at the time of Plevna, of course. Howitzers, long associated with sieges, had been in use as long ago as the fifteenth century, but they reached an apotheosis in the eighteenth century when they were widely employed in siege work. Armies employed siege howitzers and field howitzers. Interest in howitzers waned thereafter, although they continued to be used throughout the nineteenth century, notably during the American Civil War when siege howitzers with rifled barrels proved to be highly effective in destroying defences. Some of these were very big with calibres in the region of 200mm, firing shells that weighed 100kg. Paradoxically, the gradual adoption of rifled field guns between the 1850s and the 1870s led to armies abandoning smooth-bore field howitzers as they were thought to be an unnecessary expense. The increased range and power of rifled guns firing ogival shells meant that they could replicate some of the effects of smooth-bore howitzers. However, as demonstrated in the American Civil War, and again in Russo-Turkish War, field guns could not produce plunging fire which was necessary to engage entrenched defenders.

The renewed interest in and the subsequent emergence of new types of howitzer was a consequence of the trend for trench warfare to occur in the wars of the second half of the nineteenth century. The significance of the howitzer to trench warfare did not make itself clear until nearly twenty years after Plevna, however, despite the fact that by the early years of the twentieth century European armies included howitzers in their artillery trains. The battles on the Western Front during 1915 showed that the howitzer was the essential artillery piece of trench warfare. It was the lack of howitzers, especially large-calibre howitzers, which led to the development of that other quintessential weapon of trench warfare, the mortar. Like the howitzer, the mortar had a long association with siege warfare but, unlike the field howitzer, no mortar had ever been employed in anything other than siege work. The First World War was to change fundamentally the concept of mortars and their tactical employment, as well as demonstrate the crucial role of long-range guns and howitzers.

CHAPTER 3

Munitions of Trench Warfare before 1914

There is no doubt that developments in ordnance, small arms and ammunition during the nineteenth century played a significant role in the evolution of trench warfare. Firepower was the key factor. As firepower increased, so the necessity for digging in by infantry became essential if it was to survive on the battlefield. What is less well recognized is the effect that the evolution of trench warfare had on munitions. Apart from highlighting a need for ordnance capable of plunging fire, trench warfare led to entirely new types of weapons, some of which, while resembling older munitions, were, in fact, quite novel. Among these, perhaps the most important for the effect they had on warfare as a whole were the hand grenade and the trench mortar.

The widespread use of grenades in the First World War has been ascribed to no more than a re-emergence of these ancient weapons after they had fallen into disuse during the nineteenth century. Indeed, it has been generally accepted that the grenade first re-emerged during the Russo-Japanese War and that the use of grenades in the First World War merely continued the process as an inevitable progression. The evidence does not support this view, however. Not only were the grenades of the First World War quite unlike the traditional grenade, but they were, in fact, novel munitions which introduced novel concepts in warfare. Moreover, rather than having fallen into disuse during the nineteenth century, the grenade had actually remained in constant, if sporadic, use since its heyday in the early eighteenth century. The British, for example, only declared the traditional hand grenade obsolescent in 1902.

That other weapon which epitomizes trench warfare, the trench mortar, was not a development of earlier siege mortars but was, in fact, an entirely new munition. The construction of trench mortars and how they were used set them apart from the traditional siege mortar and eventually led to the first true infantry-support weapon, the light infantry mortar, the light machine-gun notwithstanding. Traditional mortars, as described in R. Forrest's *Illustrated Handbook of Military Engineering and the Implements of War* of 1858, differs from guns in having the trunnions placed at the extremity of the breech, with the thickness of metal being much greater in proportion to their calibre. Their use is for throwing shells, carcasses, etc.; and as they are fired at high elevations, generally 45°, the shells which they project make a very high curve in their flight and fall with their full gravity, nearly vertical, upon the object to be struck, breaking through the roofs of the strongest buildings, casemates, etc. ... Mortars have their range increased or decreased ... by loading greater or lesser quantities of powder, not by altering the elevation.

A good case can be made for arguing that the machine-gun, which predated the trench mortar by several decades, was, in fact, the first infantry support weapon. Indeed, the light machine-gun which came to prominence during the First World War was certainly used as a support weapon. The difference, however, was that whereas the light machine-gun was integrated into the platoon, the trench mortar remained separate from .it. Nevertheless, the light machine-gun would not have risen to prominence without trench warfare. Heavy or medium machine-guns were initially used as a form of artillery, much as the French had used the mitrailleuse in 1870–1, and as such their role could be construed as infantry support but, crucially, they remained in fixed positions, were employed in batteries and did not move with the infantry. The first trench mortars were also fixed but this was to change in 1916.

The machine-gun is often cited as a weapon of trench warfare, largely because of perceptions about its role in the First World War, but its origins predated the advent of trench warfare, although the first true automatic gun was that invented by Hiram Maxim in 1883. Hitherto, all machine-guns, such as the Gatling and the mitrailleuse, had been hand operated. While the effect of the machine-gun, including hand-operated guns, could be highly destructive to large formations of troops prior to the First World War, from a tactical perspective, the machine-gun played only an insignificant role in warfare. Indeed, some of the successes of the machine-gun in the late nineteenth century were in colonial wars against an indigenous army unskilled in modern weaponry, such as at Omdurman in 1898.

The British Army took up the machine-gun in 1891, whereas Germany did not adopt it until 1899. The machine-gun was not perceived as a decisive weapon, nor as one which might be used to support the infantry. In Britain, preference was given to conventional weapons so that few machine-guns were bought. Financial concerns rather than military ones decided the issue in Britain, but the question of whether the machine-gun was worthwhile arose in both Britain and Germany. The Russo-Japanese War was equivocal with regard to the effectiveness of machine-guns, which had little impact on the emergence of trench warfare in the decades before the First World War. One reason, of course, was their very small numbers in any army before the outbreak of war in 1914.

Some munitions were developed as a direct result of trench warfare in order to counter the disadvantages of being entrenched. Such devices included the periscope, the sniperscope – a remote-firing device fitted to a rifle to enable it to be fired from cover – body armour and trench shields. Body armour was not a new idea, of course, although it had largely disappeared from the battlefield by the end of the seventeenth century. Engineers engaged in siege work still wore armour in the eighteenth century. But the types of armour that were developed for trench warfare differed substantially from earlier armours. The periscope, a device that seems to lack any importance to warfare, was, in fact, one of those necessities for dug-in infantry, but more especially for the artillery observers of the First World War. Without periscopes, entrenched troops could not see what the enemy was doing without exposing themselves to injury or death from shellfire, but particularly from sniper fire. Periscopes enabled troops to observe from below the parapet with relative safety. Indeed, so important were periscopes on the Western Front, that dominance of no-man's-land and of the enemy's parapet was determined by which side could bring to bear the most periscopes. For this reason, periscopes were a prime target for snipers, with the added bonus that the observer might be blinded by the shattered glass when the periscope was hit.

Of the weapons devised to help overcome the deadlock of trench warfare during the First World War, three stand out: the flamethrower, gas and the tank. Although the flamethrower had been invented before the war, the Western Front provided an opportunity to test its effectiveness in battle. It was, however, largely ineffectual because the fuel lacked an essential ingredient: a thickener. Thickened fuels were invented in the 1930s and, come the Second World War, the flamethrower proved to be a highly effective device for combating bunkers and trenches. The case for gas weapons is dominated by the moral issues of using poison gas. Nevertheless, when the reliable delivery of concentrated gas clouds on to a specified target was achieved, gas was a formidable weapon against which there was no defence. While gas was introduced by the Germans, firstly on the Eastern Front in 1915, then against the French on the Western Front a few months later, the British were the greatest exponents of gas warfare and used it very effectively. One of the most effective delivery systems was the Livens projector, a type of mortar, of which several thousand would be fired simultaneously to flood a relatively small target area with gas in such a concentration that it killed instantly every living thing within a lethal zone that was often no more than a few thousand square metres.

While the tank is seen as the most significant weapon to have been devised as a direct consequence of trench warfare, it played a far less significant role in the First World War than other innovative munitions. Gas warfare as practised by the British was more decisive than the tank. The role of the tank was politicised to promote it as a war-winner when in truth it was no such thing. On the other hand, the hand grenade and the trench mortar were two weapons which fundamentally changed warfare between 1915 and 1917, more so than gas or the tank.

The hand grenade is a Chinese invention which dates from about the tenth century and was introduced to Europe in the fifteenth century. Grenades are supposed to have been first used in Europe during the siege of Casalmaggiore on the River Po in 1427. One of the earliest recorded uses of grenades in a European war is the siege of Arles in 1536 when they were used by the defenders. The grenadier as an elite soldier emerged in France during the seventeenth century and, by the 1670s, some infantry regiments had companies of grenadiers. Unfortunately, the grenadier as a thrower of grenades was vulnerable to enemy musket fire, despite the short range and inaccuracy of muskets. Quite simply, the distance a grenade could be thrown was much less than the lethal range of a musket ball. The heyday of the grenadier was the first half of the eighteenth century. Thereafter, the grenade declined in importance, while grenadier regiments survived as elite units. The grenade continued to be used during sieges, however, and remained a staple of siege work. The British, French and Russians used such grenades during the siege of Sebastopol in 1854. British troops used them again in the Sudan in 1884–5 and hand grenades of this sort were improvised by British troops during the siege of Ladysmith in the Boer War.

By the time of the Russo-Japanese War, the hand grenade had hardly changed since the eighteenth century. The grenade was a hollow sphere of iron, pottery or glass containing gunpowder which had to be ignited by means of some sort of fuse or slow match, similar to that used with matchlock muskets, inserted into the explosive. (British patent No. 303, dated 1692, is for a hand grenade made of glass but glass was certainly used for grenades before this date.) According to the *Illustrated Handbook of Military Engineering and the Implements of War*, grenades were:

> common shells, about 3 lb weight, with a small fuze and bursting charge. They are lighted and thrown from the hand; hence originally the name of 'grenadier'. They are principally used for throwing over ramparts into the ditch, when in possession of the enemy. Sometimes a number are bound up and quilted together in a canvass bag, and thrown from mortars.

Having to use a naked flame or the glowing end of a slow match to light the fuse meant that grenades were unreliable in wet conditions. Moreover, the fuses tended to burn at unpredictable rates and were not necessarily of uniform length so that a high degree of uncertainty pertained to grenade warfare. By the eighteenth century, the fuse was usually a tapered wooden tube filled with slow-burning gunpowder. Apart from susceptibility to water damage, the main problem with all these fuses was their unpredictable rate of burning which meant that handling grenades always required nerve on the part of the grenadier. The grenade might explode in his hand, or the fuse might fizzle out as he threw it. On the other hand, the fuse might burn for far too long, enabling the enemy to pick up the grenade and throw it back before it exploded. The invention of safety fuse by William Bickford in 1831 largely overcame these problems. While Bickford's fuse was originally intended to overcome the hazards of using unpredictable fuses in mines, the advantages of such a fuse to the Army were obvious. Bickford safety fuse was a jute rope containing a core of gunpowder, sealed with varnish. This fuse burned at a constant rate and was much more moisture proof than earlier types of fuse. The cast-iron, Bickford-fused blackpowder hand grenade was only declared obsolete by the British in 1902.

The unreliability of such grenades was a serious drawback which mitigated against their widespread use. However, it was the range of musket fire and, later, the accuracy of rifle fire which made grenades impractical in conventional combat situations. Thus, while they were still used in sieges, grenades were unimportant to the conduct of battles so no one was bothered by such shortcomings. No one, that is, apart from a few crackpot inventors who thought that they could solve them by devising an entirely new sort of grenade, but one which no one wanted. A percussion-fused grenade is supposed to have been invented sometime around the end of the sixteenth century, but nothing is known about it. By the middle of the nineteenth century, the suggestion that a percussion-fused artillery shell might be an improvement over roundshot and time-fused shells was being taken seriously by inventors. The percussion-fused shell became a feature of the American Civil War. The concept of a percussion-fused grenade was resurrected at about the same time but there was no incentive to produce a workable percussion-fused grenade. The Ordnance Board rejected all proposals for such a device. Captain Norton of the 34th Regiment offered one in 1828. William Parlour of the East India Military Seminary submitted another in 1834. Both grenades were rejected as 'ingenious, but not applicable to His Majesty's Service'. In 1852, the Ordnance Board rejected yet another, this time devised by William Spencer. Inventors were on a hiding to nothing in the field of grenades because there was no incentive for one to be adopted by any army.

The use of grenades at Sebastopol was in keeping with the general principals of siege warfare, so was nothing exceptional and the numbers employed were small. The French, for example, used only 3,200 grenades during the siege, a paltry figure that is indicative of their unimportance to the conduct of operations at Sebastopol. Interestingly, British troops resorted to improvisation which implies that this was a common practice. Grenades made from empty soda-water bottles were used to harass the Russian defenders from British trenches. According to Hugh Hibbert of the 7th Royal Fusiliers, these were filled with gunpowder and 'old twisted nails and any other sharp or cutting thing we can find at the time', then fitted with a slow fuse. It is unclear just how lethal these devices were or whether they were merely irritants to the Russians. Improvisation is a recurring feature in trench warfare and occurred in almost every instance of trench warfare. The British improvised grenades and body armour in South Africa while entrenched during the Boer War, for example.

The Americans had a quite different attitude to grenades during the Civil War, when at least six types of hand grenade saw service, three of them innovative.

Hand grenades were used in riverine and naval operations as well as in sieges, such as the one at Vicksburg. Perhaps the best-known grenade of the period was a percussion-fused devise invented in 1861 by William Ketchum, a New York manufacturer of farm equipment. About 90,000 Ketchums were ordered for the Union Army and Navy. The grenade resembled a dart and had to be thrown like one. The Confederates copied it, calling it the Raines, after General Gabriel Raines, who commanded the Confederate Torpedo Bureau. These grenades were unreliable and often failed to work as they had to hit a hard surface at the right angle for them to detonate. Troops sometimes spread sheets of fabric over their trenches to prevent the grenades from striking a hard surface. A similar tactic was later adopted in the First World War, notably by German troops, to counter percussion-fused grenades.

The oddest and most dangerous percussion-fused grenade was the Hanes Excelsior of 1862. This was a metal sphere of explosive surrounded by a casing which was intended to act as a striking surface for caps mounted on spikes projecting from the sphere. With no safety mechanism to prevent accidents, the Hanes was potentially lethal to anyone handling it. Not surprisingly, it was not popular. In 1865, John Adams of Massachusetts came up with an improvement to the traditional time-fused grenade. This had a friction lighter instead of a conventional fuse that had to be lit with a flame. The lighter, in the form of a wire in a tube of match composition, was attached to a strap with a loop through which the thrower put his wrist so that when the grenade was thrown the strap pulled the wire through the composition which ignited the fuse. This was a sophisticated design which had a number of novel features that addressed the problems of moisture damage and premature detonation due to a phenomenon called flash-through. This occurred when the heat of the ignited fuse was such that it travelled so rapidly through the fuse to the explosive that the time fuse was turned into an instantaneous one. It also incorporated a safety device to prevent the wire being pulled out unintentionally. While neither the British nor the Germans took much notice of the American grenades, the French copied the Adams fuse and fitted it to the 1847 model grenade, an updated version of which was still in service in 1915.

Nothing more of significance in the development of grenades occurred until the Russo-Japanese War. During the siege of Port Arthur, the Russians started improvising grenades as the British had done at Sebastopol, fifty years earlier. The Japanese quickly followed suit. These grenades made a far greater impression on the military observers from the major powers than might have been anticipated, considering the general lack of interest in grenades since the eighteenth century. The improvisations were mundane and in the tradition of improvisations – adequate but unspectacular – and followed the conventional form of grenade. The only difference was the addition of a detonator to ignite the explosive; high explosive could not be detonated by a traditional fuse.

At the beginning of 1905, the Russians devised a percussion-fused grenade which the Japanese soon copied when they found one following the Battle of

Mukden. It is unclear, however, whether the Russian percussion-fused grenade or the Japanese copy ever saw action. Neither the Russians nor the Japanese overcame the inherent problem associated with percussion fuses: they will detonate if accidentally struck. The designs were unlike the traditional grenade. The grenade had a cylindrical body, circled by a segmented lead band for fragmentation, and was fitted to a long wooden handle. Fragments from such grenades could travel up to 150 yards. The handle allowed the grenade to be thrown with more force than a traditional spherical grenade so that it went further. The Japanese copy had streamers attached to the handle to ensure that the grenade hit the ground on its fuse, rather than on its side, a refinement that had been used on the Raines in the American Civil War. These grenades were improvised in the field by military engineers. In June 1905, engineers in the Second Japanese Army were reported to be making 4,000 percussion-fused grenades.

More than 44,000 grenades of all types were used by five Japanese divisions during the siege of Port Arthur, or less than 9,000 per division, in July to December 1904. That worked out at only about fifty grenades per day per division. Japanese troops armed with grenades discovered that assaults on Russian positions were only successful when supported by rifle fire. In other words, grenades alone could not decide the outcome of an action. One British report stated that grenades had a considerable effect on enemy troops crowded together. The military observers attached to the Russian and Japanese armies reported on everything they witnessed, including the grenades, with the result that a desire was created for these 'new' weapons. Thus began research programmes in Britain, France and Germany to develop 'new' hand grenades.

In October 1904, the Japanese introduced an improvised wooden mortar. This was not a variation on the siege mortar, however, but an adaptation of a firework mortar. Yet again, this was an improvisation. While it was cheap and simple to make, and easy to transport, as a military weapon it was next to useless as it was slow to load, had a very short range and was very inaccurate. The barrel was constructed from four strips of fir, wound with bamboo cane. The 5-inch model had a range of 100–400 yards and fired a 4.5lb bomb. As with conventional mortars, range was adjusted according to the size of the bagged propellant charge. There is an instance of a Japanese mortar reportedly beating off a Russian attack with a single round. The Japanese used 103 5-inch and twenty-three 7-inch mortars at Port Arthur, firing more than 11,500 explosive bombs of which most were specially made for the mortars, as well as 519 incendiary bombs. Curiously, only the Germans seem to have been sufficiently impressed by the mortar concept to want to devise their own mortars.

A wooden-barrelled mortar was not new. Three such mortars had been improvised by Union Army engineers during the siege of Vicksburg in 1863 to make up for a lack of proper siege mortars. Logs of seasoned gumwood were fitted with iron bands at the top and bottom, then bored to calibre. They were evidently capable of withstanding repeated firings, no doubt because of the small propellant charges which placed little strain on the barrels, compared to the much heavier charge used in traditional mortars. The small charge restricted range to 100–150 yards, which was enough, however, to reach the Confederate lines at Vicksburg. Some 468 shells of 6lb and 12lb were fired from three wooden mortars over a period of 48 hours, causing about ninety casualties.

Although, in the 1880s, the British Army still advocated grenades for defence of fixed positions, it had effectively lost interest in them. However, in October 1904, the Chief Superintendent of Ordnance Factories was instructed by the War Office to design a new grenade in light of the grenades used in Manchuria. The decision to design a 'modern' hand grenade was but one in a series of decisions concerning trench warfare matériel taken by the War Office at the beginning of the twentieth century. Experience in South Africa had shown that such munitions were, indeed, necessary to an army in the field since entrenchments were an inescapable aspect of warfare. The British adopted several types of trench warfare device, including armoured trench shields in 1902 and wirebreakers in 1912. A wirebreaker was a device fixed to the muzzle of the service rifle for snapping single strands of barbed wire. Hand-operated wirecutters became standard equipment for the British Army in 1909. In the early 1900s, another new device, the periscope rifle or sniperscope, was proposed by an inventor called William Youlten. Although the British did not envisage becoming involved in siege operations, the attitude towards such devices was clearly changed by the Boer War and reinforced by what was seen in Manchuria. Nevertheless, the British considered shields, grenades and wirebreakers as unsuitable for the infantry. They were specialist munitions which needed to be handled by specialists, the Royal Engineers.

Armoured shields were no more new than body armour. Both had been in use for centuries and neither had completely vanished from the battlefield, despite the penetration characteristics of small-arms ammunition. Body armour was worn in the American Civil War, to not very great advantage it has to be said, largely because the manufacturers had no idea how to make bullet-proof armour. Yet the notion that armour could protect against small-arms fire was persuasive enough to convince many Union soldiers that it was worth buying armour from one of the several private firms that were set up at the start of the war for the sole purpose of making and supplying armour. The firms stayed in business for about eighteen months after which time it became apparent that such armour was, in fact, useless and no defence against the Minié bullet. Armour had never completely disappeared from the battlefield although less of it was worn after the widespread use of firearms in the sixteenth century. Armourers attempted to make pistol-proof cuirasses and back plates, not always successfully as some surviving examples from the seventeenth century attest. Pistol-proof armour became so heavy by the time of the Thirty Years War (1618–48) that it was often discarded (three-quarters armour weighed 80–100lb). Siege engineers often wore heavy armour during the eighteenth century and even as late as the Franco-Prussian War of 1870–1.

The idea that armour could provide protection was very resistant to the contrary evidence. Some of the earliest British body armour patents date from 1896 and 1907. Crude helmets made locally were used by the British during the siege of Ladysmith in early 1900. Again, it was the Russo-Japanese War which stimulated serious interest in armour. Both the Japanese and the Russians wore cuirasses at Port Arthur and both sides made use of portable shields as well as trench shields to protect infantrymen. The difference between these armours and earlier examples was the effort that was put into addressing the problem of how to stop the penetration of high-velocity projectiles. Here were the seeds of a new technology which would eventually lead, via the First World War, to the modern composite armours of today. Although the Germans developed mobile shields for its infantry, which it subsequently used in the opening phases of the First World War, no other nation seems to have been inspired by the armours of the Russo-Japanese, unlike the grenade which fermented a great deal of interest.

Following the end of the Russo-Japanese War, Britain, France and Germany all took up the hand grenade with renewed interest. The British were the first to adopt a new grenade in 1908. The Germans did not adopt one until 1913, the *Kugelhandgranate*. The well-known 'potato masher' design of grenade did not appear until 1915. Whereas the Germans used time fuses fitted with friction lighters to overcome the difficulties associated with flames and glowing matches, the British became enamoured of percussion fuses. In this respect, the German device of 1913 was superior to the British grenade of 1908, the percussion fuse of which was always problematical.

Initially, the Royal Laboratory at Woolwich tried to design a time-fused grenade but when Lieutenant Colonel Haldane, one of the British observers in Manchuria, brought back a Japanese percussion-fused grenade, the Royal Laboratory set about designing a percussion model. At this time, the British preferred the percussion fuse over the time fuse because it was not susceptible to water damage and, in theory, it was more reliable. However, percussion-fused grenades were inherently dangerous in a way that time-fused grenades were not; if the armed percussion fuse struck a hard surface, it detonated the grenade. Hence, a reliable and effective safety mechanism was essential if accidents were to be avoided. The safety mechanism of the British No. 1 Percussion Grenade of 1908 was quite inadequate. Here, the lack of a body of knowledge on the subject of grenades meant that no one had any idea of how to go about making an effective safety mechanism. It went further than this; no one involved with the grenade was aware that a more reliable safety mechanism was needed.

Despite four years of effort that the Royal Laboratory put into designing this grenade, only 420 had been manufactured by August 1914, which meant that the British Army could hardly be described as being equipped with grenades when it went to war. No grenades went to France with the BEF. The device was clearly not considered to be important to the kind of military operations in which the British Army envisaged becoming involved.

Meanwhile, Frederick Marten Hale, an inventor with considerable experience of explosives – he was a director of the Cotton Powder Company which supplied explosives to the mining industry and to the armaments industry – designed his own percussion-fused grenade. Over a period of several years, he improved the device and submitted it to the War Office at least four times, but it was rejected on every occasion. In 1908, Marten Hale invented the rodded rifle grenade from an idea that came to him when he speculated on the consequences of firing a ramrod out of a rifle barrel. The concept of shooting a grenade further than a man could throw one went back centuries. Attachments for shooting grenades from muskets had been used in the seventeenth and eighteenth centuries but they were unreliable and dangerous. In July 1908, Marten Hale submitted the rifle grenade to the War Office. The Chief Draughtsman at Woolwich called it 'a crazy and audacious monstrosity' that would burst the barrel when fired.

Marten Hale was a canny businessman who understood the value of patents and publicity. Not only did he patent his inventions, thereby securing a monopoly in the field of rifle grenades, a situation that was to cause the War Office and, later, the Ministry of Munitions a major headache during the First World War; but he actively promoted his inventions to the armies of the world. He was not the first inventor to stage events for prospective buyers. Hiram Maxim had done a similar thing in the 1880s with his machine-gun. However, Marten Hale was probably first to market a new weapon in the same way that a bicycle or washing powder might be marketed, advertising in the press, sending out glossy leaflets and providing press interviews, as well as sending letters to the War Office and to foreign governments. Between 1908 and 1913, Marten Hale demonstrated his grenades at the Faversham works of the Cotton Powder Company to representatives of eighteen countries, including France, Germany, Russia, Mexico and Spain. In 1910, the War Office decided to conduct trials with fifty rifle grenades. However, the Ordnance Board rejected it and the Royal Laboratory was ordered to design one. It was not successful. In October 1913, the Ordnance Board announced that Hale's rifle grenade would undergo troop trials and, eventually, his rifle grenade was adopted for service. Germany adopted a rifle grenade that same year. In August 1914, the British Army had an unopened box of fifty.

The operational debut of the rifle grenade was in Morocco in 1909 when it was used in a minor colonial conflict by Spanish forces. The Mexican government ordered 25,000 rifle grenades in 1912 for suppressing riots, but these never made it to Mexico and ended up on the Western Front in the service of the BEF. It is clear that, initially, the rifle grenade was not seen as a weapon of positional warfare. Indeed, it was not taken very seriously by the major European powers, with the exception of Germany which went to war in 1914 equipped with hand and rifle grenades, as well as mortars. It would be unwise to place too much emphasis on this apparent foresight on the part of the Germans since the numbers were too small to be significant to the conduct of operations. Indeed, the Germans were forced to improvise grenades and mortars in 1915 just as the French and the British were forced to do.

In the nine years between the end of the Russo-Japanese War and the start of the First World War, other entrepreneurial inventors turned their attention to these munitions and the number of patents granted for grenades slowly increased. Notable among these inventors was a Norwegian called Niels Aasen, whose grenades were evaluated by the British, French and German armies before and after the outbreak of war in 1914. While the British disliked Aasen's grenades, the French and German armies were so short of grenades in 1915 that both armies accepted Aasen's into service. In March 1915, the French were producing 1,500 Aasen Excelsior grenades a day and this was about to be increased to 10,000 a day.

There is no question that the First World War brought about a radical change of attitude to munitions designed specifically for trench warfare. While some were adaptations of traditional weapons, others were entirely new. These devices came to prominence because of the exigencies of trench warfare over a protracted period, which focused attention on devices intended specifically for this sort of warfare. For all practical purposes, most of these devices either existed in insignificant numbers or did not exist at all in the autumn of 1914. There had been no call for them and there was a general belief, certainly among the British, that when warfare returned to its customary mobile form, such munitions would become redundant, interest in them would wane and they would be consigned to storage. However, the converse happened and rather than become redundant, many of these munitions contributed to a fundamental change in warfare that occurred during the war.

Nevertheless, the British ambivalence to grenades prior to the First World War was not untypical of the attitude of all the European powers. There is no sense that Britain behaved with any less foresight than any other nation. Indeed, Britain opted for new types of grenade before either France or Germany. In this respect, Britain was often more enlightened with regard to new weapons than her continental neighbours. The machine-gun is a case in point. Such weapons were considered to be defensive rather than suitable for the assault, and the trench mortar was seen as no more than a poor substitute for the howitzer. Before 1915, there was no tactical system for grenades, mortars or, indeed, machine-guns, a situation that held true for all the belligerents. Germany seems to have been slightly more enlightened with regard to the tactical employment of grenades. Unlike Britain, Germany equipped its infantrymen with them rather than relegating to them to specialist use.

The Japanese light mortar was an aberration with no military future. As soon as the Russo-Japanese War ended, it was forgotten. The British believed that plunging fire was best provided by the howitzer. Germany, on the other hand, was sufficiently impressed by the concept of a small mortar that could bombard the enemy in his trenches from the front line that it set about designing small mortars for its own army. These were, in effect, scaled-down, muzzle-loaded howitzers. Germany adopted its first mortars in 1910 and 1911, but was much more interested in massive mortars that were capable of destroying the Belgian Forts.

One other element was to play a crucial role in trench warfare: barbed wire. Invented in America in 1867, by 1874 it had became a mass-producible fencing material with which to confine cattle to a rancher's land. Its military potential was quickly realized, however, but although it was used during the Boer War and in the Russo-Japanese War, it was not until the First World War that barbed wire saw widespread use. The full implication of setting up barbed-wire entanglements in front of a defended position was not appreciated until the First World War was nearly a year old. Barbed wire was to have an impact on warfare as great as any new weapon or new tactical doctrine.

CHAPTER 4

Siege of Sebastopol

When the British and French set off for the Crimea in 1854, they had no plan of action other than a vague notion of taking the naval port of Sebastopol away from the Russians to deny them power in the Black Sea. The Allies, which included Turkey, landed 53,000 troops 30 miles to the north of the port and had to march south, fighting the Russians at the Battle of the Alma (20 September) before reaching the city. They then marched another 15 miles around it to encircle it from the south and east. The Russians quickly blocked the approach to the harbour by sinking ships across the inlet from the Black Sea so that the British and French warships were unable to get close enough to bombard Sebastopol. Guns from the blockships were used to reinforce Sebastopol's defences.

The Allies then set about laying siege which lasted from October 1854 to the following September, a period of eleven months. From the outset of winter, and after a destructive storm in mid-November in which the British lost their supply ships, conditions in the trenches deteriorated for everyone, French, British and Russian alike. The trench conditions and the nature of the fighting which developed during the siege were a foretaste of what was to come in the future. The heavy bombardment of the Russian defences by the Allied guns was not in itself a departure from usual practice in a siege, but the Russian counter-bombardment, the continuous manning of trenches by the infantry and the hand-to-hand fighting in the trenches during the siege as men fought to secure ground were unprecedented. Counter-battery fire was often employed at Sebastopol, especially before an infantry assault. A number of innovative solutions to siege conditions were applied by the Russians, including the digging of rifle pits from which their riflemen could snipe the Allied troops in their trenches, and a type of fougasse mine which detonated when trodden on rather than being detonated by a fuse which had to be lit.

As British and French forces marched round to the south and east of Sebastopol, the Russian commander, Prince Menshikoff, marched the bulk of his army out the city to the north-east to meet the reinforcements that were heading to Sebastopol and to prevent his army from being bottled up. The Russian and Allied armies crossed with neither being aware of the other. On reaching the high ground on the southern side of the city, the British took the right flank, east of a ravine, leaving the French to move to the western side of the ravine and take the left flank.

Had the Allies chosen to launch an immediate attack on Sebastopol, it is possible that it would have been successful, but failing to do so and setting about laying siege worked to the advantage of the Russians who used the time to strengthen their defences. At a distance of 2,300 yards from the city, the Allies began entrenching on 9 October; earthworks for gun batteries were build almost 1,000 yards closer on the heights overlooking the city. Usually in siege work, the first trenches were opened up a mere 600–800 yards from the objective, a distance determined by the range of the heavy mortars which were sited just behind the first trenches, while gun batteries were dug about 50 yards in front of the first trenches. However, when the Allies began their siege of Sebastopol, they had no mortars. Later, as the second parallel was dug, positions for mortars and howitzers were constructed much closer to the objective. The initial entrenchments of the first parallel were completed a week later, with 126 Allied guns in place and ready for action. Trench construction did not end then, of course, but continued throughout the siege as the Allies moved closer to the city. As Hibbert of the Royal Fusiliers explained: 'Digging these trenches, parallels and zigzag approaches was in itself a hated task … The ground was hard and stony under the turf, and at the end of each day the distance covered seemed absurdly small.'

By the summer of 1855, a labyrinthine network of lines, or parallels, angles and saps covering an area of many square miles on the Allied side of the line had been dug, mirrored in extent by the Russian works opposite them. The French dug about 30 miles of trenches to a depth of nearly 2 miles, while the British dug around 10 miles of trenches.

The relative positions of the Allied forces with respect to the city did not remain static, especially when Russian reinforcements approached from the north. Indeed, while the siege was a form of static warfare in which both sides were entrenched, it was not stalemate. In truth, Sebastopol was not enclosed by the Allied siege works but was open to the north, across the Black Sea inlet on which Sebastopol was built. Moreover, Allied warships were restricted by the blockships and, hence, could do little more than harass the defenders from time to time while presenting substantial targets for the Russian guns in the forts either side of the mouth of the inlet.

Sebastopol is on the south bank of a 4-mile inlet of the Black Sea, divided by a smaller inlet and extending southwards along it; strictly speaking the town of Karabelnaya, which faced Sebastopol across the smaller inlet from its east bank, was separate from Sebastopol. The Russian defences consisted of an incomplete ring of forts and redoubts round the city and Karabelnaya, starting and finishing on the south bank of the larger inlet. The forts were joined by earthworks, but one fortified hill was left in front of these entrenchments, the Mamelon. Some of these forts, such as the Redan and the Malakoff, were to become the focus of fierce fighting in the months to come. The Russian defences were mostly in the form of earthworks, rather than stone-built structures, although some were faced with stone. The earthworks were reinforced with timber and gabions. Gabions, siege defences dating from medieval times, were cylindrical wickerwork baskets filled with earth. They were used extensively during the siege by both sides to construct parapets, earth being heaped in front of and on top of a row of gabions. Defensive structures of this sort were quick to rebuild and restructure when damaged by Allied gunfire. Sergeant Charles Usherwood of the 19th Foot noted that the Redan, which the British tried to capture on several occasions, was

> scientifically constructed ... having its traverses so arranged as to protect its gunners from any cross fire that could be brought against the work besides which the embrasures close cased by screens of sheet iron and plaited ship ropes rendered the position of the Artillery men secure against musketry, while to enable the Russian infantry to keep up a good and effective fire platforms were erected between the traverses and the Work. In addition to these advantages the enemy had also constructed barrack or guard rooms beneath the buttresses sufficiently large enough to contain a good number of men and wooden benches for them to rest upon when not on duty or on immediate guard and entirely secure from any harm

An extensive earth rampart was part of the defences, in front of which was a palisade and a ditch, a form of defensive position that would have been recognizable to Roman legionaries. Beyond this rampart, the Russians dug rifle pits from which individual riflemen sniped at the Allied troops. Conical holes, 2–3 feet or 8 feet deep and containing a stake, were arranged in rows in front of an earthwork to impede attacking infantry. Using sandbags, the Russians adapted some of the shallower ones to enable riflemen to snipe at Allied troops. In addition, other forms of obstacle were constructed, including abbatis from felled trees, chevaux de frise and various sorts of fougasse mine, each of which comprised a gunpowder charge at the bottom of a hole, provided with a fuse, usually a powder hose (a linen tube filled with black powder) or a length of Bickford safety fuse which burned at a rate of 28.8 inches per minute. Such mines came in several varieties, including the standard or Common Fougasse, an explosive charge in a hole, filled over with earth which was tamped down hard and made to blend with the undisturbed surrounding ground; and the stone fougasse consisting of a conical hole, set at an angle of 40°, near the bottom of which was a board. A 60lb charge was placed under the board and the hole filled with stones. When detonated, 3–4 cubic yards of stones were thrown 40–50 yards, spread over about 40 yards. The refinement developed by the Russians was a pressure-sensitive ignition system which avoided the hazards of lighting a fuse by hand. This consisted of two glass tubes, one inside the other, connected by a gunpowder train or hose to the explosive in the mine. The larger tube contained potassium chlorate and sugar, a simple explosive mixture (these days known as a weed-killer bomb), while the smaller one inside it contained sulphuric acid. When the glass tubes were trodden on, they broke and allowed their contents to mix and react, which produced sufficient heat to ignite the powder train.

One of the defining features of siege warfare was mining and counter-mining, a tactic that was employed extensively by both sides during the siege. Indeed, more than 5 miles of galleries were dug, while the French alone used 130,000lb of gunpowder in their mines. When the mines were detonated, there followed a race to the crater rim to take the dominant position over the enemy. Such mines were detonated by means of a powder hose, Bickford fuse or electrically using a battery, the current from which provided sufficient energy to ignite the explosive.

In September 1854, when the Allies landed in the Crimea, the combined force of British, French and Turkish troops amounted to some 51,000 men but, in six months, the figure had doubled, despite the casualties sustained in siege operations and in battles such as the Alma and Inkerman. By mid-February, the French alone had 90,000 men, compared to no more than 12,000 British troops, although the number of British guns had increased to around 300. In fact, the British had more than twice as many sick and wounded as they had fit and able men due to the dreadful conditions under which they were living, often without proper shelter. In addition, there were some 20,000 Turkish soldiers and 13,500 foreign mercenaries. The small number of British troops meant that their role in the siege diminished, while the French became the dominant partner. By early spring 1855, the British only held a small section of the line facing Sebastopol, manned by fewer than half of the 32,000 British soldiers in the Crimea.

At the start of the siege, approximately 35,000 Russians manned the defences of Sebastopol, a quarter of whom were marines and militiamen, but the rest included 18,000 sailors and 5,000 civilians. The Russians had 118 guns ready for counter-battery fire, with another 200 guns positioned to engage the Allied infantry when they attacked, all manned by 2,500 artillerymen. By May 1855, the number of Russian troops in the Crimea had risen to 170,000 but as many as 103,000 may have died during the siege.

The first Allied bombardment began on 17 October and was immediately met by a Russian counter-bombardment which destroyed a French magazine and its battery on Mount Rudolph when it received a direct hit by a Russian shell. Other French batteries were also silenced. British fire on the Malakoff redoubt destroyed many of its guns. Now was the perfect time to launch an infantry assault on the Malakoff but, because of French losses, the British declined to use this opportunity to take the Malakoff, which might well have led to the fall of the city itself. Lack of awareness of the situation and poor communications also contributed to the failure to attack. Despite being bombarded by British and French warships, the Russian forts sustained little damage by their action, although the ships suffered badly in the exchange of fire. The British artillery resumed their fire on the Russians the following day but, during the night, the heavy damage inflicted on the fortifications the previous day had been repaired so the British guns were merely repeating what they had already done. The Russians proved themselves adept at making nightly repairs to their earthwork defences so that the effect of Allied gunfire was largely nullified, and this pattern of destruction and repair was repeated many times during the course of the siege.

With the onset of winter, conditions in the trenches deteriorated. A tremendous storm, the Great Hurricane, struck the Crimea on 14 November and caused wholesale destruction across the siege lines, tearing tents and leaving men without shelter. Allied ships were severely damaged or sunk while the French and British bases, from which the men in the siege lines were supplied with food, clothing and equipment, were severely damaged and vital stores were lost. The high winds brought snow and the trenches began to flood. Without adequate winter clothing and having to subsist on poor food, British troops began to suffer terribly and ever-increasing numbers fell ill, reducing the effective strength of the British forces to such an extent that Britain ceased to play such a significant role in the conduct of the siege. The British were not the only ones to suffer, of course. French troops faired no better than the British and the Russians suffered most of all. Men succumbed to exposure, cholera, dysentery and starvation.

In the meantime, Sir John Burgoyne, Chief Engineer in the British force, saw the Malakoff as the key position in the Russian defences; he argued that if the Malakoff could be taken, then Sebastopol would fall soon afterwards. With this in the mind, trenches were dug towards to the fort with the intention of getting within striking distance of it so that it could be taken by assault. By now, the numbers of Russian defenders had been increased by troops from the Russian forces defeated at Inkerman. While it had become apparent to the Russians that their army was not going to defeat the Allies on the battlefield, they still believed that Sebastopol could be held and that the Allies would be defeated by exhaustion before its defences. The Russian chief engineer at Sebastopol, Lieutenant Colonel Todleben, set about strengthening the defences. It was at this point that he hit upon the novel idea of having his riflemen snipe at the enemy from pits located beyond the rampart in the area that would, in a later war, become known as no-man's-land. This tactic proved to be so successful that the Allies were forced to take action to stop the sniping. Night-time sorties to deal with the occupants of the pits was all too frequent an occurrence. As Sergeant Thomas Gowling of the Royal Fusiliers described it, taking

> their rifle pits was fearful work … done in the darkness of night … Rifle pits are … manned by crack shots, who tormented us considerably by picking off our artillerymen, and the sailors manning our heavy guns; if anyone showed his head above the parapets of our trenches he was almost certain to have a hole made in it.
>
> The taking of these pits was … all done with the bayonet … generally undertaken by volunteers from the various regiments that happen to be in the trenches at the time … About 100 or 150 (sometimes 300 or 400) men would be formed up at the point nearest to the pits to be assailed, all hands sometimes taking off their accoutrements. At a sign from the officers who are going to lead, the men creep over the top of the trench and steal up to the enemy on all fours. Not a word is spoken but, at a given

signal, in they all go – and in less time than it takes me to write this, it is all over; the bayonet has done its work. The defenders are all utterly destroyed or taken prisoner, while the pits are at once turned and made to face the enemy, or are converted into a trench.

In November, French engineers started mining a bastion known as the Flagstaff. The Russians became aware of the operation and set about digging a counter-mine. The French mine was in preparation for an Allied attack on the Mamelon, which was 1,500 yards beyond the Malakoff. The Russians vigorously defended it whenever it was attacked. The fortified hill remained a focus of fierce fighting for the next five months. Towards the end of February 1855, the Russians threw the French off the hill. In June, the French retook it after a heavy bombardment by about 550 guns and pushed the Russians back to the Malakoff. Unwisely, buoyed up by their success, the French then pressed on towards the Malakoff, but were repulsed with heavy losses and had to fight hard to keep hold of the Mamelon. The tables were turned and the Russians pushed towards the Mamelon. Fighting over ground with the tide of battle fluctuating in this way was typical, with the outcome often being inconclusive. And all the time, the extent of the earthworks and entrenchments was extended by both sides, both in terms of width and depth, but especially by the Allies as they worked their way towards the city.

The width of no-man's-land varied from about 150 yards to less than 30 yards, the gap tending to shorten as the siege lengthened and the Allies worked closer to the Russian redoubts and bastions. Trenches were constructed the same way as in the eighteenth century. A trench was a relatively shallow ditch, a mere 3 feet deep and 10 feet wide, with a parapet built up at the front from the earth dug from the ditch piled on top of the gabions and fascines which acted as reinforcement, with 4-foot timber stakes acting as revetments. There was no parados at the back. A British parapet might be 7 feet thick and 6 feet high, which was capable of preventing bullet penetration. As a general rule, no traverses or bays were built into the trenches to prevent enfilade or to minimize the effects of exploding shells, although some trenches were dug in zig-zags for this purpose, while some double saps were provided with traverses if they could not be zig-zagged. There were no sumps to drain water, no duckboards to walk on and no firestep to fire from. The point of the trenches was originally that of protecting troops forming up for an attack but at Sebastopol they became static positions and were permanently occupied.

There was a clear distinction between trenches and other earthworks built as part of a redoubt in which rudimentary fire steps were built into the raised structure. The parapet fell away to a substantial ditch in which chevaux de frise, or an angled palisade (known as a fraise), might be positioned to impede attackers and leave them vulnerable to small-arms fire. Beyond the ditch, the ground sloped away in a glacis.

The Russians constantly harassed the Allied troops with grapeshot and if any soldier was imprudent enough to show himself above the parapet he was immediately fired upon. Equally, the Allies harassed the Russians who suffered huge losses when they were engaged in building work. The Russian riflemen were considered to be crack shots capable of shooting off a finger if one were poked above the parapet. Sandbag loopholes allowed the enemy parapet to be observed to some extent, but vision was limited. The enemy could also be sniped through them. During quieter periods, it was not uncommon for men to provoke a Russian to stick his head above the parapet so that he could be shot at. Sometimes, a white flag would be hoisted aloft to signify a temporary local truce and Russian and British soldiers would climb out of their trenches to see what was going on, feeling safe in the knowledge that, so long as the flag remained visible, no one would open fire. But as soon as the flag was lowered, everyone made a frantic dash for the safety of their own lines as though it were a deadly game of tag. As soon as the men jumped back into their trenches, the firing would erupt in earnest and woe betide anyone left in the open.

This sort of fraternization was not uncommon between the British and the Russians. As the siege progressed, and especially during the hardships of the winter, a degree of fellow feeling developed between enemies, born out of universal suffering. As would be discovered sixty years later on the Western Front, when soldiers had to endure harsh conditions, awful weather and shot and shell, with little control over their own destinies, a strong sense of common cause arose among ordinary soldiers and, indeed, some officers, a sense which extended not merely to allies but also to enemies. The notion that the soldiery were all brothers only separated by their different uniforms who, under different circumstances, might otherwise be friends, did not find expression in quite the way in which it was made very public in the First World War, however. There was no public expression of fellow feeling, partly because it would take the rising political awareness and the increasing power of the workers across central Europe during the latter part of the nineteenth century, and into the early twentieth century, to suggest that soldiers were, indeed, alike, irrespective of whose uniform they wore. While this is often viewed as a socialist idea, common cause among enemy soldiers was much less political in origin than it was akin to a form of the Stockholm syndrome.

While the British were prepared to acknowledge the suffering of the Russians, any sympathy they might have had was tempered by the dreadful injures Russian guns inflicted on friends in the same regiment. The French were much less keen to fraternize than the British, who seemed to adopt a nonchalance about short armistices which allowed brief encounters in no-man's-land, during which snuff and cigars were exchanged. The Turkish soldiers hated the Russians, a deep-seated animosity derived from many years of conflict between the Russian and Ottoman empires.

During the winter, the trenches were cold. Wet snow lay thick in December and January and frostbite became a problem. Indeed, it was often fatal. Men died of hypothermia. Sometimes, it was necessary to make those who were dangerously cold run about and exercise vigorously to warm them before it was too late. The British, in particular, had no winter clothing or mud-proof footwear. Often cold and wet through, with no means to get warm and dry, men had to endure 24 hours of piquet duty in the trenches with only 12 hours rest between stints. When the temperature began to rise, the snow thawed and the trenches became full of mud which in places came up to the knees. The troops on both sides now looked more dead than alive so bad were the conditions under which they all had to live and fight. Often, the men had no proper shelter because their tents had been lost in The Great Hurricane, although some fortunate officers had the luxury of a house with a fire or a stove. Although new drafts of men arrived to replace the sick and the dead, they were too inexperienced to be of much use and they were quickly exhausted by having to undertake digging details to repair and extend the entrenchments. Those men who had endured the siege for several months learned how to pace themselves so that they had some energy available to jump to it when an alarm was raised. Even when out of the trenches, ostensibly resting, there was no rest as the men had to be ready to answer a call to arms whatever the time of day or night.

Following William Russell's reports in *The Times* about the conditions at Sebastopol and the indifferent manner in which the quartermasters were addressing the issue of winter clothing and equipment, so scandalized were the government and the public that the quartermasters were forced to act more sympathetically. Equally, the general officers began to take more of an interest in the welfare of their men, but there was little that could be done to ease their appalling conditions. With hindsight, it was, perhaps, evident to the Allies that they should have been less cautious and attacked Sebastopol immediately upon their arrival, instead of laying siege to it, thereby avoiding the misery that ensued. But by December 1854, it was far too late for that. The public responded to Russell's reports and began sending clothes to the offices of *The Times* to be dispatched to the Crimea, as well as money. There is doubt that Russell raised public awareness of the dreadful conditions at Sebastopol. However, the poor organizational arrangements in the Crimea, and the long-held view among quartermasters that they had first pickings of whatever came their way, meant that very little of the public's largess initially found its way to the men in the trenches. However, by the end of February, the British were better clothed than they had been earlier in the winter.

The need for artillery capable of plunging fire was addressed with mortars. Robert Mallet, a civil engineer, inventor and seismologist – he coined the term seismology – devised a huge mortar for the British at Sebastopol. It was intended to be made in easily transportable sections which could be assembled in situ. His mortar weighed 43 tonnes and had a 36-inch calibre. The siege ended before his invention could be built and he had to wait until 1857 to find out if it would successfully fire its 2,400lb projectile. It did, to a distance of 1.5 miles. Had the

Mallet mortar been used at Sebastopol, it would have caused unprecedented destruction. Instead, the British had to make do with smaller mortars but these were very effective, nonetheless. Brass mortars came in a variety of calibres, from 10 inches down to 4.4 inches, the former having a range of 1,300 yards, the latter a mere 800 yards. There were also longer-ranged iron mortars in calibres of 13 inches, 10 inches and 8 inches, which fired shells out to 2,700 yards, 2,500 yards and 1,700 yards, respectively. Such mortars were crucial to the bombardment of the Russian positions. The reason the iron mortars had longer ranges than the brass ones was down to the fact that larger propellant charges could be used with iron mortars because they were better able to withstand the higher pressures.

These were all smooth-bore muzzle-loaders which fired common shell and carcass. A carcass was an incendiary, essentially a shell punctured by three holes and containing a flammable composition so that flames blazed from the holes. Common shell was simply a hollow sphere of iron containing gunpowder and fitted with a time fuse. The usefulness of common shell depended entirely upon the fusing which determined the accuracy of the time delay. The object was to get the shell to detonate as it arrived at the target, for which an accurate time fuse was essential. By the time of the Crimean War, the Boxer fuse, invented in 1849, was in service; this could be relied upon to burn for a specified period before detonating the shell. The Boxer fuse consisted of a gunpowder-filled wooden cone into which a number of small radial holes had been bored, each one set at specified time interval. Connected to these holes was a second narrower channel also filled with powder. The holes were blocked with clay and, before the fuse was fitted to the shell, one of them was poked open according to the required time delay. When the gunpowder burned down to hole, a flash went through it to the narrower channel and into the explosive in the shell, detonating it.

The mortars took part in a ten-day heavy bombardment over Easter 1855 during which the Russians lost 6,000 men. But the Allies did not make the infantry assault the Russians anticipated, largely because of political wrangles between commanders and their governments, all conducted by telegraph, over how operations ought to be conducted at this stage of the siege This led to the resignation of the French field commander, General François Canrobert in May. He was replaced by a veteran of the wars in Algeria, General Jean Pélissier, who, fresh to the siege, brought new vigour to the task of taking the city. Rather than attack Sebastopol's supply lines in accordance with directives from Paris, he decided that it was time to storm the city. But first, the defences had to be reduced by yet another bombardment. This started at 3pm on 6 June and continued until sunset the following day. This preceded an attack by the French on the Mamelon and by the British on the adjacent Quarries. A fourth bombardment started eleven days later as a prelude to yet another attack on the Russian positions.

Rockets were widely used at Sebastopol by the Russian, French and British armies. They were mostly of the Congreve type and were used to harass the enemy, and to supplement the artillery during a bombardment. The British also experimented with some of the more modern Hale rockets. The launching tubes were usually made from stiff leather. Rockets were fired by hand at low elevations so that they would travel through enemy troops rather than descend on them from above. They were somewhat unpredictable and none were particularly accurate, with angular deviations far in excess of artillery shells (typically 40 yards in 1,000 yards), as they flew with erratic trajectories. Nor did they carry much of a payload. But their effect was sometimes greater than their explosive power because of their psychological impact. They shrieked in flight and threw out great quantities of sparks in a trail of white smoke. They could be quite deadly without exploding, killing men as these passed through a column of troops, as occurred at the Alma. Ranges varied from a mere 600 yards (12-pounder) to 1,000 yards (6-pounder), considerably shorter than the ranges achievable by artillery. Up to 500 rockets a day were produced in Britain during the Crimean War, although not all of them would have been fired at Sebastopol, of course. Rockets were fired elsewhere in the Crimea, including at the battles of the Alma, Inkerman and Eupatoria (February 1855).

Features of the siege of Sebastopol were trench raids and working parties. The latter were essential to the maintenance and repair of trenches damaged by enemy fire. British infantrymen reported to the Royal Engineers who provided them with the tools and instructions on how to proceed. Such parties were unarmed so had to be protected by another party of infantrymen, although later, working parties took their arms with them and piled them nearby. The guard party had to be ready to deal with any Russian sortie that might try to stop the working party. Under such circumstances, the working party had to retire to safety. According to orders on 2 October 1854:

> The guard will be posted in rear of the working party and near to it, if possible under cover of the fire of the place, if not, they must lie down in order of battle with accoutrements on and each man with his arms close by him: One party not less than one third of the force absolutely on the alert all through the night, making it alternatively ready for an immediate rush upon the enemy.

Working parties also adapted captured enemy trenches by reversing the position of the parapet. Such work was always a chore but the men received an extra ration of rum. The size of such parties and their accompanying guard parties was large in the early days of the siege. Sergeant Usherwood recorded that on 11 October 1854, for example, orders were for:

> 400 men at the Engineers' park in front of the Powder Mill [a windmill surrounded by a wall] at 4.30 pm to be furnished by the Light Division.
> The covering party of 1000 men from the 3rd & 4th Divisions.
> 3rd Division 300 men and 4th Division 600 men as Working parties.
> Covering parties 2000 men.

The following night, the numbers required were:

> Green Hill Works or sailors' Battery 600 men of 3rd Division
> 4th Division 200 men to be relieved by equal numbers at midnight, this party to be further aided by 100 seamen with ship's Carpenters [for the timber shoring] – Covering party 1000 men 4th Division – Frenchmen's Hill Works, 400 men of the 2nd Division to be relieved by an equal number at Midnight. Covering party 1000 men 2nd Division.

While digging trenches was hard physical work, the guard parties did not have it easy. Such parties might have to begin their stint at four in the morning and remain on duty until the same time the following day. The duty was sometimes reduced to 12 hours, but it had to be repeated four nights out of every seven, which was exhausting, especially in the freezing winter conditions. It was hard to stay awake and men sometimes fell asleep, the punishment for which was death if they were caught. And, of course, working parties retrieved the wounded and buried the dead.

Each regiment was expected to have one company always ready to turn out at a moment's notice should the Russians launch an attack. Night sorties by both sides were not uncommon, the object of which was to enter an enemy position, kill or capture whoever was in it, and retire before reinforcements could intervene. At the beginning of the siege, there were skirmishes between Russian and Allied piquets. Alarms in the night often resulted in heavy exchanges of fire, sometimes to no purpose. During the winter, some British and Russian soldiers came to an understanding at night, whereby those detailed for night duty would get out of their respective trenches and walk about freely in the open just to keep the circulation going, exchanging looks rather than shots. When British manpower was at its lowest during the winter due to the high rate of sickness among the troops, night work was sometimes nine days out of every ten. In the spring and summer of 1855, men might be detailed to occupy rifle pits in no-man's-land at night. The frequency of trench duty varied in the spring and summer of 1855 but it usually came round every third day.

Manning the trenches required a continuous and substantial presence of troops which involved rotating regiments into the line and out again. On one day in February 1855, for example, the 2nd Brigade Light Division provided troops for the trenches from the evening onwards for the next 24 hours: 100 men from the 19th Regiment, seventy-seven from the 77th, 167 from the 88th men and fifty-six from the 90th, totalling 400 men; the 88th Regiment provided fifty men for night piquet duty, to be replaced by men from the 77th the following morning, who would themselves be replaced by men from 19th the following evening. On another occasion, towards the end of March, the Light Division provided 1,200 men. Clearly, a degree of planning and organization was required if the transitions were to work smoothly. Manning strengths and dispositions were determined by the number of able-bodied men available for duty, as well as by the requirement of a given circumstance.

Fighting developed in three phases during an assault on a Russian position. First came the bombardment, then the assault by column and, if the attackers managed to get in amongst the defenders, a fierce hand-to-hand battle ensued in which the bayonet and the sword were the principal weapons. The column attack, in which a mass of men in close order pressed into the enemy and thereby broke him by weight of numbers and sheer determination with the aid of the bayonet, presented an unmissable target for gun batteries firing grape, which could cut down swathes of men at a time, and for Russian rifle fire. Hence the need for counter-battery fire before the assault to neutralize the enemy guns. Such bombardments were not always successful, however, leaving the Russian guns and gunners relatively unscathed. The Allied gunners often claimed greater success in these tasks than was born out by the reality encountered by the attacking infantry. Provided the infantry survived the grapeshot and enemy small-arms fire, they had to deal with the abbatis and chevaux de frise in front of the Russian positions before they could engage the enemy with the bayonet. When the British attacked the Redan on 17 June 1855, they were unable to cross the chevaux de frise or haul them aside. Those who tried were shot down.

During the course of the siege, the Allies mounted several assaults on Russian redoubts, notably the Malakoff and the Redan, while the Russians launched counter-attacks when they lost ground. In February 1855, Prince Gorchakov, who had replaced Menshikoff as commander of the Russian field army, made a feeble attempt to attack the British supply base at Balaklava, resulting in the Battle of Eupatoria in which the Turkish Army threw back the Russians. In August, Russian forces launched a major assault on the Allies to break the siege and reach Sebastopol by attacking from the south and east. The five-hour Battle of Traktir Bridge was a heavy defeat for the two Russian corps which engaged 37,000 French and Sardinian troops on the high ground above the River Chernaya. The Russian casualties were 3,200 dead and 5,000 wounded, while the total Allied losses were 1,700. The siege would not be broken by Russian attempts at relief and now it could only end one way. The question was how long the Russians in and around Sebastopol could continue to hold on. No longer did they believe that they could prevent the Allies from taking the city.

Allied attacks on the Russian positions were carried out with vigour and great courage by the infantrymen who had to cross open ground between the lines and scale the slopes of the redoubts. Unfortunately, coordination between French and British assaults on neighbouring strongpoints was often lacking. A case in point were the assaults of June 1855 when the objectives were the Malakoff and the Redan, adjacent redoubts of considerable defensive strength and capable of mutual support. This operation proceeded in two phases, the first of them on 7 June when the Mamelon, the White Works and the Quarries, the Russian outer defences, were taken. The fighting was hard and the Russians launched more than one counter-attack, so the price of the operation was high. While the Russians suffered 8,500 casualties, the Allies lost about 6,900 men in one day of fighting over a relatively small area of ground. Allied artillery fire and Russian counter-fire did not abate for several more days.

The second phase, in which the French assaulted the Malakoff while the British attacked the Redan, was a costly failure, largely because the Russians had reinforced the Malakoff and Redan following the Allied successes of a week earlier. The British had to wait until the French had taken the Malakoff before launching their own attack but were caught in crossfire when the French failed. The weight of Russian fire was too much for the French or the British to overcome by sheer courage alone. A surprising number of individual soldiers penetrated deep into the enemy positions but were then cut off. When it was obvious that the attack had failed, these isolated men lay low until they could find their way back to the British line. Assumed to have become casualties because of their failure to retire with the others, these returnees became known as 'resurrectionists'.

In any assault on a redoubt, it was not enough merely to cross the open ground between the Allied line and the Russian earthworks. Once reached, the attackers had to scale the Russian positions while under fire. Usherwood recorded that, in the 17 June attack on the Redan, the British force consisted of 100 riflemen in a covering party, seventy-two men carrying wool sacks, followed by:

> 400 men of 23rd & 34th Regiments under Lt. Col. Lysons together with sappers and seamen carrying ladders to be formed in the quarries and in the Russian trenches to the right of them which have been appropriated, leaving room on the left for a detachment of the same strength from the 4th Division, and the support which will be composed of 800 men from the 7th, 33rd, & 34th Regiments. These will be immediately followed by the working parties consisting of 200 Rifle Brigade – 100 from the 23rd Regiment and 100 from the 34th Regiment.

The attack was in five columns and each man was detailed to carry twenty additional rounds of ammunition in his haversack. On another occasion, the attack was in three columns and only ten extra rounds per man were carried. Certainly in the later assaults, the men dispensed with their shakos, donning forage caps instead, and removed other accoutrements which might otherwise impede them.

Right from the outset of the siege, the fighting was often at close quarters, which made it all the more ferocious. The socket bayonet was the main weapon. Its 17-inch blade was easily bent in the fighting, not so much when it penetrated but rather when it was withdrawn, as this was rarely done smoothly due to the victim turning and falling after being stabbed. The butt of the rifle was also used but sometimes men resorted to their fists and feet, or even to throwing stones when ammunition ran low. During an attack, especially when troops had to hold ground taken against strong counter-attacks, ammunition had to be brought forward in barrels, mostly by volunteers. Private Hughes of the Royal Fusiliers was awarded the Victoria Cross for his actions under fire during the British attack on the Quarries at the beginning of June 1855. He twice crossed open ground to bring barrels of ammunition to the men in the captured Quarries, smoking his pipe the whole time.

There was, surprisingly perhaps, always a problem with deserters and the failure to take the Redan was attributed by some to deserters who had gone over to the Russians in the days before the attack. Desertion, it seems, was a likely response to punishment meted out for misdemeanours large and small, although quite why deserting to the besieged Russians was considered a good idea is unclear. It was believed that the deserters revealed details of the forthcoming attack but it seems unlikely since the ordinary soldier was not privy to such information. No doubt the low morale of the troops at the defeat fostered such ideas.

In the assault on the Malakoff and the Redan, the Allies suffered 4,000 casualties, but the Russians lost 5,400 men. During July and August, Russian losses averaged about 350 men every day, despite the fact the Allies did not launch another serious assault until the beginning of September. At such a rate of attrition, the Russians were losing the battle for Sebastopol. Attrition was a tactical ploy adopted by the Allies, not chance. Artillery fire was constant and relentless, and on 19 August 1855 Light Division orders stipulated:

> that musketry fire should be kept up day and night from the advanced trench, Officers in command of parties will give their best attention to this essential duty, the object by night is to prevent the enemy coming outside to repair the damage done to his work. Therefore constant dropping fire with small parties firing vollies now and then at the edge of the ditch and embrasure will prevent this eventuality. The object by day is to keep a well directed fire into all embrasures though principally those from which Artillery is firing.

The final assault on the Malakoff and Redan began with a three-day bombardment, followed by a continuation on the day of the attack, 8 September. Unlike previous attacks, this one was well planned and well executed, although no new tactics were applied to the taking of these positions. It all came down to coordination and cooperation between the different elements engaged. This was achievable through the synchronization of watches, the first time this had ever been done. This time, the French took the Malakoff and the British the Redan with supporting fire by the French from the Malakoff when the British were initially repulsed. As was observed after the battle when standing in the Redan, the Malakoff was, indeed, the key position in the Russian defences and when it fell, the Redan was bound to fall as well. Although the Russians fought hard, with much of the fighting hand-to-hand, they were pushed back and on the 9th the Allies entered Sebastopol. The Allies lost 10,000 men in this assault, while the Russians suffered 13,000 casualties.

It is worth noting that the phrase forever associated with the British on the Western Front of the First World War, 'Lions led by Donkeys', was first coined in 1855 by the magazine *Punch* with reference to the British Army in the Crimea. As observed by Sergeant Gowling of the Royal Fusiliers:

More than half the officers did not know how to manoeuvre a company – all, or nearly so, had to be left to non commissioned officers – but it would be impossible to dispute their bravery, for they were brave unto madness. The writer has seen them lead at the deadly bayonet charges, and at the walls and bloodstained parapets of Sevastopol, as freely as they would have led off in a ballroom.

Most of the elements that are usually associated with trench warfare were features of the siege of Sebastopol. While the entrenchments were still very much of the form and structure that the sappers, engineers and infantrymen of the sieges of the war of Spanish Succession would have recognized, a number of new developments emerged. The construction of shelters and accommodation by the Russians in their redoubts was a foretaste of what was to be familiar on the Western Front sixty years later. The introduction of rifle pits and their subsequent joining together to make trenches was new. While counter-battery fire was not innovative, its importance in this sort of warfare was made very clear, and infantry assaults could not succeed without a preliminary bombardment to disrupt the enemy's ability to fight. This lesson was forgotten after the Crimean War until about 1916; the notion of artillery fire to suppress the enemy's ability to fight before an assault was replaced by the doctrine of destruction, made manifest in the battles on the Western Front of 1915 and 1916.

In the Crimea, the column assault on a fortified position was shown to be very vulnerable to sustained fire from enemy infantry and enemy artillery firing anti-personnel rounds. No tactical solution to avoid high casualties emerged, however, largely because the fighting at Sebastopol was conducted in the manner of a conventional siege. While the importance of mortars was made evident during the siege, no attempt was made to invent new weapons to overcome the difficulties posed by the trench warfare which developed as the siege went on. Raids, or sorties, patrols in no-man's-land, stands-to, night vigils, hand-to-hand fighting in trenches with the bayonet as the principal weapon and sniping, while not in themselves new, together formed a different sort of warfare, namely trench warfare. Trench warfare at Sebastopol and the miseries it brought were the future of warfare, not a dying vestige of siege warfare. Sebastopol was not seen by contempories as the dawn of a new form of warfare.

CHAPTER 5

Trench Warfare in the American Civil War

Five years after the end of the war in the Crimea which had witnessed the emergence of trench warfare as a mode of fighting distinct from siege warfare, another war erupted, this time on the other side of the world. Trench warfare would assert itself during the American Civil War, not only in sieges – such as those at Vicksburg and Petersburg – but as a development of open warfare. More significantly for future wars elsewhere, the form and structure of the fieldworks in America were more advanced than those built in the Crimea, reflecting not only the impact that rifled small arms and rifled artillery made on warfare but also a different philosophy with regard to entrenching compared to Europe. Indeed, in America, the importance accorded to the pick and spade in warfare as a whole predated the Civil War by two decades.

Many of the features that came to be associated with the trenches of the Western Front in the First World War were present during the Civil War. There were, of course, similarities with the entrenchments in the Crimea and the use of palisades, ditches, abbatis and chevaux de frise were common to both wars, but the entrenchments in America became more sophisticated than at Sebastopol and were used differently. Indeed, Union General George McClellan had been an observer at Sebastopol and his experience influenced his actions with regard to entrenchments in the Civil War. Moreover, while the trench fighting in the Crimea had been confined to the area around Sebastopol, in America trench warfare developed independently in several different locations and did so spontaneously, sometimes arising from siege but also from an inability to breach temporary earthworks thrown up as a standard feature of open battle. Here was the start of temporary entrenchments becoming semi-permanent positions. This battlefield development was apparent as early as the First Manassas in 1861 when, as a matter of course, troops dug temporary rifle pits and trenches for protection before the battle.

The development of trench warfare in America was due to a number of contributing factors, not the least of them being the indoctrination of officers at West Point, the US Staff College, in the importance of digging in at the earliest opportunity. While the Union and Confederate armies both made extensive use of rifled muskets and breech-loading rifles firing the Minié bullet, as well as rifled artillery, firepower was incidental to the attitude of general officers to the pick and the spade. Without official sanction to dig in on the battlefield, the troops on neither side would have dug trenches for the simple reason that they would have had neither the tools nor the opportunity to entrench. This approach set the Americans apart from the Europeans and may be attributed to the influence of Dennis Hart Mahan, a military engineer and one of the instructors at West Point. From 1830 onwards, Mahan taught the technical aspects of military science, including fieldworks, to many of the cadets who were to play significant roles in the Civil War. And Mahan advocated digging in as a routine measure on the battlefield.

In this, Mahan was merely taking his cue from the French. In the nineteenth century, the French were viewed as the leading exponents of modern tactical thinking, although one of the most influential tacticians was, in fact, Swiss, Antoine-Henri Jomini, who had served under the Napoleon. The French were keen advocates of the attack, and their tactics focused on how to achieve this efficiently and successfully; yet they also held that strong fortifications were crucial. While Jomini and other influential European tacticians who adhered to the French model were avidly followed in translation in America, a different slant was provided by Mahan who, as an engineer, emphasized the fortification aspects of the French tactics. The consequence was a tactical approach to battle that presented a dichotomy: attack yet dig in as well seemed to be the model put forward. Thus, the idea that digging in was a direct consequence of increasing firepower on the battlefield is somewhat undermined by Mahan, whose approach was followed slavishly by his contemporary, General Halleck. However, it is evident that the practice of entrenching occurred long before the introduction of rifled artillery or rifled muskets. Examples of digging in can be found in the wars against Napoleon, for example. The significance of such entrenchments lay in their purpose. Prior to the American Civil War, entrenchments were intended to impede an attacker rather than protect the defender. A shift in the balance of this relationship occurred largely because of the rise in firepower, so protection for the defender became the main point of entrenching. The problem lay in the unavoidable consequence that, by digging in, the attacker turned himself into a defender while in the process of attacking. It became very obvious early in the American Civil War that direct assaults on defensive positions, in which the defenders were armed with rifles, could not be successful if the attacking infantry had to cross a lot of open ground before they could engage the enemy with the bayonet.

This same dilemma had faced the armies at Sebastopol but, because they were conducting a siege of more or less traditional form, no attempt was made to address the problem. In America, however, the problem could not be ignored and this contributed to the rise in the use of entrenchments in situations that were not siege but battle. As a consequence, two opposing tactical dilemmas emerged: how to cross the open ground over which a deep lethal zone made massed infantry assault very costly, which reinforced the practice of entrenching as part of the process of battle and prevented a speedy resolution on the battlefield; and how to engage an entrenched enemy while your own forces were also entrenched. The development of situations in which stalemate arose, when siege was not the intention, was an obstacle to decision on the battlefield, especially as the war progressed. Thus, a means by which the deadlock could be broken without causing huge numbers of casualties became a priority by the middle of the war. At the same time, entrenchment by attacking troops became the norm so that the fluidity of mobile warfare was interrupted.

It is clear that the predisposition for armies to adopt trench warfare as a mode of fighting rather than engage in open battle was attributable neither to technology nor to any inadequacies concerning tactical doctrines relating to the assault, although inadequacies were certainly there. There is also the point that, at least as far as the Union was concerned, industrial might provided munitions on a huge scale, which contributed to the effect of firepower. There is no doubt that firepower played a significant role in the development of trench warfare, but only after trench warfare had become an accepted mode of fighting; and its role has tended to be overemphasized. Firepower in the Civil War did not in itself lead to trench warfare. Rather it evolved from caution and a military engineer's interpretation of the role of entrenchments, views that were expressed verbally to cadets at West Point and more widely disseminated via his treatises. Such views were readily accepted and reiterated by others. As already pointed out, the use of defensive works by armies in the field to avoid being taken by surprise had a long history, but in America such entrenchments became an end in themselves. Equally, the massed armies of essentially armed civilians also contributed to a rise in trench warfare due to the fact that such men were less skilled tactically in the assault than the much smaller number of regulars. This meant that the enlisted and conscripted men were more prone to digging in to protect themselves from hostile fire when a more vigorous assault might otherwise carry the enemy position. Their caution was reinforced by the growing emphasis placed on the value of entrenchments by the officers in command. This became a vicious circle. However, these factors were not necessarily additive and their individual effects varied enormously according to circumstances.

Put simply, the desire for individual infantrymen to dig in and return fire from a position of safety, rather than press on through the enemy's fire to engage him at the point of a bayonet, was not discouraged. Indeed, by the middle of the war, commanders tended to have less stomach to fight battles by direct confrontation of masses of men because of the numbers of casualties which it caused. Part of the trouble was the poor understanding of the translated French tactics by individual commanders of regiments engaged in a battle. Indeed, there was a tendency to misapply completely what was set out in the manuals and launch an assault in such a way that it played to the strengths of the firepower of the defenders rather than diminished them. Each commander made his own interpretation of his orders within the overall plan of attack, using his take on the tactical methods set out in the manuals. Consequently, there was often a lack of cooperation and coordination, with chaos and disorder often resulting. Digging in became a much safer alternative to protracted battle. Instead, protracted stalemate ensued.

This inevitably gave rise to the notion that warfare in the 1860s was heavily biased towards the entrenched defender. In other words, assaults were bound to fail because the defence was too powerful. In fact, assaults tended to fail for other reasons, not the least being the tentative manner in which they were launched and carried through. Impregnibility of strong defence became a self-fulfilling prophecy. Thus, indecisive stalemate became the preferred mode of fighting for many, but not all, commanders. This raises the question of whether the nature of the fighting in the American Civil War and more especially the rise of trench warfare during the war, can be seen as an inevitable change in the way in which wars were being fought. And, indeed, whether the American Civil War did provide a foretaste of wars to come.

The first thing to consider is the nature of the entrenchments dug by both the Confederate and Union armies and compare them with those dug in the Crimea. The most obvious difference between the trenches of the American Civil War and those at Sebastopol was the American use of logs to provide loopholed head cover to enable riflemen to shoot with relative safety. No such protection was provided for entrenched troops in the Crimea. Clearly, such cover was only feasible if there were areas of woodland nearby. Various forms of head protection were set on top of the parapet. One consisted of a loopholed or notched baulk of timber set along the top of the parapet, the apertures allowing riflemen to fire on attacking infantry without exposing themselves to enemy fire. A similar effect was achieved with a head log supported at its ends between two sets of four small stakes driven into the top of the parapet. Head logs were first used by Union troops of XII Corps at Chancellorsville and Gettysburg in 1863. They used head logs again in 1864 during the Atlanta Campaign. It would appear that the use of a log in this way was particular to these troops. The log rested on two baulks of timber called skids, set between the stakes and extending back to the rear of the trench. The skids had two functions: firstly, to allow a narrow gap between the log and the parapet through which the riflemen could shoot; and secondly, to prevent the log from being rolled on to the men in the trench if it was hit by roundshot or a shell – in such an event, it rolled over the timber baulks rather than into the trench. A third form of parapet protection consisted of sandbags arranged to form loopholes in much the same way as they had been used in the trenches at Sebastopol.

The form or profile of a trench in the American Civil War was not very different to that of a trench at Sebastopol. Again, there was no firestep and no parados. A trench comprised a ditch and a raised bank to the front of it, the parapet, which sloped away in the direction of the enemy. Sometimes a ditch was dug in front of the trench, the earth from which being used to build up the parapet. To shoot through an aperture, the riflemen leaned against the sloping inner face of the parapet to steady his aim. Although timbers were not used as head protection at

Sebastopol, their use in America was an obvious alternative to sandbags when there was a plentiful supply of trees. In this sense, such timber protection did not represent a new departure.

The trenches were made more robust with addition of gabions and wickerwork and timber reinforcements, along with fascines, as in the Crimea, and these tended to be used in the sieges as tradition dictated. These earthworks were mostly intended to protect men from small-arms fire rather than from artillery. Only in sieges did this latter requirement become a desirable feature of some elements of the fortifications, due to the more prolonged nature of a siege in which the enemy shelled the attacker and vice versa. The defences constructed in America followed the European models in form, although the Americans used more timber in the construction of shelters and blockhouses, some of which resembled the archetypal log cabin that is forever associated with settlers. The Russians had built similar structures in some of their redoubts for the accommodation of the troops manning them. The construction of bomb-proof structures within siege lines was not entirely a departure from the European model since the Russians had built bomb-proof shelters in their redoubts. However, the extent of their use in the Civil War and the form they took went beyond European practice. Indeed, the American bomb-proof shelters were akin to the dugouts of the Western Front. Thus, the dugout was fifty years old by the time of the First World War. Typically, bomb-proof structures were intended to protect magazines from shellfire, but they were also used to shelter troops during bombardments. The form varied, but in general they were below ground level and reinforced with timbers and a deep layer of earth. Some, however, were essentially blockhouses with additional reinforcement. And, like blockhouses, bomb-proof shelters were usually provided with loopholes to enable the occupants to fire on their attackers.

Such structures that were above ground level resembled the ferroconcrete blockhouses of the First and Second World Wars. Indeed, towards the end of the war, the Americans built casemates to house cannon and these too resembled the steel-reinforced concrete casemates of the world wars, especially those built along the Atlantic Wall and the West Wall. Again, the Americans made full use of timber in their construction, as well as a lot of earth to make them bomb-proof. Their design was borrowed from those in permanent stone-built fortifications in which they were, of course, well known. But their use in fieldworks during the Civil War was novel. Had ferroconcrete been invented by the time of the Civil War, it is highly likely that some siege works would have included ferroconcrete blockhouses and casemates. Normally, artillery and mortars were placed in embrasures built into the siege works, constructed in much the same way as the British, French and Russians had done at Sebastopol. Thus, the American siege works differed only in detail from those at Sebastopol.

One aspect of defence which had not appeared in the Crimea was the wire entanglement. Barbed wire had yet to be invented but smooth telegraph wire still presented a considerable obstacle when stretched between trees to form thick entanglements. The Confederates used wire in this way at Bermuda Hundred during Grant's Overland Campaign of 1864. Besides wire, similar obstacles to those employed in the Crimea were used in America. Such obstacles as chevaux de frise, abbatis, pits, palisades and fraises were used in siege operations rather than in conjunction with trenches dug in the field as a prelude to or during battle.

The rifle pit which had been employed so successfully by the Russians at Sebastopol was also used in the Civil War and these, too, were more associated with siege operations than entrenchments on the battlefield. Nevertheless, they were also used on the battlefield, notably by the Army of the Tennessee, commanded by Sherman, in 1864. These pits, initially only large enough to protect one man, tended to be dug wherever it was possible to take advantage of existing natural cover, such as a rock or a fallen tree. Subsequently, they were extended sideways so that several pits were joined up to form a trench. This was all done under cover of darkness and in front of the main trench line. The Russians had done the same thing at Sebastopol. Indeed, both in the Crimea and in America, digging was always done at night, preferably with the protection of a skirmish line, the pits or trenches being covered by brushwood or some other material to hide them.

In most respects, fieldworks and siege works constructed in America were essentially the same as those built at Sebastopol, although the bomb-proof dugout or shelter was more widely used during the Civil War than in the Crimea. The use of wire entanglements was a new development, but the main difference between the entrenchments in the American Civil War and the Crimean War lay in how they were used, especially on the battlefield. As already discussed, unlike the Russians, British or French, the Americans had a predisposition to use entrenchments in battle, although their use was derived from European practice. The Americans simply took the tactical use of entrenchments in a different direction. Indeed, so wedded to the trench were American troops that some generals, the Confederate General Hood especially, bemoaned the fact that soldiers would not get on with a battle because they insisted on digging in. Hood, Sherman and Sheridan all condemned digging in because it prevented their troops from closing with the enemy on the battlefield, so that a decisive outcome was often lacking. While the soldiers may have felt themselves to be protected from enemy fire when in a trench, this very sense of self-preservation also dissuaded them from fighting at close quarters. Thus, there was a tendency to engage in firefights rather than in bayonet charges.

It is clear that trench fighting developed in two ways, namely as an element of siege but also as an element of battle. While the sieges were in many respects similar to the siege of Sebastopol, in that Civil War sieges developed along traditional lines, the use of entrenchments in battle was not only a new departure but one which promised to reinforce the notion that firepower and mobility on the battlefield were mutually exclusive. The Confederates became particularly adept at digging formidable entrenchments within 24 hours of halting, especially during Grant's Overland Campaign in 1864. This dichotomy was to reappear again in

Manchuria during the Russo-Japanese War of 1904–05, and more dramatically on the Western Front during 1915 and 1916. Essentially, it came down to an argument over whether firepower could be overcome by manpower if the infantryman was imbued with sufficient élan. That firepower could be overcome, inevitably and invariably, was a battle philosophy embraced by the French, in particular, during the course of the nineteenth century and one which they still held to be valid during the first two years of the First World War. Curiously, while the American tactical approach to battle was based on the French model, they also took to heart the notion of fieldworks as an essential element in warfare.

The earliest clashes in the Civil War gave an indication of how the nature of the fighting was likely to develop. While it was not immediately apparent to those involved in the fighting that entrenchments would become essential features of many battles, nevertheless, the fact that trenches were made ready before the start of battle gave a clear indication that traditional forms of open battle were less likely to occur than siege-like fighting. Indeed, there was no reason at the start of the war for anyone to assume that battles in the Civil War would turn out to be so inconclusive. The sense of cautiousness that a dependence on entrenchments created was a major factor in the lack of decision in battle during the Civil War. The Battle of Big Bethel, fought on 10 June 1861, provides a good example of the way in which entrenchments and excessive caution led to the wrong conclusions being drawn by the participants. This, the first battle of the war, was not trench warfare, of course, but it did demonstrate a reluctance for close battle on both sides, and a preference to go to ground rather than face hostile fire. However, it would be entirely misleading to suggest that this reluctance manifested itself in total avoidance of close combat. On the contrary, there were many fiercely fought close-combat encounters within battles.

The 1,200 Confederate troops at Big Bethel, Virginia, had been positioned to prevent Union forces from advancing along the Virginia Peninsular. At the beginning of June 1861, they were approached by 3,500 Union troops in two columns under the command of Brigadier General Pierce. As the Union forces got closer, the Confederate troops withdrew to a redoubt they had built beyond Marsh Creek, not far from Big Bethel, and waited. The Union troops advanced upon the redoubt but were suddenly confronted by volleys from the men concealed in the trenches and were beaten back. Part of the Union force then tried to outflank the Confederate positions but they too failed and the Union troops retired in disarray, leaving the Confederates where they were. There were seventy-nine Union casualties of whom only seven were fatal, while the entrenched Confederates lost only one man, with seven others wounded. The Confederate troops did not even remain in place after the Union troops fell back but withdrew a few hours later.

The conclusion drawn from this was that entrenched troops presented an insurmountable obstacle on which an assault would founder, especially when they presented disciplined fire. What it actually demonstrated was the chaotic discipline and poor tactical sense of the Union troops, as well as a reluctance to press home an attack, while on the Confederate side, a reluctance to engage in a stand-up fight, resorting to fieldworks for protection, meant that an opportunity to inflict a more serious blow on the Union troops had been missed, again through poor tactical sense.

The Battle of Manassas, or First Bull Run, fought six weeks later on 21 July, was a much larger encounter involving 18,000 troops on both sides, with thousands more in reserve. This, too, involved entrenchments when there was no sound reason to rely on them in what was supposed to be, and should have been, a battle of fire and manoeuvre. Again, entrenchments were dug by the troops of the Confederate Army of the Potomac before the battle with every intention that the fight should be one in which the Confederates defended a piece of ground rather than engage the enemy in battle. The Confederates dug rifle pits and entrenched themselves along the River Bull Run, then fell back to these positions as the Union troops approached. They also laid abbatis in front of their positions. This time, the Union forces were also prepared to dig defensive positions of their own, a rather curious way of advancing on and attacking an enemy, and before the start of the battle, they built a redoubt to hold the right flank. It is clear that the notion of battle in the sense of manoeuvring to engage an enemy, then advancing on him in column and firing, following up with the bayonet, was not how the armies on either side intended to fight but preferred to defend or take ground instead.

The result was a farce. When the Union troops advanced to clear the abbatis, they were comprehensively beaten back by the Confederate fire and no attack was actually launched by the Union troops. Yet again, they fell back in disarray and fled the field. The casualties suffered on both sides were correspondingly higher than those inflicted at Big Bethel a few weeks earlier. The Confederates lost just under 2,000 men, of whom nearly 400 were killed, while the Union Army lost about 1,600 of whom 460 were killed, but almost as many men were captured as were wounded and killed. This only served to reinforce the belief that entrenchments were essential to battle and that attackers would always fail to take the enemy position. In consequence the Confederates built ever bigger and stronger fieldworks to defend Manassas Junction, which they subsequently abandoned in March of the following year.

While neither of these encounters – they hardly qualify as battles – degenerated into trench warfare, because one side gave up and left the scene before this could develop, nevertheless, it is evident that as soon as both sides decided to stay and fight over a piece of ground, trench warfare was bound to follow. Equally, it is clear that it had little to do with firepower and everything to do with tactical approaches to the conduct of battle. Unfortunately, the failure of the Union troops to conduct themselves with greater fortitude and better tactical sense at Manassas again led to the conclusion that firepower and fieldworks were the key to victory on the battlefield. It was hardly surprising, then, that siege should become a major factor in the war, since army commanders were already predisposed to fighting from defensible positions.

Indeed, the development of siege-like warfare on the battlefield was an inevitable escalation of defence and counter-defence. The notion of mobile battle began to diminish as a desirable mode of operation. The Battle of Williamsburg in May 1862 showed how siege-like some of the operations were becoming. When McClellan advanced towards Richmond after the disaster of Manassas and found that he had to deal with Yorktown, he lay siege in order to counter the considerable earthwork defences which the Confederates had built around it, mostly since the Battle of Manassas. He spent a month constructing siege lines from which to engage Yorktown's defences, only to find that the Confederates abandoned them almost as soon as the first Union guns opened fire. General Johnston, the Confederate commander, took his troops out of Yorktown and fell back to a fortified position at Williamsburg. The Union Army pursued them and the fighting that followed was a mixture of open battle and ground-taking operations. This time, however, it was the Union troops occupying two abandoned Confederate redoubts on the flank who repulsed a Confederate attempt to take back the position from where the Union troops had started to shell the Confederate positions. Once again, the impregnable nature of well-defended earthworks was impressed on all those involved.

It should be stressed, however, that the use of earthworks in battle and especially for artillery was nothing new, nor indeed different from the accepted tactics. Indeed, as already mentioned, earthworks had been used for artillery in the English Civil War some 200 years earlier. What set the actions in America apart from those in England in the seventeenth century and, indeed, from those on the continent of Europe during the eighteenth century, was the emphasis right from the start in the American Civil War on fighting for ground rather than to defeat the enemy in battle, although this was to change in 1864 during Grant's campaign. While this may seem improbable given that the war was not about territory, nevertheless, it is evident that much of the fighting was not about destroying or defeating the enemy but about denying him ground. This was not, of course, the intention of any commander but because of the reliance on digging in at every opportunity, the impetus to close with the enemy was often absent so that commanders contented themselves with taking ground away from the enemy, convincing themselves that they had achieved victory in so doing. This sort of action did little to diminish the fighting capabilities of the South, although it played to the strengths of the North in that it permitted the industrialization of the war to proceed, and indeed accelerate. The process of industrialization was to have a profound effect on the trench warfare that was to develop later in the war.

While it would be misleading to suggest that all operations during the Civil War, large or small, had a basis in holding or taking static lines, nevertheless, this was a dominant feature of many battles as the war progressed, even when such ground contests were only minor aspects of the main fight. The year 1863 was dominated by siege operations in which trench warfare of the form seen at Sebastopol began to emerge as a principal mode of warfare. Moreover, battles such at those at Chancellorsville, Gettysburg and Chickamauga all involved some degree of entrenchment. Sieges, such as those at Vicksburg, Knoxville and Chattanooga, became more akin to the sort of trench warfare seen on the Western Front in the First World War than to sieges of the past, such as those at Saragossa (1808), Cadiz (1810) and the operations at the Lines of Torres Vedras (1810) during the Peninsular War; not to mention the storming of Cuidad Rodrigo and Bardajoz in 1812, or, indeed, the sieges during the Greek War of Independence 1823–8, or even the siege of Pueblo during the US-Mexican War of 1846–8, the war in which many of the principal commanders of the Civil War learned their craft.

Nevertheless, battlefield tactics evolved during the Civil War to deal with the problem of taking entrenched positions. The tactic of skirmish lines was well known and had been used in the Napoleonic Wars. This was developed into a raiding style of attack, a tactic that re-emerged during the First World War, although it is unclear whether this simply evolved during the Civil War by chance due to a favourable combination of local circumstances, or whether it came about by conscious design. The raiding technique was a form of infiltration by small bodies of men detailed for the task, a few hundred at most, and was usually carried out at night. The object was often to take prisoners. When extended to larger formations, such as a brigade, success depended on favourable weather conditions, such as fog, to conceal the infiltrators from the enemy, or had to be carried out at dawn. Such tactics proved to be very effective in overcoming entrenched troops. The difference between the raid of the American Civil War and its Western Front cousin was considerable, however, so that they bore little resemblance to each other, tactically or operationally. Nevertheless, the Civil War raid used the same principals as the raids of the First World War, namely planning, stealth and dispersal.

Infiltration and raiding techniques in the Civil War were developed in direct response to the problem of dealing with entrenched troops. Such techniques were all very well but infiltrators and raiders could not take an enemy position by themselves as their numbers were too small. To take advantage of the confusion they caused, the main force had to follow up and pass through them to engage the enemy when they were at they most vulnerable. This tended not to happen simply because the infiltrators themselves did not follow through, but fell back to report on the strengths of the enemy positions, which rendered the exercise somewhat redundant. Thus, the tactical value of raiding and infiltrating was not generally understood. Generally, even brigade-sized infiltration groups were only used to take prisoners and gather intelligence, rather than as part of a major assault. Nevertheless, such techniques brought both the Confederates and the Federals tantalizingly close to a new form of assault; they just did not know it.

The first action in which the Confederates entrenched their entire frontage facing a Union army before engaging the enemy was at the Battle of Mine Run in November 1863, forcing a stalemate, but it was during the campaigns of 1864 that trench warfare developed significantly beyond the construction of earthworks for protection to become a mode of warfare. This was due in part to Grant's tactic of maintaining contact with Lee's army. Here was a contradiction, however. On the one hand, firepower was not the cause of trench warfare but its effects were heightened because of it, drawing out battle into slogging matches of attrition in which high casualties were an inevitable consequence. The issue of the effects of firepower in forcing men to dig in are still contentious, as it pertains to the arguments about whether tactical change is led by technological change or whether technology is incidental to other factors which bring about change. However, it is the combination of firepower with tactical doctrines which decides the nature of battle, not firepower alone. If evidence is required that this is a dynamic relationship in which the balance decides whether mobility or stalemate ensues, you have to look no further than the Western Front in which this dynamic was eventually resolved. The dilemma of whether to opt for firepower or mobility was an issue that dogged tactics throughout much of the nineteenth century and remained unresolved well into the First World War.

While it has been argued that the soldiers of the Civil War dug in so readily because their officers had learned this approach to battle at West Point, and the manuals reinforced the idea, the effect of firepower and the issue of caution on the battlefield arising from an unwillingness by troops to close with the enemy, gives rise to the notion that the shock of combat reduced their ability to fight so that they dug in. There is no question that compared to European armies of the period, American troops showed a far greater readiness to entrench. Whether the European soldier was hardier and more resilient, less of an individual and more willing to obey orders, compared to the American soldier, is questionable. However, the discipline in European armies of the time was probably much tougher than in the American armies of the Civil War. The armies of the Civil War were not professional, being militarized civilians more than professional soldiers. This inevitably had an impact on how such troops conducted themselves in battle since most would have received no more than a few months training before being sent on a campaign or into battle. On the other hand, those who survived their first combat would have learned a great deal from the experience which would have enhanced their ability to fight. Which brings us back to the fact that digging in was an American way of war and had little do with firepower or experience on the battlefield.

The apotheoses of entrenched warfare were the Overland and Atlanta Campaigns conducted by the Union in 1864. These two aggressive operations, the former under General Grant who commanded the Army of the Potomac, the other General Butler's Army of the James, were designed to operate cooperatively in a pincer to capture Richmond and thereby crush the South. They are usually described as relentless pursuits of the Confederate forces which were trying to halt the Union armies. However, this is a little disingenuous since entrenched warfare was the usual mode of battle in both campaigns, rather than open battle of manoeuvre and shock assault. Indeed, so firmly established was the notion of entrenching that the fieldworks put up by both sides as preludes to battle, especially in the Overland battles, were unprecedented in the war and were only exceeded by those constructed at sieges such as Vicksburg and Petersburg. Spotsylvania and Cold Harbor, major battles in the Overland Campaign, were engagements which few European soldiers would have recognized as battles at that time. Indeed, these battles were, in many respects, more similar to the First Battle of Ypres and the First Battle of Champagne in 1914 than they were to Inkerman (1854) or Sedan (1870). However, such comparisons can only be taken so far because there were many more differences than there were similarities. Not the least among the differences was the terrain of the Wilderness which, although mostly flat, was wild, heavily wooded and crossed by large rivers, whereas European battlefields tended to be farmland or open countryside. Indeed, the fighting in the Wilderness resembled that in the Hürtgen Forest in late 1944 and early 1945; the Wilderness favoured defence as the woods and the heavy undergrowth presented a real obstacle to progress if Grant's troops left the roads and went overland. Lee used this to full advantage by entrenching the Army of Northern Virginia at strategic locations along the 60-mile route of the Army of the Potomac. It was at these locations that the main battles occurred.

A major factor in the entrenching of the Overland battles was Grant's need to remain in contact with his enemy. Thus, for the Confederates not to entrench would have been foolhardy as that would have left them vulnerable to a surprise assault by the Federal troops. Equally, the Army of the Potomac entrenched so that its troops could get as close to the enemy was possible, then engaged them in small-arms fire and generally harassed them. Not only did this put pressure on the Confederates but it allowed the Union troops to do so without launching assaults on the Confederate positions, while presenting a threat to do just that. The Union trenches were only temporary expedients from which the next attack would be launched, while those of the Confederates were intended to be much more of an obstacle. Lee's intention was to impede or stop Grant's progress and, whereas Grant would have preferred open battle, Lee took advantage of his situation and used entrenchments as barriers to Grant's army. In this respect, the fighting was more about attrition and taking and holding ground. The Confederates were primarily interested in making the campaign so costly for Grant that it would end in failure.

It is worth noting that although both the Confederates and the Federals had large engineer contingents, most of the fieldworks built during the campaign were dug by ordinary infantrymen, albeit under the guidance of the engineers. This was to be a recurring theme in later wars in which trench warfare figured prominently, especially on the Western Front. It is also worth noting that one of the tasks of the engineers was to observe, survey and record the enemy's fieldworks. Clearly, along with maps, which at this time were less than reliable despite the tremendous efforts that were put into creating new ones during the war by both sides, specific information about the location, form and extent of enemy fortifications was crucial to an assault or, indeed, to a successful defence.

The trench systems that were constructed at Spotsylvania and Cold Harbor, for example, resembled the networks that were subsequently constructed in the Russo-Japanese War and on the Western Front. Nevertheless, much of the entrenchments were hastily prepared and trenches were sometimes no more than scrapes in the ground with some timber, stones or earth piled up in front to form a rudimentary parapet. Similarly, Confederate artillery was placed in advanced positions, sometimes without infantry support, but protected by logs and hidden with brushwood, although in the Battle of the Wilderness, the trees were too dense and the undergrowth too thick for artillery to operate effectively. In the series of engagements that were the Battle of the Wilderness, most casualties were caused by small-arms fire. The vegetation hindered both Confederate and Federal alike.

When both sides entrenched, a no-man's-land between the opposing lines was created, although there were no real instances of either side trying to dominate it except by rifle fire, which was a poor substitute for patrolling and raiding. However, it was usual practice to put a line of skirmishers into the no-man's-land to prevent the line being hit by a surprise attack at night. Sometimes, as at Cold Harbor, skirmishers were sent out into no-man's-land in broad daylight to deal with enemy snipers, not always successfully.

Of particular significance was the creation of a salient at Spotsylvania as this pertained to the holding of ground, rather than to a convenient jumping-off point for an assault. Indeed, salients by their very nature make their occupiers more vulnerable than if they are holding a more linear front line, especially as they tend to attract more attention from the enemy on three sides because they mount operations to pinch out the salient. The Mule Shoe salient at Spotsylvania, held by Lee's Confederates, proved to be costly ground for Confederate and Federal alike.

One of the problems that Grant's men faced when attacking their well-entrenched enemy was uneven resistance. This often left the attackers' flanks exposed when they tried to exploit a local success. It happened time again when a body of Federal troops succeeded in breaching the Confederate line, allowing them to make a deep penetration of the enemy positions, only to discover that friendly troops to their left and right had failed to keep up or had been repulsed, leaving them isolated. The breaking-in troops ran the risk of being cut off, killed and captured once the Confederates realized they had a group of Federals behind their lines. There was no choice but to withdraw such as happened during Federal attacks on the Confederate position at Laurel Hill during the fighting at Spotsylvania in 1864. This sort of action, whereby local success could be rapidly converted into a costly failure, was a feature of trench warfare and by no means unique to the Overland Campaign of 1864.

Many of the battles of the Overland Campaign tended to be dragged out for around ten days in a series of violent engagements which were often inconclusive, due in part to Lee moving his forces about the battlefield to wherever they were most needed. However, the protracted nature of the battles, such as Spotsylvania, which lasted eleven days, and Cold Harbor which lasted ten, reflected the fact that they were centred on trench warfare rather than on fire and manoeuvre in open country.

The fighting in the Mule Shoe salient at Spotsylvania epitomized the bloodiness of trench warfare. The Mule Shoe was dug by men of General Richard Ewell's II Corps on 8 May, in the dark, although troops continued to work on it for the next three days. They used whatever tools that were to hand as there was a shortage of spades. Its outline trace was dictated to a large extent by the nature of the terrain which rose towards the north; it was essential to deny the higher ground to the Federals but the presence of Union troops nearby meant that the line had to turn south again. It was a quadrilateral strongpoint, at the apex of an arrowhead position that extended back several miles on each side. One of the corners of the Mule Shoe formed the apex of the whole position, pointing north towards the oncoming Army of the Potomac. The base of the salient and the quadrilateral was not dug until several days into the battle, as a last line of defence for those inside the Mule Shoe. Within the salient there were two unfortified houses and one reserve line running across the width of the salient, and half way down it. A short support line ran parallel with part of the north-west facing line which projected slightly from the line of the north-west face of the salient.

It was a high-risk strategy to build such a position as the Mule Shoe because it would be both the focus of attack for the Union forces and vulnerable to assault from three sides. Indeed, the extent of its vulnerability was not apparent to its builders as they built it in the dark, but in the cold light of day Confederate and Federal alike could see that the Mule Shoe was a potential death trap for those inside it. Moreover, it was too big. At its widest, it was more than a mile across and nearly a mile in depth, so that the area inside the salient was about 1 square mile. While fallen trees were used for the parapet, the entire work was hastily put together and it lacked strength in depth. Indeed, it lacked real substance along its entire trace as it had no reinforced sections and work to strengthen it continued during the battle. By the time of the second assault on the Mule Shoe on 12 May, the Confederate positions had been strengthened by the addition of traverses built from earth reinforced with logs. Traverses consisted of 20-foot banks build at 40-foot intervals along a trench to divide it into bays, so that it was no longer one continuous parapetted ditch, thereby offering some protection against enfilade. Traverse and parapet were 3–4 feet wide but gave no more than about a foot of protection in height for a man standing in the trench. Moreover, the trenches were not built to the same standard everywhere and some areas were considerably weaker than others.

The Union troops did not simply launch an assault on the Confederate positions when they made contact. On the contrary; they dug in and formed a trench line facing the Confederate trenches. And they, too, continued to reinforce their positions during the fighting. Once it became clear that the entrenched armies were not going to decide the issue quickly, the problem of holding the line had to be addressed. It was all very well entrenching but the entire contingent of a regiment or a brigade could not be expected to remain on duty in the trenches day and night with no respite. So began the night watch by a detail of the troops, the rest being awoken just before sunrise to stand to in case of a dawn attack.

The first assault on the Mule Shoe was made by Colonel Upton with 5,000 troops from twelve regiments on the west face of the Mule Shoe. Unfortunately, the point chosen for the attack had a support line 100 yards behind it which had gone undetected. The support line acted with the front line to funnel any attacker to the north against the apex of the position, rather than into the open ground inside the salient. Tactically, this section of the salient was a poor target. A supporting attack by 1,500 men under the command of Brigadier General Mott was launched on Upton's left flank but, due to confusion, it was launched too soon and too far north of Upton's intended attack and was repulsed with ease.

Upton attacked after a half-hour artillery bombardment, the first wave his men crossing the 200 yards of open ground to the Confederate position too quickly for the Confederates to respond and, with the support of the second wave, they broke in, capturing 1,000 men including the Confederate commander of that section of the Mule Shoe. Now Confederate reinforcements came up and, although the support line was abandoned, Upton's men were contained. A quick counter-attack left Upton with nowhere to go but back whence he came, and he retreated. The break-in never became a breakthrough and it was all over in less than an hour. The failure of the attack illustrated the problems of breaking through trench lines which the enemy was prepared to defend vigorously. Moreover, it highlighted the fact that flank support was essential to success. In this short fight, Confederate casualties were 1,500 men – the prisoners taken by Upton were released in the counter-attack – while Upton lost 1,000 men, all three waves of attackers having been committed along with Upton's reserves.

The execution and outcome of Upton's assault was open to interpretation and Grant chose to see it as a partial success. He decided that a larger attack of the same sort would succeed. Here he was reinforcing failure, however, because he ignored the flank support element of Upton's failure to convert break-in into breakthrough. Neither did he consider how the break-in troops might be reinforced to exploit a breach. Instead, sheer weight of numbers was supposed to carry the day. The attack was to be made with 20,000 men at dawn on 12 May. Lee misinterpreted the movement of Federal troops forming up for the assault and drew the conclusion that Grant was breaking contact to move further south, so he began withdrawing artillery and infantry from the salient ready for the pursuit, thereby leaving some areas of the line very weak. But suspicion that the noises detected by Confederate piquets heralded an attack led to the order to withdraw being rescinded at the last moment. When the assault came, the guns were being returned to their former positions.

The attack went in against the apex. Crossing open ground, the Federals reached the abbatis which were 50 yards deep and started clearing them without hindrance. The Federals swarmed over the parapets into the trenches, sweeping all before them in fierce hand-to-hand combat. This was bayonet work, yet some men resorted to using their rifles as clubs, indicating a lack of proper training with the bayonet. The morning drizzle made many of the rifles misfire. While the Federals succeeded in getting into the apex of the salient, those attacking on the left flank in the same place as Upton's earlier assault were held, the support line playing a significant role in this. When the Confederates counter-attacked, the Federals were pushed back. A situation developed in which the two enemies were separated by a single traverse and there followed what might be described as classic trench fighting, some Confederate troops moving from traverse to traverse, engaging in savage close fighting with the Federals. Nevertheless, the Federals now held about a mile of the line. The Confederates lost twenty-four guns and the Federals had taken 1,000 prisoners.

While Grant's faith in the power of numbers to carry the day appeared to have been justified, discipline and order among the Federals began to break down. Scattered groups advanced towards the reserve line and were met with rifle fire. They beat a hasty retreat. Counter-attacks pushed the main Federal force back up and out of the salient. In the meantime, another assault on the line by fresh troops failed. The Federal troops were now mostly outside and on the wrong side of the parapets, while those still in the trenches were effectively cut off. After about six hours of fighting, the situation was confused. Confederate and Federal reinforcements added to the chaos but the Federals were held. It was at this juncture that Confederate troops dug the base of the quadrilateral, known as Lee's Last Line. Some trenches became overcrowded because the reinforcements had nowhere to go. Stalemate developed. Neither Federal nor Confederate troops sheltering in a traverse or on one side of a parapet could move; rifle fire was too intense and anyone venturing round an enemy-held traverse or over a parapet was likely to be shot or bayoneted.

To make matters worse, the constant rain turned the ground into a quagmire. The mud was especially bad in the trenches due to the constant tramping of many boots in the overcrowded conditions. Indeed, in many places it was ankle deep, but in others it was knee deep. Water pooled in every hollow and hole in the trenches, in the traverses and on the open ground. The fighting in the trenches of the Mule Shoe lasted 21 hours. It only ceased because of the rain, the mud and exhaustion. Early the next morning, the rain had turned to fog which obscured everything. The result was stalemate. No one on either side could move without attracting close-range rifle fire, although the rain made many muskets misfire. This was a protracted firefight between desperate infantrymen.

Although a few guns were brought into action to fire canister, the conditions were not suitable for artillery. Several Coehorn mortars were set up to fire into the Confederate trenches in the West Angle of the salient, but the correct range was difficult to achieve and most bombs either missed entirely or landed in friendly positions. Nevertheless, the mortar was an indispensable weapon to trench warfare, proving its worth at the siege of Petersburg and at the Battle of Cold Harbor.

Indeed, improvised mortars had been used to great effect by Federal troops at the siege of Vicksburg the previous year. The Confederates tried with some success to improvise mortars at Cold Harbor while they awaited the arrival of Coehorns from Richmond. The Federals used Coehorns to support an attack on more than one occasion at Cold Harbor, which proved so successful that the Union commander demanded more of them. While only eight were available for operations against the Mule Shoe, the Army of the Potomac had forty before the Overland Campaign was over.

The rates of fire by individual infantrymen were unprecedented. It has been calculated that some Confederate troops fired 500 rounds during the 21 hours of the stalemated fighting, amounting to one shot every 150 seconds by each man, while some Federal troops fired 350 rounds over 11 hours, a shot every 115 seconds. Normally, these weapons needed cleaning every twenty-five rounds because of the fouling caused by black powder, but there was no way that Federal or Confederate could accomplish this trapped in the trenches. The Federals just did not bother and carried on firing, while the Confederates sent their weapons to the rear to be cleaned, cleaned ones being passed forward to replace them. And, of course, such rates of fire expended ammunition almost faster than it could be brought forward. Resupply was no easy matter and various means had to be improvised, usually involving men passing ammunition pouches by hand in a chain, the last man flinging it into the trench.

Much of the firing was done blind, muskets being angled over a parapet, the firer using his thumb to pull the trigger in the hope of hitting an enemy on the other side. To counter this, the barrel of any musket that poked over the parapet was pushed skywards so that the shot missed. This was tiring work, both physically and emotionally. Remarkably, some men tried to engage the enemy by clambering over the parapet to shoot but this was an almost suicidal act and not enough men tried it to be in any way useful. The weapon that none of them had but which would have been an effective trench-clearer was the hand grenade. While grenades were used in riverine actions and during the sieges of Vicksburg and Petersburg, for example, none were supplied to armies engaged in supposedly mobile battle. Here was a prime example of stalemate being exacerbated by lack of suitable tactics and lack of suitable weapons for trench fighting. Indeed, Brigadier General Pendleton, Lee's artillery commander, wanted 2,000 hand grenades at Cold Harbor because he believed they would be useful for clearing trenches and for supporting an attack on Federal trenches. There is no evidence that the grenades were ever supplied from Richmond. Nevertheless, Pendleton was right to argue that grenades would be useful in trench warfare. The trouble for both the Confederate and Union armies was the unreliability of the grenades of the period. Had they been available, the experience of grenades elsewhere in the Civil War suggests that they would have been of dubious value and were unlikely to have been decisive in any engagement in which they were used.

Not everyone was content to let the fighting descend into chaos and attempts were made to organize counter-measures to deal with the stalemate. None of these amounted to anything, however, due to lack of enthusiasm by men to expose themselves to almost certain death. One idea proposed by a Federal officer involved detachments of fifty men going over the top to take a traverse, this being repeated by several detachments to clear the enemy trenches, but the scheme was deemed suicidal and abandoned. What no one seems to have considered is a coordinated assault overground and round a traverse to drive the enemy out. However, this was not a tactic that could be improvised as it required extensive training. For that to happen, a need for such a tactic had to be identified and hitherto no such need had arisen.

The battle for the salient ended in the early hours of 13 May, when the Confederates pulled back to Lee's Last Line. The carnage on the battlefield was unlike any other during the Civil War, with corpses piled high in the trenches, many of them shredded by countless bullet hits. It took days to clear the area of the thousands of dead. There were many more wounded on both sides. The total casualty figure came to about 17,000. Not only was the fighting in the salient bloody, but it was inconclusive; the battle at Spotsylvania continued for another four days. As far as the Confederates were concerned, the salient was a mistake and of no military value, while, for the Federals, their attacks on it were ill-conceived and badly executed. At Spotsylvania, the Union troops did most of the attacking, while the Confederates mostly defended from their entrenchments. This helped foster the impression that it was a bloody business to attack fortified positions because the defender had the advantage, although it was more a case of Lee not choosing to attack rather than choosing to fight on the defensive. Lee would have liked to have taken the offensive to Grant but he was not prepared to repeat the mistakes made by Grant in attacking well-entrenched troops.

The reason the assaults on the Mule Shoe were so costly yet inconclusive was due to bad planning rather than because of the inherent strength of the Confederate positions. In particular, there was no understanding of how to exploit break-in. This was a tactical issue and one that was especially pertinent to trench warfare. Battlefield tactics of the time were essentially linear in that bodies of men approached an objective in lines or waves, a tactic which was not suitable for engaging entrenched troops. An attack failed as soon as the lines hit the enemy parapet and each successive wave then became a disorganized rabble which could not then act according to the linear doctrines of the time. Hence, failure was built in and success was entirely dependent on the willingness, or its lack, of the defenders to stand and fight. The question of using linear tactics to attack entrenched troops was an issue that would remain unresolved until 1917.

Following a series of engagements a state of mutual siege arose when the Army of the Potomac encountered the Army of North Virginia in the region of a crossroads known as Cold Harbor. Once again, the Union troops entrenched immediately they discovered the Confederate trenches. And once again, attacks on

Confederate trenches were all frontal assaults, executed in waves. A major Union assault was launched on 3 June. Wherever Union troops faltered as they were hit by Confederate fire, they dug in. When some Federal troops crossed no-man's-land, broke through the defensive palisades, mounted the parapet of the Confederate trenches and jumped in to engage in hand-to-hand fighting, all semblance of order was completely lost. Some managed to break into the Confederate positions and advance towards the enemy rear. Yet again, a timely counter-attack pushed them back. In other places, close-range fire destroyed the massed ranks of the attacking Union troops. Rather than either side making any kind of progress, however, stalemate began to develop. The casualties were even higher than during the attack on the Mule Shoe: some 3,500 Federals in one hour of fighting. It was a deeply traumatic defeat, the cause of which was poor planning as well as Grant's persistence with engaging the Army of North Virginia in a series of head-on assaults.

The significant difference in this battle, however, was that the Union troops dug in where they were stopped, rather than falling back to their original positions. Because this was done by a large number of troops, a new line of trenches, closer to the enemy line, was dug. In many places, the depth of no-man's-land was now no more then 40 yards. The new Federal line was soon as strong as their start line had been and as strong as the Confederate trenches in front of them. Although it had never been Grant's intention that his troops should lay siege to the Confederates, that is what happened for the better part of ten days. Part of the reason for this eventually was Grant's decision to transfer his focus of operations to Petersburg. For several days during the first week of June, both the Confederates and the Federals reinforced their trenches and, in some places, dug rifle pits in front of their main positions, which were then extended to form trenches, but the Federals were especially assiduous. Networks grew on each side as communication trenches were dug, redoubts were built and bomb-proof dugouts were added. Some trenches zigzagged to avoid being enfiladed, while some communication trenches were covered to conceal movement forward to the front line. Gun emplacements were also constructed and tunnels were dug out to piquet posts so that troops could move to and from them safely. The secondary lines in the trench networks were essential because of the range of rifle bullets. Anyone throughout the entire depth of the defensive area was vulnerable to hostile fire, so it was essential that trenches were dug behind the front line. Some were no more than shelter pits and short trenches, unconnected by communication trenches to the main entrenchments. Some trenches were deep enough for a man to stand upright without exposing his head, while others were no more than shallow scrapes. This became, for a short time, mutual siege and, hence, the embodiment of trench warfare. Meanwhile, artillery, mortar and rifle fire was exchanged sporadically throughout the construction process. Snipers or sharpshooters positioned themselves at loopholes and picked off the enemy as he exposed himself working, crossing poorly constructed earthworks or out in the open, including at night when the moon shone. Their activities never ceased, partly because they were never short of targets and partly because the lines were so close; 125 yards or even 40 yards were not uncommon.

Part of the process was to engage in conventional siege operations and it was with this is mind that the Federals began digging towards the Confederate lines and constructing parallels. The purpose of this was to get the troops closer to the enemy before launching an assault. Most of this work was done on the southern flank of the line, but it was carried out all along the Federal line. While the men dug, the Confederates fired on them, day and night. In a significant deviation from conventional practice, much of the digging of saps towards the Confederates was done without the use of a sap roller which, once detected, rather gave the game away, because the Federals were so close to the Confederate positions. Instead, men went over the parapet in the dark and dug without the protection of the roller, towards the enemy, back to the Federal line and outwards to form a parallel. Although this was not in itself novel, since the method was clearly set out in the manuals, it was unusual and set a precedent that was to be repeated on future battlefields elsewhere.

During the night of 5 June, a detachment of the US Engineer Battalion, aided by infantrymen, began the preliminary work on a mine under the Confederate line. The following night, they started excavating the gallery. But the mine was never finished. After several days, and before the entrenching and mining were finished, Grant ordered all siege work to stop. The focus of attack was now to be Petersburg. For the next five days, both Confederate and Union troops remained in their lines and the dead remained where they had fallen. In the summer heat, the bodies rapidly decomposed and the smell soon became overwhelming. On 7 June, a truce was agreed whereby the dead in no-man's-land could be buried without hindrance from either side.

It is clear that the idea to start siege operations was not well considered as the area in which the two armies were entrenched was bounded by rivers which allowed little room for manoeuvre. Crossing the River Chicahominy to the south would be self-defeating and gain Grant nothing. Worse than this, however, was the nature of the ground over which the siege works were being advanced. The Confederates held the higher ground so could look down into the Federal positions and, indeed, fire into them; the Federals had the disadvantage of having to fight uphill. A similar problem, but on a much larger scale, was to beset the British and French in the First World War.

While it would be stretching a point to claim that the ten-day period of trench warfare at Cold Harbor was unique to Civil War battlefields, nevertheless, it is true to say that the men on both sides lived, ate, worked and slept in the trenches. The officers had it slightly better than their men as most had access to tiny shelters, or dugouts, out of the front line. This period of stalemate was a significant development in trench warfare, one which was noticed at the time, drawing direct comparisons with other battles, and especially with sieges. However, there was no sense that mutual siege of this sort was a foretaste of the future. Just one week of mutual siege highlighted the practical difficulties of supplying entrenched troops with essentials such as water, food and ammunition. Water was a particular problem because without it life was unsustainable, let alone military operations. Indeed, no satisfactory solution to supplying it in large quantities was found and some men were forced to dig down to find wet clay from which some wetness could be forced. Salvation came in the form of a night-time rain storm which flooded the trenches, thereby highlighting another problem, that of draining water away. At dawn, the stand-to was normal routine and units were rotated from the front line to the support line every 24 hours, a matter of necessity to allow men to rest for 48 hours, although sometimes lack of manpower did not allow rotations and men had to stay in the line until the operations at Cold Harbor ended.

The conditions were not good. Most of the narrow trenches were cramped and overcrowded making sleep next to impossible. There were no proper latrines and the men had no opportunity to wash because of the lack of water. It is not surprising that such conditions encouraged lice, while the unburied dead, who lay all around, attracted rats. Men became ill with typhoid and dysentery due to the unsanitary conditions. All were under constant stress as there was little respite from the firing or the bad conditions, while only the bomb-proof shelters offered any degree of safety. A spontaneous phenomenon that was to be repeated many times during the First World War occurred, despite the short duration of the mutual siege: the brief live-and-let-live truce. Not only did some men on both sides suddenly stop shooting, but they effectively stopped warring to the extent that others could enter no-man's-land or expose themselves above the parapet without attracting hostile fire; ordinarily, such bravado would be fatal. One reason, no doubt, for these spontaneous acts was stress. Nevertheless, the morale on both sides remained high, although the Federals were less buoyant due to their failure to take the Confederate positions and because of their consequently high casualties. There was inevitably a higher loss among officers and NCOs because they led from the front.

While the siege of Petersburg was not the stalemated mutual siege of Cold Harbor, the development of trench warfare here did present other facets that were to emerge again during the Russo-Japanese War of 1904–05, and on the Western Front of the First World War. In particular, the firing of a large mine under the Confederate line and the subsequent battle to secure the crater was a feature that, although not in itself unprecedented, was given a different significance. A Federal mine had been detonated under Confederate positions during the siege of Vicksburg in 1863 but this had been in keeping with traditional siege. Moreover, the day-to-day routine of trench life at Petersburg, rather than being merely a modernized version of what had happened during sieges of the past, foreshadowed future wars. Petersberg was not perceived as such at the time because it was a siege not a battle. Nevertheless, the fact that stalemate and mutual siege had occurred at Cold Harbor, ostensibly a battle, made it inevitable that siege and battle would merge again in the future and the routines of siege would be adopted.

The Petersburg mine was begun in mid to late June 1864 after the Army of the Potomac had forced the Confederates to fall back from their original defensive positions, which had been built between August 1862 and March 1863, to a new line nearer to the town. Outnumbered by seven to one, the Confederates at Petersburg were overwhelmed by Grant's initial assaults on the outer defences but, once the Confederates were in their new positions, they managed to hold off the Union attacks which had begun to lack momentum. So began the siege which was to last until the end of the war in April 1865. The mine gallery, dug at a depth of 50 feet to avoid detection, was eventually 511 feet in length. It took about forty days to excavate the gallery and build the explosive chamber 20 feet beneath the Confederate line. The chamber, set at right angles to the gallery so that it was aligned with the Confederate line, was 75 feet long. It was packed with 320 barrels of gunpowder which amounted to 8,000lb (more than 3.5 tons).

The mine was blown early in the morning on 30 July, killing around 300 men and producing a crater 170 wide and 30 feet deep. However, the firing of the mine did not go according to plan due to poor fusing and it exploded at 4.44 am, an hour later than planned and after dawn rather than just before. This would not have mattered but for the fact that the firing of the mine was the initial phase of a major assault on the Confederate lines and there was a real possibility that failure of the mine would not only lead to casualties among the Federal troops, but ultimately to failure of the entire enterprise which held the prospect of a significant advance on Petersburg. The assault on the crater was to be carried out by a division of black troops who had been specifically trained for the job, while two other white divisions acted in support on the flanks. The significance here is that troops received training for two weeks before the assault, specifically for the task of taking control of the crater and advancing beyond before the Confederates had time to recover from the shock and mount a counter-attack to deny the crater to the Federals.

For all the good planning, the execution of the assault was a disaster, mainly due to the Union general, Meade, in command of the attack, losing his nerve. He prevented the trained black troops from carrying out their task because he was afraid that if the attack failed, which he anticipated would happen, high casualties among black troops would lead to a public and political outcry. Untrained troops, therefore, led the assault on the crater and did all the things which the trained troops would have avoided, such as occupying the hole rather than racing for the rim. Moreover, they waited for 10 minutes after the mine was blown before leaving their trenches. The Confederates mounted a counter-attack and slaughtered the men in the crater, who were sitting targets. Although the Confederates were thrown back by Federal reinforcements, another counter-attack pushed them back. Hand-to-hand fighting continued for several hours, the crater ending up in Confederate hands. Meade lost 3,798 men, of whom 504 were killed, while 1,413 became prisoners or were missing; Confederate losses were approximately 360 killed and 730 wounded, with about 400 captured or missing, including those lost when the mine exploded.

This was an object lesson. Firstly, training was of crucial importance in operations where specific tasks had to be carried out. When such an operation was given to troops untrained in the specifics of the objective and how it was to be achieved, the result was costly failure. Untrained troops tended to do what they perceived to be the obvious and the least dangerous. Secondly, the crater of a blown mine was the key to dominance of the enemy in the locality, and whichever side took the rim carried the day and dominated their foe both physically and psychologically. Thirdly, planning and coordination of all the elements in a complex enterprise were essential for success. Deviation beyond a certain point brought failure. The mine operation satisfied none of the criteria for success, although the potential for success had been there from the outset. Indeed, Meade managed to snatch defeat from the jaws of victory, largely because he had no faith in the enterprise, not because it was boldly planned.

While the stalemate at Cold Harbor caused men to live below ground level instead of above it for ten days, the siege of Petersburg led to a truly troglodyte world for the men on both sides of no-man's-land. Here, the labyrinthine networks of trenches, bomb-proof shelters and redoubts surpassed in scale and sophistication every other trench system constructed in the course of the Civil War. Of all the trench systems built in the war, those at Petersburg most resembled what was to appear on the Western Front fifty years later. It is not surprising, then, that the manner of their construction and maintenance bore similarities. The use of details of infantrymen as labourers to do the work under the supervision of engineers was commonplace. The weather often caused major problems. Parapets and revetments collapsed and trenches flooded when it rained hard; when the temperatures fell below freezing the ground was too hard for spades to penetrate.

It was at Petersburg that the trench raid came of age. They were often carried out just before dawn. The stand-to was a routine of life in the trenches and piquet lines. Piquets located in advanced trench posts in front of their own line had to endure 24-hour stints of observation and sniping while remaining under cover before being relieved at night as quietly as possible. In early 1865, some Federal sharpshooters were armed with target rifles fitted with telescopic sights. Sniping led to many head and neck wounds which were often fatal, as well many hand and wrist injures due to accidental exposure above the parapet. While, in some parts of the line, sniping was vigorously pursued, in others, it was stopped because it was deemed to be unhelpful. Theoretically, ending sniping activities encouraged the enemy to do likewise, thereby establishing by tacit agreement a live-and-let-live system of co-existence. While the justification for adopting a less aggressive disposition towards the enemy was that it reduced the number of casualties, nevertheless, the establishment of a quiet sector was a more complex issue than mere peaceful co-existence with an enemy. Indeed, live and let live was not an issue of logic at all but rather one of passivity based on the idea that if you left your enemy alone he would leave you alone. This completely failed when the troops opposite were an aggressive unit uninterested in making life easy. Moreover, the notion that casualties were reduced when such a system was adopted was to some degree self-delusion.

In some instances, live and let live went beyond an unspoken agreement not to engage in aggressive acts and became actual fraternization. While this was actively discouraged because it dampened the offensive spirit, it was never eradicated. Men from one side would enter the trench of their erstwhile enemy and generally act as though they were friends. And on Christmas Day 1864, an unofficial truce arose spontaneously in some places along the front line. That sort of thing made it all the more difficult to return to normal hostilities.

The issue of lack of training and motivation in relation to the rise of trench warfare is both seductive and misleading. On the one hand, there is no question that replacements were not the best trained, the most effective or the most highly motivated of troops in the Union armies, the Army of the Potomac in particular. Draftees and so-called bounty-men certainly lacked the motivation to put themselves at risk in battle if they could avoid it. To suggest as some historians have done that this was sufficient reason for them to dig in and engage in trench warfare, rather than face open battle, is to ignore the fact that trench warfare was far from safe as a mode of warfare and, indeed, placed troops under greater stress than open battle. Survivors hated trench warfare and were bitter about the loss of friends in a form of fighting which they thought was pointless. Similarly, the idea that the more experienced survivors of the fighting wanted to dig in because they were weary of fighting is contrary to battlefield experience in Europe. Moreover, it implies that command and control were largely absent from the Civil War battlefield because it suggests that men dug in irrespective of what higher command might want.

Trench warfare encouraged attrition, which in many ways increased the risk of becoming a casualty, rather than decreased it. There was a predisposition to dig in, and the shelter of a ditch and a parapet of earth was compelling but this was a top-down instruction, not a ground-up resort of last refuge. The issue of training was crucial as demonstrated by the débâcle of the crater battle at Petersburg but to suggest that men dug in because they were not better trained to do otherwise is quite the wrong conclusion to draw from the events of the Civil War. Indeed, the 'not better trained' idea and the 'experienced survivor resort' idea are contradictory.

Trench warfare was, in many ways, a descent into disorder and chaos from a command and control perspective, as well as from the perspective of the man in the trench. Armies engaged in trench warfare became stuck in what often turned out to be a pointless slugging match from which one side usually disengaged after a period of time. Grant recognized this in his Overland Campaign. Here was a crucial element in whether trench warfare was an inevitable consequence of various factors coming together or whether it was, in fact, avoidable. There is no question that during the Civil War armies that became bogged down in trench warfare lost their momentum and their focus. To regain it, breaking off contact to re-engage somewhere else was essential. That it was possible to break contact and re-engage suggest that trench warfare was a mode of fighting that occurred from choice not accident.

The trench warfare of the American Civil War was far from pleasant and conditions were often as bad as those at Sebastopol and, indeed, as those that would occur on the Western Front in the First World War. Nevertheless, it was quite unlike the trench warfare of the First World War. This was entirely down to the nature of the weapons with which the two sides fought. Or rather, it was because the armies lacked some particular weapons that had yet to be invented, which subsequently made major contributions to the nature and conduct of trench warfare. In the Civil War, the infantry engaged in firefights, sometimes had to withstand artillery bombardments and occasionally had to face infantry assault on their positions. The weapons which they lacked in the trenches would not only help to define trench warfare but would become the very munitions by which the tactics of trench warfare were developed. Indeed, some of these weapons were invented as a direct response to the demands of trench warfare. The most important of these were the hand and rifle grenade and the trench mortar. While the hand grenade was used during the Civil War, it played no significant role; the rifle grenade and the trench mortar did not come into existence until the first decade of the twentieth century. Indeed, the seeds of these munitions were sown during the Russo-Japanese War in Manchuria and they were to bear fruit in the trenches of the Western Front.

While the trench warfare of the Overland Campaign sapped the strength of Lee's army and prevented Lee from engaging in more ambitious attacks on the Union elsewhere, the issue of whether Grant was right to adopt his continuous contact policy rather sidesteps the question of how he went about achieving it. There is a sense that consequences of entrenching were not appreciated by either Grant or Lee simply because entrenching was an accepted practice. In this sense, trench warfare was a natural development of this process. However, trench warfare was not merely siege warfare transplanted to the battlefield. Nor was it simply a matter of continuous contact. Indeed, trench warfare required different tactical thinking if it was to achieve victory by means other than attrition. Such thinking was not considered simply because the object of trench warfare was, at that time, attrition. It did not come about through an inability to outflank in mobile warfare. It came about by intention. Trench warfare in the Civil War was a failed attempt to engage in a different form of fighting to defeat an enemy who had proved himself to be adept at battles of manoeuvre.

CHAPTER 6

The Russo-Japanese War, 1904–05

In the forty years that separated the American Civil War from the Russo-Japanese War, a great deal of change occurred in military affairs. While the tactics of the early twentieth century were still rooted in ideas that owed their origins to the wars of Napoleon, they were no longer the tactics of the column and massed assault. The Franco-Prussian War of 1870–1 saw to that. Nevertheless, tactical thought had not kept pace with munitions design; armament technology had outstripped tactical doctrine so that there was a serious mismatch between tactics and the capabilities of the weapons that now equipped most armies. The munitions of the early twentieth century were, in effect, over-designed for how they were intended to be used. Within twenty years of the end of the American Civil War, infantry had given up their single-shot, muzzle-loaded rifles for breech-loading, magazine-fed rifles. The lead Minié bullet had been superseded by the jacketed spitzer and black powder had been replaced by more powerful, smokeless, nitrocellulose propellants. At the same time, breech-loading rifled artillery became the norm, replacing all muzzle-loaders. No gun had fired roundshot since the 1860s; now they fired ogival shells with high-explosive fillings detonated by sophisticated fuses. The full capabilities of these munitions were not fully realized, however, largely because few opportunities had arisen for their employment. The Boxer Rebellion in 1900–01 and the Boer War of 1900–01 provided clues to the firepower of such weapons but it was not until the Russo-Japanese War that Western armies began to appreciate how warfare might be about to change because of the technological advances of the last thirty years. Such clues were, of course, open to interpretation and each government tended to have its own slant on the evidence presented to it but, without exception, everyone agreed that warfare would not follow the pattern observed in Manchuria.

The favoured tactical doctrines at the start of the twentieth century all emphasized the crucial importance of élan. Indeed, the spirit of attack was at the heart of tactical thinking. While élan had been fostered throughout the second half of the nineteenth century, its apotheosis was the first two decades of the twentieth century. By the end of the nineteenth century, no army with pretensions to military modernism eschewed the primacy of attack as the means to victory in war; taking the offensive and seizing the initiative would lead to victory over a cautious, defensive posture. At the heart of such thinking was an unbreakable faith in the dominance of men over machines. The attack would always succeed provided the troops went forward with enough of the attacking spirit. There was no suggestion that men would act with caution by digging in or by pausing in the face of the enemy. Firepower was no substitute for spirit. There was precious little in the way of solid evidence that such an approach to battle could ever carry the day, however. The American Civil War provided only ambiguous evidence that defensive firepower could stop an assault. Indeed, there was a certain degree of European superciliousness over the way the Americans had conducted themselves in the Civil War. A similar superior view was taken of the Russians, who were categorized as preferring defence over attack, and the Japanese, who were regarded as aggressive upstarts.

The relationship between technology, firepower and tactics was not quite that simple, however. The effects of technology on firepower, although not fully understood at the end of the nineteenth century, did not inevitably lead to tactical failure on the battlefield; these munitions were used tactically in much the same way as their less powerful predecessors had been employed. Hence, the effects of firepower were somewhat negated because the tactics did not exploit the strengths of these munitions. At the time of the Russo-Japanese War, the general view among military officers was that increased firepower of modern weapons worked in favour of the attacker, rather than to the advantage of the defender, a view that was the opposite of that held by American officers during the Civil War. The same evidence was used to support contrary views, however. That these munitions had greater potential for tactical change was not really appreciated before the Russo-Japanese War, although some thinkers, Ivan Bloch among them, had been forecasting the end of war because the power of modern weapons would make war impossible for anyone to win. At the same time, the notion that armies should approach each other, skirmish and the weaker one fall back to prepared defensive positions was a view held by some officers, implying that the concept of trench warfare was well established, if rarely put into practice by European armies.

The Russo-Japanese War is usually held up, with the benefit of hindsight and not a little reverse logic, to have been the precursor of the First World War. Here were two 'modern' armies, although the Russian Army was less modern than the Imperial Japanese Army, engaging in all-out war with weapons and tactics that were not so very different from those of the major European powers and the result was stalemate. Surely, this was the way of modern warfare. The flaw in this simplistic view of the events in Manchuria is the obvious fact that trench warfare arose from a siege, that of Port Arthur, a siege that was embarked upon by the Japanese as just that, a siege. In the way that the five-month siege of Plevna in 1877, during the Russo-Turkish War of 1877–8, was a deliberate act by the Russians, so the siege of Port Arthur was a strategic act by the Japanese. However, whereas the Russian siege of Plevna, which also led to trench fighting, is largely ignored in the evolution of trench warfare, the investment of Port Arthur is held up to be a significant step towards what was to happen on the Western Front a few years later. It is a moot point. The difference between the sieges was their military usefulness: Plevna was pointless whereas Port Arthur had a strategic purpose.

For about four years before the outbreak of war, Japan made plans to attack Russia in order to assert her own authority in the Pacific and ensure her dominion over Korea. Port Arthur, located on the tip of the Liaotung Peninsular in Manchuria, was Russia's only naval base in the Pacific that was ice-free all year round. Without it, Russia would be powerless across the whole of the Pacific. Essential elements of Japan's strategy were the destruction of the Russian Pacific Fleet and the capture of Port Arthur. With these objectives achieved, Japan could then embark on a land campaign without the Russian Navy interfering with her supply lines. While the surprise attack by the Japanese Navy on the Russian ships moored in Port Arthur was a success, the capture of Port Arthur by the Imperial Japanese Army did not proceed quite so smoothly.

There were marked similarities between the war in Manchuria and the war in the Crimea, fifty years earlier. In both cases, the objective was the capture of a Russian naval base, to which end the bases in question were besieged, while a number of land battles were fought in direct consequence of the sieges. And in both instances, trench warfare emerged from the means by which the strategic objects were pursued by the aggressor. In neither instance was trench warfare adopted by choice, except insofar as siege and trench warfare were facets of the same process. Indeed, it is quite plain that the Japanese had never considered the possibility of trench warfare arising during the war and, consequently, they had no tactical doctrine for how to conduct it, other than by conventional siege methods, and no specialist weapons with which to fight it. The same was equally true of the Russians.

Whereas the trench warfare at Sebastopol and that which occurred during the American Civil War gave rise to neither new tactics nor new weapons, trench warfare in the Russo-Japanese War began a process of change that was to reach its climax in 1918. Tactically and technologically, the consequences of the Russo-Japanese War were profound. One reason for this was that the fighting in Manchuria was monitored and reported on by Western military observers to such an extent that nothing went unrecorded. Certainly as far as the British were concerned, everything from sanitation to tactics, from munitions to telephony, was noted down. Significantly, these reports became the basis of an official history of the war. While the Americans had sent observers to the Crimea and the European powers had sent observers to the American Civil War, the degree to which the observers in Manchuria scrutinized, noted, annotated, described and tabulated whatever they saw was unparalleled. While the reports by British observers of the American Civil War were treated by the War Department as accounts of some interest but for the 'no action necessary' tray, and the conclusions made by one American observer about Sebastopol had a direct effect on how he conducted siege operations in the Civil War, the reports from Manchuria were treated much more sagely. The only problem with this assiduous reportage was the lack of proper analysis of the information gathered so that much of it was presented in a fairly raw state, although the subsequent official history made it look otherwise. This, too, would have consequences. The tactical power of the machine-gun and the value of indirect artillery fire, while noted, were not emphasized so that they were dismissed by faint praise. Rather than a failure of insight, this was a failure of analysis.

The reports acknowledged the rise of trench warfare but recorded the means by which it was fought as though such a mode of fighting had never arisen before. While it was noted, it was also dismissed as atypical of sophisticated warfare, the implication being that such an occurrence was to be expected from the likes of Russia and Japan: the former, a lumbering giant which preferred defence over offence; the latter, an emergent non-European upstart with pretensions to military power but unversed in the ways of proper warring. Such views were never quite expressed explicitly, but the tone of many of the reports suggested that European armies would not resort to entrenching because they understood the spirit of the attack. This, of course, conveniently side-stepped the fact that the aggressive and often fanatical Japanese assault was, indeed, in accordance with the much-vaunted principal of élan. The observers then turned a blind eye to the failure of the massed infantry assault on entrenched, well-armed and determined defenders. If there was an object lesson to be noted it was the effect of firepower on massed infantry, especially when faced with barbed-wire obstacles. This was the first major war in which barbed wire was used extensively and its usefulness was duly noted.

Although the Japanese persisted with the suicidal frontal assault by massed infantry throughout the war, their awareness of the inability of their infantry to take Russian positions without incurring very high casualties led to some changes in tactics. These changes were mostly with respect to the assaults on the defences of Port Arthur. In addition, the Japanese tried to reduce their casualties by introducing body armour and armoured trench shields. The Russians supposedly ordered 100,000 sets of body armour from an Italian firm, although it is unlikely that it was ever completed. They also used trench shields similar to those employed by the Japanese. It is likely that the Japanese copied the Russians. The effectiveness of such armour was limited. The British had noted the need for trench shields following the Boer War, while body armour had been available during the first eighteen months of the American Civil War. Where the Japanese differed from the British and the Americans, however, was in their experimentation with various armours, the results of which led to a number of innovations. A principal discovery arose from observing what happened to thin armour plate when struck by a high-velocity bullet. Even when the range was too great to penetrate the metal, typically in the region of more than 100 yards, the impact had sufficient energy to cause a spall of metal to fly off the opposite face of the shield with the real risk of blinding anyone close behind it. Indeed, in the case of body armour, the spall could penetrate the clothing and skin of the wearer. This discovery led to the development of an early form of composite armour: a layer of a tough flexible material was adhered to the inner face of the armour to prevent spalling.

Both the Russian and the Japanese armies took very seriously the idea of portable infantry shields. Moreover, the Japanese fitted armoured shields to some of their field guns, one of the first nations to do this. Indeed, the European powers followed Japan's lead and, by 1914, most guns had shields that were capable of protecting their gunners from small-arms fire. The reason for their adoption was simple. Artillery was positioned so that the gunners could fire by direct line of sight, which meant that they had to be able to see their targets and, consequently, were close enough to enemy infantry to be targeted by them. Moreover, while 15 per cent of casualties during the Russo-Japanese War were caused by artillery shells, most of the other 85 per cent were caused by small-arms fire. Hence, shields and body armour were logical solutions to try to reduce the number of casualties. After the Battle of Mukden, a shield fitted to one 3-inch gun was found to have been struck eighty-six times, seventy-nine of them being bullet impacts, while another shield was found to have received twenty bullet hits.

Portable shields used by the Japanese had a wide range of uses, including: protecting men detailed to cut barbed wire with hand-held cutters; officers engaged in reconnaissance close to Russian trenches, a tactic which was frequently used to ascertain the strengths and weakness of the Russian trenches before mounting an assault; and men digging saps or trenches in no-man's-land. They were also used for observation from Japanese trenches, the observer peering through two small eye holes in one model of shield, or a narrow slit in another model. They saw fairly widespread service with Japanese engineers during the siege of Port Arthur and were used by some infantry at the Battle of Mukden. These shields were no lightweights, however. One type weighed some 25lb while another model weighed about 37lb. A lighter one was at the experimental stage when the war ended. Despite their evident cumbrousness, the shields provided significant protection against small-arms fire despite being only 0.4 inches thick. One Japanese shield used at Port Arthur received forty bullet strikes. Significantly, the proper use of portable shields required appropriate training in cooperating with other infantry, especially troops detailed as hand-grenadiers, or bombers. Without coordinated cooperation between shield users and other infantry, the shields were more of a hindrance than a help.

While only 109 body armours were made in Japan, a further 115 were made by Japanese engineers at Port Arthur. Although the total of 224, averaging seventy-five per division, is not significant in terms of the numbers of soldiers engaged in the siege, the fact that such armour was considered at all is noteworthy. Body armour had not been officially sanctioned in European military operations since the Franco-Prussian War, when some siege engineers wore armour. The numbers of portable shields and trench shields used by the Japanese Third Army at Port Arthur exceeded 1,660. Again, this is not a large number considering the size of the Third Army, which by July 1904 had increased to 80,000 men, although not all of them would have been engaged in operations that required the use of shields, of course. However, the Russo-Japanese War was the first conflict in which armoured shields of this sort were employed to counter small-arms fire and shrapnel.

The entrenchments constructed by the Russian and Japanese engineers during the siege of Port Arthur were similar to those built during the American Civil War. There were, however, several important differences, although the principals behind their form and construction were the same and had changed little from the sieges of the eighteenth century. The trenches built in the field before battles such as Mukden, while similar to those at Port Arthur, were constructed on quite a different principal. Indeed, their purpose differed from that of the trenches built during the battles of the American Civil War. While the purpose of protecting troops from small-arms fire and shrapnel remained unchanged, the Japanese developed a more aggressive approach to entrenching. The lethal range of rifles then in service across the world meant that anyone in the open at 1,000 yards could be killed by a single round. Although such an aimed shot would require a marksman, troops in the open at 600–800 yards would be shot down by massed rifle fire before they reached the trenches. At a steady 6 m.p.h., or steady jog, it would take 2.5 minutes to cross 400 yards in which time 100 riflemen could fire 2,500 rounds. Although mass infantry assaults were carried out by Japanese infantry, the cost was very high.

During the Battle of Nanshan in May 1904 and the Battle of Liaoyang, fought between 25 August and 3 September 1904, the Japanese infantry made repeated frontal assaults on strongly held and well-made Russian trenches through barbed-wire entanglements. The Japanese losses at Liaoyang were 23,000 while the Russians lost 19,000. The outcome was inconclusive and, had the Russian commander recognized that this was not a Russian defeat, it is clear that stalemate would have followed. Instead, Kuropatkin withdrew.

The Japanese entrenched as part of their assault tactics. To this end, Japanese infantry were also provided with two empty sandbags which they filled when they went to ground and used as extemporized cover. The difficulty of digging into frozen ground in the winter meant that hastily dug trenches were far shallower than had they been dug in the summer. Rather than persist with massed infantry assaults over open ground, although the Japanese never actually abandoned this tactic, part of the process of assaulting Russian positions was to attack in stages, each stage bringing the infantry closer to the main Russian line. While this was similar to the tactic employed by the Army of the Potomac in 1864 at Cold Harbor, the Japanese took the idea much further. Indeed, wherever they stopped, they dug in, so that they held the ground they had taken, yet kept advancing. The process was a mixture of rapid movement forward above ground, followed by methodical digging, resulting in trench warfare, until the Japanese were ready to mount another assault. Remarkably, Japanese infantry were trained to dig while prone, to which end they were equipped with a lightweight entrenching tool. This process of digging forwards was similar to the siege technique of constructing parallels but, whereas parallels were dug from saps, ensuring that the diggers remained below ground level as much as possible, the Japanese technique required their infantry to forego the saps. Hence, they were trained to dig lying down.

Clearly, the Japanese were aware of the need to avoid unnecessary casualties but not, it seems, at the expense of attacking spirit. Time and again, aggressive Japanese tactics defeated the Russians but the cost to the Japanese was often very high. Yet, despite the casualty balance usually settling in favour of the defender, who was usually Russian, there were occasions when the Japanese suffered fewer casualties than the Russians, despite attacking well-defended entrenchments. After the Battle of Sha-Ho, 5–17 October 1904, both the Russian and the Japanese armies were exhausted and dug in. The Russians lost 40,000 men while the Japanese lost 20,000.

The formation of front-line and reserve trenches, and how they should be manned were issues which had no definitive answer during the war. The Russians tended to avoid packing too many troops into their front-line trenches because these were likely to be bombarded by Japanese artillery, whereas one British observer was of the opinion that this was a bad idea. He felt that those in the reserve line would be hit by the same rifle fire and gunfire as those in the front line because the Russians built the two lines too close together. The Boers in South Africa had sparsely manned their trenches, largely because they lacked the manpower to do otherwise and, while they could inflict casualties, they could not mount counter-attacks. They suffered relatively few casualties themselves with this tactic. Thinly manned front-line trenches made much better sense than packing them with men in the hope that an opportunity for a counter-attack would arise. The same British observer also suggested that trenches should be narrow and have no parapet as the latter evidently acted as a target for artillery. It is clear that the front line was intended to be the only effective line for defence, while the reserve was no more than what its name suggests, a place for the reserves. Such a trench system had no depth and could be penetrated with ease provided the Japanese could reach the front line.

The barbed-wire entanglements which the Russians put in front and on the flanks of all their entrenchments, both in the field and before Port Arthur, were innovative. While the military use of barbed wire dated from at least 1888, no army had employed it in front of trenches in quite the way devised by the Russians in Manchuria. The Americans used barbed wire in the Spanish-American War of 1898 but only as corral fencing, while the British put it in front of some trenches during the Boer War, as did the Boers, but only in single strands. The Japanese also laid out barbed wire in front of their trenches and in this they may have copied the Russians. At Port Arthur, the Russians set up wire 100 yards in front of their trenches, using two sets of wooden posts, while at Tieh-Ling, whence the Russians fell back after their defeat at Mukden, they set up three lines of wire only 25 yards in front of their trenches. The Japanese tended to site their wire 60 yards in front. The wire was stretched along the posts in the manner of a fence and across from one line of wire to another, thereby creating an obstacle that could not be crossed easily; had to be cut by the attacker. Some Russian barbed-wire obstacles consisted of a single strand through abbatis, while others were in the form of 6-foot squares staked out in three rows of posts. The difficulties in doing sufficient damage to any such entanglements to enable attacking infantry to get through became all too apparent to the Japanese who found that wire was very resistant to artillery fire. They resorted to issuing hand-operated wire-cutters to the infantry, 808 sets being issued in the Japanese Third Army during the siege of Port Arthur. They also devised a so-called roller grenade.

The roller grenade was an explosive device on the end of a bamboo pole that could be extended by attaching additional 15-foot lengths of bamboo up to about 120 feet in total. The bomb was in the form of a cylinder attached via stub axles to a U-shaped piece at the end of the pole. The axles allowed the cylinder to roll as it was pushed along the ground and under the wire. The bomb came in two sizes, 22lb and 44lb, and was fired electrically. Described by one British observer as a device for 'destroying the enemy's cover close to their trenches', the roller grenade was more likely intended for blowing holes in wire entanglements rather than destroying 'cover', although their size suggests that they could have been employed as small mobile mines. These devices were improvised by Japanese engineers in the field, conceived as a solution to a specific problem no one had encountered before the siege of Port Arthur, such as the inability of artillery to destroy barbed-wire entanglements. During the bombardment of 203 Metre Hill, a key position in the defence in Port Arthur, 4,000 230mm shells were fired at the Russian trenches, which destroyed the wire but the Japanese infantry had a hard time crossing the cratered ground. The Japanese also tried sapping under barbed-wire obstacles, although this was only feasible when the wire was well in front of the Russian lines and it was a very labour-intensive way to deal with barbed wire.

The Russians nearly always sited their trenches on high ground so that the Japanese had to attack uphill. They were wise enough not to dig trenches along ridge lines but 20–50 yards lower down the forward slopes, although they ran into problems when guns in such locations had to be withdrawn because of Japanese advances which threatened to overrun the position. Both the Russians and the Japanese constructed loopholed parapets using sandbags, and both constructed concealed positions for machine-guns. A notable feature of all the entrenchments, Russian and Japanese, was how neatly they were built, with parapets that were uniform and traverses that conformed to a parade-ground mentality. This implies that troops from neither side had engaged in prolonged trench fighting. As would become painfully evident on the Western Front, neatness indicated inexperience in the trenches. The simple truth was that neat lines enabled the enemy to locate trenches and spot movement in them. Anyone who unwisely showed even a small amount of his head above a level parapet was quickly spotted. Snipers were adept at taking snap shots at such targets.

The extensive use of entrenchments in Manchuria was not what European observers expected to find and they tended to dismiss fieldworks as indicative of the 'Russian character' for fighting on the defensive, a prejudice that was not supported by the evidence. As for the Japanese, entrenching supposedly went against their peacetime training which emphasized the offensive in the European style of war. Yet, at the start of the war, 50 per cent of Japanese infantry were provided with an entrenching tool of some sort, such as a shovel, pick or hatchet, which rose to 66 per cent by the war's end. The Japanese trenches 'were not remarkable for … excellence of construction and detail' and were noticeably less well constructed than those built by the Russians at the start of the war, but this was excused as being due to their lack of practice rather than policy. There is no question that the Japanese constructed stronger fieldworks as the war progressed, which is indicative of the increasing importance of trench warfare in Manchuria. Indeed, the Japanese evidently copied the Russian entrenchments in form and structure.

While the Japanese incorporated what might be termed assault entrenching in their tactics, when building prepared positions of a more permanent nature, the earthworks were much more traditional in form and purpose. These were akin to the fieldworks that had been constructed prior to battle since the eighteenth century and took little or no account of the firepower of modern weapons which equipped the Russian and Japanese armies in Manchuria. Japanese defensive fieldworks were in the form of connected redoubts, or strongpoints. They lacked support lines and the whole scheme lacked depth since a position was but one line of fieldworks.

The redoubts were triangular in form, presenting an obtuse-angled front to the enemy. These faces were 100 yards long, while the base was 150 yards, giving a depth of 50 yards. They were spaced 2,000 yards apart and manned solely by infantry, each with a garrison of up to 600 men. The redoubt was defended by several machine-guns in enclosed positions, or caponiers. The redoubts were linked by trenches, some of which were provided with parapets, thereby turning them into fire trenches. Wherever possible, natural features such as streams, ravines and ridge lines were incorporated into the general defensive scheme, with villages being incorporated as well if the line ran through them. While neatness of line in the construction of fieldworks was much applauded by British observers, the Japanese always tried to conceal their trenches by ensuring that the background was not skyline, against which all movement would be highlighted. The Russians also concealed their trenches whenever possible. At Mukden, the Japanese got to within 300 yards of the Russian first line before they became aware of the Russians. This also indicates the good fire discipline of the Russian troops. In addition, shrapnel-proof covers were built over some of the trenches which further concealed them. These were in the form of roofs on short stilts so that all-round vision was not compromised. In some instances at Port Arthur, strips of canvas were later attached to the rear of these covers because it was discovered that the aperture which they created highlighted any movement inside the trench.

The issue of concealment of the entrenchments so that the enemy was unaware of their location became more important as the war progressed. It is evident that fields of fire and firepower, rather than shelter alone, were primary concerns. Shelter from enemy fire only became the main function of a trench when troops were forced to dig in during an assault. This was pertinent to infantry positions as well as to the siting and concealment of artillery. Camouflage and location, especially when trenches and emplacements were dug in a hilly area, were key to the effectiveness of the defence. By digging deeper than was customary, it was possible to obviate the normal necessity of a raised parapet to provide sufficient cover. Hitherto, trenches had not been dug deep enough to allow a man to stand upright without being seen. Every effort was made to avoid leaving the evidence of dumps of excavated earth or a raised parapet to indicate the presence of a trench. This applied to both the Russians and the Japanese. Machine-gun positions were especially hidden because when located they were subjected to artillery fire to put the guns out of action.

Japanese trenches were provided with extensive traversing, built in the same manner as the traverses used in the American Civil War, so that each bay had space for no more than two or three riflemen, although some had room for up to eight. The defensive value of the Japanese entrenchments was very limited because they only dug one line without any reserve lines. To a large degree, this reflected the Japanese focus on always taking the offensive and launching aggressive infantry assaults. Had the Japanese opted for defence in greater depth, not only might the Russian field guns have been unable to hit the deepest lines, but the Japanese artillery, if positioned in a second or third line, would not have been able to hit the first line of Russian trenches. That the depth of no-man's-land was increased to minimize the effects of artillery on the trench line did nothing to help the infantry when it came to an assault, as they now had a great expanse of open ground to cross to reach the enemy, which very much aided the defence. The Russians had plenty of time to shoot down the massed Japanese assault troops.

The Russian lines were more complex trench systems than those created by the Japanese, which reflected the fact that the Russians had the advantage of time to construct defences on their own territory. They constructed defensive fieldworks in far greater depth than the Japanese who, generally speaking, were less concerned with defence than the Russians simply because they were on the offensive, although it would be misleading to imply that the Russians never embarked on offensive operations. Indeed, at Sha-Ho and Mukden, the Russians launched assaults on the Japanese which very nearly succeeded. The Russians dug more than one line of trenches so that when the Japanese overran one, they were then faced with another which was defended equally tenaciously as the last one. The British observers did not appreciate the value of having several trench lines arranged in parallel and assumed that the intention had been to present fire from all the trenches at the same time. It was noted, however, that this was not possible when the Russians were entrenched on relatively flat terrain as at Chang-tu, which implied that there was a different reason for successive trench lines. While it is not entirely certain that the Russians even contemplated a doctrine of defence in depth, nevertheless, successive lines provided depth whereby Japanese assaults could be stopped because they were unable to break through them. However, despite heavy losses, the Japanese pressed home their assaults.

Rifle fire from determined troops in such entrenchments was quite capable of stopping even the most aggressive Japanese assault. The Russians defending one redoubt during the Battle of Mukden inflicted as many 3,000 casualties among the Japanese, who got no closer than 280 yards. Yet, the Russians left behind only fifteen dead when they withdrew. Indeed, it was only because of the general Russian withdrawal that the redoubt was given up. While this clearly illustrated the suicidal nature of any assault on well-prepared positions manned by determined troops, it also illustrated the importance of artillery by its very absence. There is no question that had the redoubt been subjected to an artillery bombardment before the infantry assault, Japanese casualties would have been far fewer. Indeed, when Russian guns hit Japanese trenches before an assault the effective resistance to their assault was significantly reduced.

The trace of Japanese trenches was often zigzagged to minimize the effect of artillery fire and, by the end of the war, they were usually dug to a depth significantly greater than the height of a man so that troops could remain upright when moving along them. Typically, there was at least 18 inches of headroom below the parapet which was only raised about 6 inches above the natural ground level to avoid easy detection. Such trenches could be more than 11 feet across at their widest; the inner faces sloped towards a narrow walkway that ran the length of the trench, along one side of which was a gutter to allow water to drain away. The interior of a trench was usually stepped on the forward face. The Japanese usually put a shelf or elbow-rest along the inner face of the parapet to aid shooting. At Port Arthur, where the Japanese went about digging siege works with methodical persistence, Russian artillery hardly bothered their working parties, or the infantry in the finished trenches. The Russians tended to fire 37mm Hotchkiss multi-barrelled cannon and Maxim machine-guns at the engineers who sheltered behind armoured shields as they worked. The Hotchkiss rounds penetrated the shields with ease and were a serious nuisance. The only effective defence against the 37mm rounds was a wall of sandbags, 4 feet thick, built on the parapet of a finished trench. Shielded loopholes had to be built in to enable the Japanese to fire on the Russians. The Japanese were also harassed by Russian sorties which ventured forth, often at night, to throw hand grenades into their trenches.

Russian trenches were built to a slightly different pattern and evolved during the course of the war. The first trenches at Port Arthur and typical of those at

Nanshan were little more than 4-foot-wide shallow ditches, provided with parapets of slightly greater height than the ditch was deep, giving cover of only 4 feet 6 inches. A variation on this profile was to provide notches in the parapet as rudimentary loopholes. When the Russians were forced to dig trenches quickly, the ditch-like quality was especially evident, but they were often slightly deeper and narrower than those dug at leisure. The parapet was correspondingly lower so that the depth of cover remained about the same. The trenches on 174 Metre Hill, a crucial element in the defences of Port Arthur, fought over for five days in August 1904, were slightly deeper and provided with traverses every 15 feet. The parapets were deeper and were again crenellated or notched, although some parapets were given loopholes instead. The 174 Metre Hill was an object of the second Japanese assault on Port Arthur, with much of the fighting being done at night, the Russians illuminating their attackers with searchlights and rockets. The Japanese infantry were cut down by the Russian Maxims so that they lost 15,000 men in reckless frontal assaults, while the Russians lost 3,000. Significantly, the Japanese had no heavy artillery at this stage.

By September and October 1904, some communication trenches at Port Arthur were being converted to act as supplementary fire trenches to provide flanking fire to support the front-line trenches. To this end, loopholed bays were built into the front face of the trench, at 8-foot intervals, and a sandbag traverse was built up behind each bay. These trenches were some of the first to be provided with a recognizable fire-step which had been added, no doubt, because they were much deeper than the original front-line trenches, being some 6 feet deep, the parapet providing a further 2–3 feet of cover. Hence, the riflemen manning the bays would have been unable to see over the top without the firestep to stand on. The step was 2 feet 6 inches higher than the floor of the trench. The greater depth reflected the original purpose of allowing troops to move about completely out of sight of the enemy, but also the increasing role of Japanese artillery and its heavier guns.

The most sophisticated trenches were developments of these converted communication trenches. Dug to a depth of 10 feet, these also had a 3-foot parapet and a parados to the rear. They had overhead cover for about half the width of the trench, made up of a wooden platform with a foot of earth to provide protection from shell splinters to those manning the loopholes. Unlike the earth fire-step of the converted trenches, these had raised wooden platforms, 4.5 feet wide, to stand on. Beneath the platform, again fabricated from wood, were what one British observer likened to 'cubby-holes … where the garrison could live in almost complete security'. This was a little fanciful and demonstrated the naivety of many observers in matters of trench warfare. While it is possible that some of the so-called cubby-holes might have provided storage areas, it seems improbable that there would have enough room to accommodate a man, who would have to be constantly on his hands and knees in a very tight space.

The Japanese had great difficulty taking trenches such as these and they had not devised suitable tactics before the war ended. During an attack on a gun battery fronted by trenches of this type on 30 October 1904, one group of Japanese assault troops crossed the last 40 yards from their own assault trenches and jumped into the deep trench, while the main body continued up the hill to the battery 150 yards further on. Once in the trench, the Japanese were confronted by the realization that they had to move in single file along it to pursue an enemy who was no longer in a trench which zigzagged every 15 yards. None of the Japanese could bring their rifles to bear, apart from the leading soldier, but the traverses prevented him from seeing a single Russian. Worse, the Japanese could not get out of the trench. Having fallen back when the Japanese approached the trench, the Russians now took the initiative and fired on the trapped Japanese, throwing grenades and burning oil-soaked rags in amongst them. The wooden structure of the trench caught light and the exploding grenades caused mayhem. The Japanese were all killed, isolating those who had advanced on the battery. The attack was a complete failure. Two further attempts were made to take the trench in November and they both failed. On each occasion, the Japanese managed to get into the trench but then could not move along it and the same scenario of the Russians tossing in hand grenades was replayed. What no one explained, however, was how the Russians were able to escape from the trench while the Japanese were trapped in it. The answer probably lay in scaling ladders which the Russians took with them each time they climbed out of the trench.

The significance of what the Japanese had experienced in this trench was quite lost on them and, indeed, on the Russians as well. Moreover, none of the observers seems to have grasped it either. It was evident to everyone, however, that in the evolution of the trench, deeper was not only better but crucial to the survival of the occupants in the face of hostile artillery fire. Hence it was clear that, in the future, trenches were likely to be of the form which the Japanese had signally failed to capture from the Russians. This should have raised questions about why the Japanese had experienced so much trouble with capturing and holding this trench. Its depth meant that ladders were needed to get out of it, while its narrowness allowed its occupants to move only in single file, and its traverses prevented enfilade of the entire trench. It is significant that the Russians used hand grenades to deal with the Japanese in the trench and threw them into the trench rather than along it. Here was the first instance of a new form of trench warfare in which men might not only be expected to fight along a traversed trench, but have to do so with grenades. The tactics of taking trenches by frontal assault had already been shown to be costly but this experience demonstrated that some means of fighting when in them needed to be addressed, otherwise no one would ever succeed in holding a newly captured trench.

The role of the hand grenade in the fighting, both at Port Arthur and elsewhere in Manchuria, caught the attention of all the observers. While the hand grenade had never actually gone out of use since its heyday in the eighteenth century, although it had certainly lost favour among all the armies of the Western world, the apparent revival of this ancient siege weapon was seen as a revelation. There is no question that the grenade saw more action during the Russo-Japanese War than it had in the American Civil War or at Sebastopol. However, whereas many of the grenades used in the American Civil War were innovative devices that addressed the shortcomings of the traditional type of grenade, this was hardly true of the grenades used in Manchuria. All of the grenades used in the Russo-Japanese War were improvised on the spot by Russian and Japanese engineers, utilizing the materials that were to hand. Not one was manufactured in a factory.

The Russians at Port Arthur extemporized eight types of grenade, but also used the traditional spherical iron bomb of which the fortress had a sizeable stock, but which was expended quite quickly. Japanese engineers extemporized only two grenade designs, fabricating them from the tin linings of biscuit boxes. At first, the Russians over-estimated the length of Bickford fuse, so that the Japanese had time to extinguish the fuse before the grenade detonated, or to throw it back. Learning from Russian experience, the Japanese made sure that their fuses burned for about 7 seconds, so that the grenade exploded about a second after it arrived. While the Russians had some traditional grenades at Port Arthur, the Japanese had no grenades when they went war. That both sides extemporized them can be attributed to the Russians merely following usual practice in siege warfare, while the Japanese copied the Russian example. In early September 1904, a Japanese unit complained that it had no grenades with which to respond to a Russian assault on their positions, indicating that the Japanese did not employ grenades as a general rule but copied the Russian grenades when they were encountered in battle. There was no sense of innovation or novelty about devising and using such grenades as they were all in keeping with the traditional type of grenade. Typical throwing distance for any of these bombs was 20–25 yards.

In the spring of 1905, the Russians devised a percussion-fused grenade, an example of which was found by the Japanese after the Battle of Mukden. The new grenade had a long wooden handle so that it could be thrown further than the time-fused grenades. Clearly, the issue of throwing range had occupied the minds of the engineers; a handle increased the moment of inertia as the grenade left the thrower's hand, thereby increasing its momentum so that it travelled further. However, it had to be thrown upwards at a high angle to ensure that the device landed on its head, thereby operating the percussion fuse. The Japanese copied the Russian grenade but it was never used operationally. It was claimed to have been invented by the Chief Engineer of the Second Japanese Army but this was hyperbole. Both the Russian and the Japanese percussion grenades had cylindrical bodies encircled by a segmented lead band, which was supposed to produce more fragments than the time-fused designs. The Japanese grenade used streamers to act like a tail and ensure that the grenade landed head first, an approach that had been tried in the American Civil War with the Confederate copy of the Ketchum grenade of 1861. The streamers, however, must have caused drag which would have negated any range advantage that the handle might have imparted.

Implausibly, the Japanese claimed to have experienced no accidents with their percussion grenade during 'practice'. Accidental detonations due to carelessness and inexperience after the grenade had been armed, which was done by inserting the detonator and setting the cap to 'live', were typical mishaps that occurred with percussion-fused grenades. Furthermore, the grenade might not explode because it had been incorrectly armed. These disadvantages became apparent to the British when they experimented with percussion-fused grenades after the Russo-Japanese War. The Russians disliked them because they were dangerous to handle, so it is likely that few were ever used operationally; they preferred to improve methods of ignition for time fuses to make them more reliable. Once armed, a percussion-fused grenade will detonate whenever it strikes a hard surface, including when dropped or accidentally bumped against something. Perversely, the same grenade might fail to explode when used in action because it hit the ground at the wrong angle. They were unsafe and unreliable. Lethal fragments from the Japanese percussion-fused grenade could travel up to 150 yards. It is evident that many of the time-fused grenades were much less lethal because they produced few fragments when they exploded, relying more on blast for effect. Approximately 6 per cent of miscellaneous casualties in the Japanese armies for the first year of the war were probably caused by grenades.

In excess of 44,000 hand grenades were available to the five divisions of the Japanese Third Army in the course of the siege of Port Arthur from July to December 1904; that is, about fifty grenades a day per division. In June 1905, the engineers of the Second Japanese Army were reported to be making 4,000 percussion-fused grenades but these were probably never used operationally. Grenades were certainly used in much of the fighting besides that at Port Arthur, so that more than 44,000 grenades were used operationally by all the Japanese divisions in Manchuria.

While reports of the operational use of grenades implied some sort of tactical system, none was ever developed for grenades. Both the Russians and the Japanese relied upon the initiative and courage of the individual throwers. There was little sense of coordinated action with respect to other riflemen, despite the fact that grenades were used in support of operations, rather than as the principal arm in an assault. As in the American Civil War, the small numbers of relatively unreliable grenades indicate that they were used on an entirely ad hoc basis. Grenades were thrown by Russian defenders at their Japanese attackers, while attackers, Russian or Japanese, threw grenades into trenches. On some occasions, the Russians rolled grenades downhill into the Japanese saps, which the Japanese countered by fitting wooden gratings over the saps so that the grenades rolled across, or fitted wire mesh to a parapet to prevent the grenades dropping into the trench. However, no grenade exchanges appear to have occurred and no system for bombing along a trench was developed.

The Japanese discovered that aggressive attacks on Russian trenches using grenades were only successful if the operation had supporting rifle fire, yet no tactical system to maximize the cooperation between grenade throwers and riflemen was ever devised. This reflected their unimportance to infantry tactics as a whole. The numbers did not appear insignificant to the observers, however, who regarded their apparently widespread use as a major feature of the war in Manchuria.

A major problem for the Japanese was that entrenching tended to slow the momentum of an attack so that mobility was lost. The issue of mobility was somewhat overshadowed by the fact that they persisted with massed frontal assaults on Russian positions. The problem of converting break-in to breakthrough was never satisfactorily addressed because the fighting often came down to head-on slugging matches once the armies engaged each other. This was partly because the extensive use of entrenchments tended to tie the armies down. As with the American Civil War, there is the question of whether entrenching was used effectively or whether it became an obstacle. The Japanese did not often attempt to outflank the Russian positions when they had the opportunity such as at Mukden because both armies entrenched before the battle, leaving little option but for both the Russians and the Japanese to make frontal assaults. The same was true of the battles of Liaoyang and Sha-Ho. The success or failure of an assault came down to how aggressively the attackers pressed on in the face of heavy opposition. Inevitably, the attacker suffered very high casualties. The attacker's objective was to establish superiority of fire over the enemy, but it is questionable whether this was ever truly achieved in Manchuria when facing a determined defence, especially in light of the higher casualties suffered by the attacker on almost every occasion. While this may appear to support the idea that modern weapons with considerable firepower presented an insurmountable obstacle, neither the Japanese nor the Russians changed their massed infantry assault tactics to negate the effect of defensive firepower. Such assaults were carried out in waves, one after the other crashing against the enemy. Indeed, the Japanese believed, as did the British observers, that when an assault was pressed home it would always overcome defensive firepower. After all, wars were not won by armies fighting on the defensive.

The light mortar devised by Japanese engineers at Port Arthur in October 1904 may well have been in response to a Russian wrought-iron 'bomb gun' used against them. The Russian mortar was an extemporized version of the traditional mortar, while the Japanese mortar was a variation of the Japanese firework mortar. In February 1905, the Russians experimented with a light, horn-shaped mortar supposedly made of aluminium. A contract for 100 mortars and 10,000 rounds of ammunition had been placed with an engineering firm in St Petersburg, but the weapon does not seem to have materialized in a tangible form. The value of the light mortar lay in its portability, which meant that it could be sited in forward trenches to bombard the enemy trenches. Towards the end of the war, an engineer with the Japanese Third Army, Nakamura, took this a stage further and devised a more compact mortar that could be taken forward in an assault, the first mortar ever to be designed with this in mind. The mortar weighed only 36.5lb which, when broken down into its component parts, would not have proved too difficult for one man to carry in a specially designed backpack. Its designer also worked out suitable tactics for the mortar, but the war ended before it could see action, so the tactics remained untried and entirely theoretical. The Japanese even considered raising a specialist mortar corps and, had the land fighting not ended with the Battle of Mukden in February and March 1905, they might well have pressed ahead with this.

The operational value of the Japanese wooden mortar is debatable, however, since it was highly inaccurate, had a short range and was very slow to load and fire. Indeed, the bombs moved so slowly in the air that they were easy to see, making the task of dodging them tiresome but not impossible. Nevertheless, the improvised mortars were sufficiently well regarded by the Japanese for them to make and use operationally 103 5-inch mortars and twenty-three 7-inch mortars, while the destructive power of the 11,500 bombs and shells clearly made some sort of impact on the Russians. But whether all this amounted to operational success for the Japanese at some level is open to question since none of the mortars affected the outcome of any of the fighting. The effect on Russian morale was emphasized but this seems more like wishful thinking than reality. What is significant, however, is the recognition by both the Russians and the Japanese that a weapon which could be brought up close to the enemy line, capable of dropping explosive bombs into their trenches, was highly desirable since none of the artillery could perform this function.

At the start of the war, Russian and Japanese artillery mostly fired from prepared battery positions and mostly by direct line of sight to give close support to the infantry. This not only made the guns and their gunners vulnerable to small-arms fire but also to counter-battery fire. This vulnerability eventually led to the widespread adoption of indirect fire, whereby the guns were concealed on the reverse slopes of hills, which meant that gunners could no longer see their targets. Target locations and the fall of shot had to be relayed to guns, often by telephone, the first time such a system had been used. The pros and cons of indirect fire had been discussed since the end of the nineteenth century, while favourable evidence for adopting it as a general principal was apparent from the Greco-Turkish War of 1897 and the Boxer Rebellion three years later. The Russians were well aware of its advantages but in 1904 preferred to shoot by direct line of sight. The Japanese, who were keen to modernize and Europeanize their military, were probably influenced by the ideas of General Moritz Elder von Reichold who, in 1897, advocated indirect fire as a way for guns to avoid being subjected to counter-battery fire. The Japanese applied the tactic first but the Russians were quick to follow. There is no question that the value of indirect fire was amply demonstrated in the Russo-Japanese War. Nevertheless, artillery was still deployed en masse from time to time, but it paid a heavy price on such occasions.

Indirect fire meant that the infantry became even more vulnerable as their own guns had no means by which to locate and fire on concealed enemy batteries, which could engage the attacking infantry with impunity. If concealed guns were able to shell guns sited for direct fire, the latter were usually decimated, a fate that befell 180 Japanese guns at Shou-Shan-Pu on 28 August 1904. In this, the Russians were also aided by the longer range of their artillery. The Japanese often employed massed artillery, as on this occasion and at Ta-Shih-Chiao, but if they were discovered by the Russians there was a serious risk of annihilation. Massing was a pragmatic solution to the problem of command and control of the artillery in battle.

Counter-battery fire was an important element of the artillery tactics in Manchuria. Although artillery accounted for only 15 per cent of casualties in the war, this comparatively low figure disguises the suppressive effect of artillery fire. There is no doubt that artillery encouraged both sides to dig in for protection. The problem for artillerists was their ammunition. The traditional role of artillery was to support the infantry, in which capacity it often fired anti-personnel rounds, usually in the form of shrapnel. Such shells consisted of a carrier shell containing lead balls held in a resin composition, and a burster charge. A time fuse detonated the shell when it was in the air so that a cone of balls was fired downwards. Fired on soldiers who were out in the open, shrapnel was very destructive, but as soon as they dug in it was far less so. Then, the only effective round was a high-explosive shell fitted with a percussion fuse so that it detonated on impact and destroyed the earthwork defences. Moreover, high explosive was the only effective ammunition for counter-battery work. The relative composition of ammunition was, however, initially weighted in favour of anti-personnel work.

The figure of 15 per cent also conceals the fact that this is an average figure that takes into account all the fighting, including battles and the siege of Port Arthur. The power of artillery in the war is better illustrated by the fact that 50 per cent of casualties during the siege were caused by artillery. Initially, the Japanese had no heavy guns at Port Arthur but, by October 1904, heavy siege artillery had arrived, including eighteen 280mm howitzers which fired 500lb shells 10,000 yards. All told, the Japanese fired 35,000 of these shells during the course of the siege. At the height of the siege, the Japanese had 474 guns of various calibres engaged in bombarding the Russian defences. Thus, while the battles elsewhere in Manchuria were principally traditional infantry-versus-infantry battles in which artillery played a supporting role, the fighting at Port Arthur became an artillery-dominated slugging match in which the Russians eventually suffered 31,000 casualties and the Japanese 58,000. Although this was a Japanese victory, because the Russians surrendered in January 1905 after five months of bitter fighting, the Japanese losses were almost twice those of the Russians.

Not only was artillery becoming the dominant power on the battlefield but the role of the infantry began to change. Rather than the artillery supporting the infantry, it became necessary for the infantry to protect the guns. This was especially true in the battles away from Port Arthur. When the attacking Japanese infantry were several thousand yards away from Russian guns, the guns were quite capable of holding off the assault without the protection of their own infantry, as happened at Ta-Shih-Chiao when six Russian batteries held the Japanese infantry at 3,300 yards, at which distance they had to dig in. An artillery duel was conducted at this distance before the infantry were engaged.

The duration of artillery bombardments varied. In September and November 1904, the preliminary bombardments of Russian positions at Port Arthur lasted 6 hours and 3 hours respectively before the infantry assaulted but in October the Japanese subjected the Russians to a four-day bombardment before an assault. Japanese artillery had the serious disadvantage of being outranged by Russian artillery which meant that, in order to engage the Russian guns, the Japanese had to come closer and risk destruction, so the advantages of indirect fire were immediately apparent to them. This sometimes became necessary in order to destroy Russian Maxim emplacements.

Unlike the Japanese, the Russians had long been interested in the power of the machine-gun and had experimented with a version of the Gatling as long ago as the 1870s. In the 1890s, they experimented with the British-made Maxim and, in 1902, secured a licence from Vickers to manufacture the guns in Russia. In 1904, General Alexei Kuropatkin, GOC of Russian forces in the Far East, ordered 246 tripod-mounted Maxims and 411 carriage-mounted Maxims, but received a mere sixteen of the former and forty-six of the latter. Indeed, on the eve of war, the Russians had only sixty-four Maxims but by July 1904 the Russian defenders of Port Arthur had sixty-two. By 1906, the total number in Russian service had risen to 944, distributed in 118 machine-gun companies each with eight guns, with one such company in each division. The Russian-made Maxim was updated in 1905 and again in 1910. The Maxim was very reliable and capable of firing thousands of rounds without jamming. It was, however, heavy, weighing 107lb when mounted on a tripod and as much as 537lb when mounted on a wheeled carriage which was supposed to make it easier to transport. Neither version, however, was easily transportable; hence, it was a weapon which the Russians used solely for defence, in which role it was highly effective. During one assault on a Russian redoubt defended by two Maxims, a 200-strong Japanese company, advancing in skirmish order, was completely annihilated at a range of 300 yards within 2 minutes of the guns coming into action.

The Japanese, who had no machine-guns in 1904, were impressed by the effect of Russian Maxims on their infantry assaults and needed little persuasion to adopt the machine-gun. They opted for the French Hotchkiss, which was lighter than the Maxim, weighing only 27lb, including its tripod. They manufactured it under licence in Tokyo. Within six months, each Japanese infantry division had ten machine-guns and every cavalry brigade had six. Unlike the Russians, the Japanese experimented with taking machine-guns forward during an assault, a tactic made feasible by the lighter Hotchkiss. The limiting factor was logistics; there was a serious problem bringing forward enough ammunition to sustain a gun which fired 500–600 rounds a minute. An effective tactic sometimes used by the Japanese was long-range supporting fire, shooting over the heads of their attacking infantry. This sophisticated technique of indirect fire was not pursued, however.

The gas-operated Hotchkiss was not as reliable as the recoil-operated Maxim and tended to jam more often, sometimes as often as every 300 rounds. Nevertheless, when the Russians attempted mass assaults on the Japanese positions defended by Hotchkiss machine-guns, the outcome was predictable. Yet, time and again, both the Russians and the Japanese persisted in frontal assaults on well-defended positions. In the battles of Liaoyang, 203 Metre Hill at Port Arthur and Mukden, for example, Russian Maxims were especially effective and caused the Japanese very high casualties. At Mukden, the Russians had only fifty-four Maxims in action, while the Japanese had 254 machine-guns. When combined with barbed-wire entanglements which halted or impeded an assault, the effect of the guns was accentuated. Indeed, barbed wire and machine-guns were an especially deadly combination, particularly when the guns were sited to provide crossfire.

Unlike his European counterparts, the Japanese soldier was trained to be more than a rifle-and-bayonet man. Indeed, he was trained to create earthworks which, certainly in the British Army, were the responsibility of the engineers. The Russian soldier was, in many respects, the antithesis of the Japanese soldier, and was trained to assault in massed ranks, to not return fire while advancing and to shoot in volleys, even when entrenched. By the end of the war, the injunction on returning fire when advancing on the enemy was ignored and independent fire when entrenched became more common, but the Russian soldier was given much less freedom of action in battle compared to his Japanese counterpart. The destruction wreaked by Russian Maxims led to the Japanese making their elimination a priority in battle. During the second assault on Port Arthur on 6 September 1904, a preliminary artillery bombardment lasting 6 hours failed to silence the Maxims in the Waterworks redoubt so that field guns had to be brought even closer to engage them. Because of the greater emphasis placed on individual courage in the Japanese Army, rather than collective bravery inculcated almost as a drill, which typified the Russian Army, some Japanese soldiers went to extraordinary lengths to destroy Russian machine-guns. At Mukden, two mountain guns were manhandled into position to silence a Maxim facing the Japanese 5th Division. These incidents highlighted a particular problem: how to deal with hostile machine-guns. No satisfactory solution was found during the war, although artillery fire was the only effective option.

Following the failure of the second Japanese assault on the defences of Port Arthur at the end of August 1904, Japanese engineers set about sapping and mining operations. The first mines were detonated in November under the counterscarp of the Sung-Shu fortress. Another three were fired three days later under the fortress of Erh-Lung. One of the largest mines, containing 4,000lb of explosive, was detonated under the Chi-Kuan fortress in December; the Russians lost 800 men and what was left of the fortress was captured a few hours after the mine was fired. Ten days later, two more mines were detonated under Erh-Lung. On 31 December, more mines were blown under Sung-Shu, the last remaining redoubt to stand in the way of the Japanese, killing most of its garrison. Port Arthur surrendered on 2 January 1905. The mine fired at Petersburg in 1865 had contained gunpowder, but the Japanese mines all contained high explosive which was far more powerful. The Japanese did not have it all their own way. The Russians counter-mined, sometimes successfully, although often not. Inevitably, Russian and Japanese miners met underground and fought each other with spades and pistols. And every time mines were detonated, the Japanese rushed forward to try to take the ruins of the fortresses. Sometimes, the Russian survivors fought tenaciously, fire from their Maxims often proving decisive, and forced back the Japanese.

While mining was an ancient feature of siege warfare, the Japanese were the first to use high explosives and fired many more mines than had ever been detonated in any siege hitherto. The Russo-Japanese War was the first in which the machine-gun and barbed wire were used. While the Gatling gun had seen action in the American Civil War, it was not a true machine-gun. Barbed wire had only ever been used as a form of military corral fencing; no one had used it to create obstacles in front of fortifications. The effects of these two innovations were profound, although not all the European observers, nor indeed the American observers, appreciated the full implications of their introduction to the battlefield. The war also demonstrated that the positioning artillery close to the front line, so that the guns could engage targets by direct line of sight, was outmoded and very costly. Indeed, the advantages of concealing the guns to fire indirectly were more than amply proved. The destruction wrought by concealed Russian guns on Japanese batteries should have been sufficient to give other armies cause for thought. Indeed, the importance of counter-battery fire to the outcome of battles during the war should have led the European powers to conclude that direct fire was no longer a feasible option, especially as the role of artillery was superseding that of the infantry as the dominant force on the battlefield. The infantry were forced to dig in, not only to protect themselves from small-arms fire, but from the guns firing both shrapnel and high explosive. The firepower of artillery, rather than encouraging mobility, encouraged immobility.

Perversely, immobility was also encouraged by the infantry tactics used by the Japanese and the Russians. The consequence of continued massed infantry assaults that were destroyed by machine-guns, rifle fire and artillery was that the survivors dug in. Rather than fall back, the Japanese tried to dig in where they were stopped, although that was not always possible. The routine of digging in for protection was well established at the time of the Russo-Japanese War. Unfortunately, the means by which mobility and momentum could be restored had yet to be considered. No one had realized that assaults based on frontal attacks by massed infantry encouraged stalemate. Moreover, the prevailing philosophy among European armies, even after the Russo-Japanese War ended, was that if an attack failed it was because of insufficient spirit, insufficient numbers of infantrymen in the attack, or poor leadership. The notion that the attack had failed because of the employment of massed infantry in a frontal assault, which was then destroyed by massive firepower, did not seem to sink in, even when the effect of counter-battery fire from concealed positions was readily acknowledged. The problem of indirect fire was keeping control of the batteries which required good communications. The use of the telephone, although the wires tended to get cut by artillery fire, and an early use of radio by the Russians, showed the way forward. However, indirect fire was dismissed by most European powers as inappropriate to the infantry-support role of artillery and the sort of war for which they trained and anticipated fighting. None of the European powers imagined that they would find themselves in a position of having to fight a war from entrenched positions, largely because so much emphasis was placed on the attack and élan.

The apparent rise of the hand grenade during the war made a big impression on the military observers, all of whom believed that they were witnessing a new aspect of warfare. Indeed, the reports about grenades all give the impression that they were used in huge numbers. Only 44,000 hand grenades were used by the Japanese during the siege of Port Arthur and, while there are no figures for the numbers used by the Russians, it is safe to assume that they may have used up to three times as many more. But this would still only be 132,000 over a five-month period, or 26,400 a month and the Russian garrison was some 40,000 strong. If half were engaged in the fighting each month, this amounts to about one grenade per man per month, which hardly constitutes a high expenditure of grenades. When compared with the numbers grenades manufactured and used in the First World War, the numbers used in Manchuria were paltry.

Nevertheless, the numbers not withstanding, the consequence of the apparent widespread use of grenades in Manchuria was that the British and German armies went away with the idea that 'modern' grenades were essential to a 'modern' army. Thus, in the years immediately following the end of the Russo-Japanese War, Britain and Germany devised new grenades. As far as the British were concerned, the grenade was a specialist weapon which only specialists should be trained to use, namely Royal Engineers. However, the British had no clear idea how they would use them should the need arise. It is evident that, in Manchuria, grenades had been used on an entirely ad hoc basis, their principal purpose being the destruction of the enemy occupying a trench. Grenades may have been used on troops in the open but as a general rule this would have been discouraged because of the danger to friendly troops. The explosion and grenade fragments would have been far more deadly in the confined space of a trench. Indeed, in one instance, a Japanese soldier was supposed to have been decapitated by a grenade. This may well have been a freak event since none of the grenades used by the Russians or the Japanese were capable of producing a lot of lethal fragments; most of the effect would have been blast. While the so-called roller grenade was no doubt devised to destroy barbed wire, it is likely to have been used against trenches as well when circumstances permitted. It is worth noting that the hand grenade was used offensively as well as defensively. The Japanese, for example, certainly threw them into Russian trenches they were attacking. Similarly, the Russians threw grenades into trenches they had just lost to the Japanese. Such trenches became death traps.

The war also saw the first instances of trenches deeper than the height of a man from which infantry fought rather merely used as a safe conduit to the fire trenches. Such trenches need a raised platform to enable the troops to fire over the parapet, which led to the first instances of fire-steps. Hitherto, fire trenches had tended to be much shallower to enable a man to see and engage the enemy as he approached. While the Russian trenches were formed in parallel lines that consisted of a fire trench, support and reserve lines, the Japanese only dug a single line which reflected the relative short range of their artillery compared to the Russian guns and the fact that the Japanese anticipated to be always attacking and rarely defending. The Japanese hardly ever had to be concerned about a Russian break-in being converted into a breakthrough; their single trench line was never intended to act as a barrier, but merely as shelter for the troops from Russian fire.

While the use of grenades in Manchuria was no more than a modern take on the traditional use of grenades in sieges, the introduction of bomb-throwing guns or light mortars was novel. Their main benefit was their ability to throw a bomb further than a man could throw one. However, they were very inaccurate and could not be relied upon to send a bomb to the same spot twice. The explosive power of the bombs was small and their effect was undoubtedly more moral than material. Again, these mortars made an impression on some observers out of proportion to the impact on the fighting, although the British were not so impressed with them that they wanted to devise mortars of their own. The Germans, on the other hand, were persuaded to devise small mortars for use in trenches for infantry support. These did not enter service until 1911 and 1913. The key here was that the crude bomb-throwers devised by the Russians and Japanese were intended to be infantry-support artillery. While it is true that artillery had traditionally fulfilled the role of infantry support, no mortar of any description had ever been employed in this role before. In this sense, the mortars were, indeed, novel but in other respects they were simply crude expedients.

Nevertheless, the rise of so-called infantry-support weapons, into which category the machine-gun also fell, was a new departure in warfare and this was directly attributable to the rise of trench warfare in Manchuria, which was itself attributable to the increase in firepower available to the infantry and artillery. This was a self-perpetuating engine of cause and effect fuelled by the inability of both sides to get away from the idea of massed infantry making frontal assaults on defended positions. Stalemate and mutual immobility arose as soon as one side dug in because the other side immediately followed suit. Battle was conducted from static positions.

CHAPTER 7

The First World War, New Problems and New Solutions

The popular view that the First World War epitomized the 'futility' of war, that it embodied the stupidity of obstinate generals who wilfully sacrificed their men and that the horrors of trench warfare could have been avoided, is one that is very resistant to any evidence to the contrary. Indeed, the notion that the First World War, the Great War, the War to End all Wars, was an aberration in which warfare descended into a kind of madness in which men were slaughtered in their thousands for a few square yards of ground, is a view derived not so much from the actuality of what happened but from popularist versions of it fostered by memoirs published ten years after the war. Not least among those who claimed that the war had been generaled by the incompetent, but fought by heroes, was David Lloyd George, who fostered the view that so many deaths had not only been unnecessary but avoidable had the generals, Haig in particular, paid heed to his wise council. In the face of such 'evidence', it has always been very difficult to disprove such 'truths' as unnecessary sacrifice and futility. The anti-war sentiment is very much a British issue, however. The French, for example, do not hold such views even though they suffered many more casualties than the British. The First World War was far from futile and the very antithesis of an aberration in military affairs.

There is no question that the First World War was unlike any previous war. Its scale and its intensity, the industrialized totality of the war and the four-year mutual stalemate that existed along the Western Front, the principal focus of the war, made the First World War unique in the history of warfare. However, unique does not equate with aberrant any more than stalemate equated with stasis. Indeed, not only was the stalemate on the Western Front entirely predictable, although not inevitable, but the constant efforts by both sides to resolve it and restore mobility, while working to prevent each other from attaining that mobility, ensured that the Western Front was constantly changing. The dynamics of this process of change were complex but, by 1917, effective solutions to stalemate were being developed. By the spring of 1918, a new form of warfare had evolved. The nature of warfare was fundamentally altered by the need to overcome the stalemate of trench warfare on the Western Front. So profound were these changes that they formed the basis of the tactical doctrines employed in most armies across the world thereafter. It is a simple truth that this could not have occurred had the generals been quite so stupid and the fighting quite so pointless as the myth of the futility of the First World War dictates.

Predicable though the stalemate of the Western Front might have been, there is a gulf of difference between foreseeable and avoidable. While it is true that no army went to war in 1914 with the intention of remaining entrenched for four years, neither was any army trained to avoid this happening. Indeed, in some ways, the policy in all armies of entrenching when halted tended to be counter-intuitive to the doctrine of always attacking, since to be entrenched was to be on the defensive. It was believed that entrenchments would be no more than temporary because the army would not remain where it halted; it would move on in order to engage the enemy in a more fluid mobile battle. Armies trained for fluid manoeuvre and mobile battle; they did not train to fight from static positions. There was no thought among the British or the French armies about siege. The very idea was anathema to the long-established doctrine of the assault. Armies were trained and equipped for the assault. Hence, in the British Army, for example, ammunition for the 13-pounder and 18-pounder field guns, its principal field artillery, was mostly shrapnel because their target was anticipated to be enemy infantry advancing over open ground, rather then enemy guns or, indeed, enemy infantry who had dug in.

Despite the preconceptions of the armies before the outbreak of war, the First World War was an artillery war rather than an infantry war like the Russo-Japanese War had been. Throughout the war, the dominant force on the battlefield, especially on the Western Front, was artillery. This was reflected in the casualty figures: 60 per cent of all casualties were caused by high explosive fired by artillery and trench mortars. Compared with the 15 per cent of the Russo-Japanese War, it is clear that the firepower of artillery had not only increased by a factor of four over the previous ten years but its role was in the process of changing. The process of change was not simply a matter of scale, in that the number of guns was increased. More importantly, it was a tactical change brought about by a more scientific approach to gunnery. By 1918, gunnery had become highly sophisticated and was no longer a matter of engaging targets which the gunners could see.

That the fighting on the Western Front was an artillery war, rather than one dominated by infantry-infantry combat, can be gauged by the changing ratio of guns to infantry in the BEF as the war progressed. In August 1914, the BEF had 410 guns of all calibres but few heavy guns and no howitzers. By the time of the opening of the Somme campaign on 1 July 1916, the fifteen divisions of the Fourth Army had 1,493 guns, including heavy howitzers and 15-inch railway guns. At the end of the war in November 1918, the BEF possessed 6,406 guns, a fifteen-fold increase since 1914. These numbers represented a doubling in the ratio of guns per

1,000 infantrymen in the BEF, rising from 6.3 in 1914 to 13 in 1918. There was an even bigger increase in the French Army, where the ratio went from 4 in 1914 to 13 in 1918, while in the German army the ratio went from 6 to 11.5. Both the French and German armies were bigger than the BEF and, therefore, had more guns. At the end of the war, the French and German armies both had about two and half times as many guns as the BEF, about 15,500 each. At the same time as the number of guns increased, the BEF grew from 400,000 in five infantry divisions and one cavalry division in August 1914, to about 3.5 million men in sixty-one infantry divisions and three cavalry divisions, an 8.75-fold growth in manpower. In 1918, the Royal Artillery boasted more personnel than the entire BEF of 1914, some 520,000 men. While the number of artillery soldiers was always fewer than the number of infantrymen, the scale of the increase indicates just how important artillery had become to the conduct of the war.

One of the most numerous of British guns was the 18-pounder, used to fire shrapnel and high-explosive shells. This gun fired about 100 million shells during the war, most of these from 1916 onwards. The French equivalent of the 18-pounder, the 75mm (the famous *soixante-quinze*), had a rate of fire of fifteen rounds a minute, as fast as a well-trained British infantryman could aim, load and fire his rifle. Such a rate of fire was, of course, a technical feasibility rather than usual practice. For one battery of six guns to fire at only ten rounds a minute would have required a prodigious quantity of shells to sustain such a rate for any length of time. This presented a huge logistical and, indeed, manufacturing, problem. For the British, such rates of fire were simply not possible until 1916. The infamous shell scandal of 1915, which brought down the government of the day and gave birth to the Ministry of Munitions, meant that British guns were often forced to fire no more than a few rounds a day. There was also the matter of barrel wear. High rates of fire wore out barrels very quickly. Worn barrels led to inaccurate shooting and to rounds falling short. Hence, the higher the rates of fire, the bigger the ammunition logistical challenge and the more replacement barrels were needed. Merely because a gun could fire faster than its predecessors did not automatically make it a more effective gun.

British guns ranged from the 18-pounder, the most common type, to 15-inch railway guns which could fire a shell up to 20 miles. One of the deficiencies of British artillery was the lack of heavy-calibre howitzers. The pre-war British Army had seen little requirement for weapons which were unlikely to be employed in the sort of battle for which the BEF trained, namely one of manoeuvre and infantry assault in open country. Trench warfare required these guns because of the need to destroy trenches and deep dugouts which were immune to all but the biggest shells. Their numbers began to increase slowly from 1915. The ideal ratio of heavy guns to field guns was 1 : 2, but this was not achieved until after 1916. In 1914, the BEF had six heavy batteries but by 1918 this had increased to 440. Similar problems with numbers of guns, and heavy guns in particular, existed in other armies, but it was perhaps the British Army that was least prepared for trench warfare in matters of artillery, while the Germans had a higher ratio of large-calibre guns to smaller guns. Their 420mm howitzers, the largest guns in the world at the time, had been specifically designed to reduce the Belgian forts during the opening phase of the war.

At the outbreak of war, the French possessed some howitzers but almost half of their medium and heavy guns were obsolescent. French tactical doctrine had emphasized the assault, to which end their artillery was designed to aid movement and rapid fire so that its firepower would provide shock and thereby overwhelm enemy artillery in counter-battery fire. The French, no more than the British, were equipped or trained for static warfare and had neither the guns nor the ammunition for trench warfare. On the other hand, German artillery had paid particular attention to howitzer technology and the Imperial German Army went to war in August 1914 with many more howitzers than the British or the French. German superiority in howitzers was magnified by their employment to fire indirectly on enemy positions. Indeed, the howitzer which, by its very design, was intended to fire at a high trajectory, lent itself very well to indirect fire. Moreover, the howitzer was much more suited to dropping heavy shells into trenches. Field guns were not designed for plunging fire.

A number of factors affected the way in which artillery was employed during the war, not least being technological innovations, not only in artillery and ammunition, but also in other fields such as aerial photography and map-making.

It is a truth not widely appreciated outside academic circles that the infantry of 1918 was not the infantry of 1914. In 1914, all infantry in all armies was trained solely to use the rifle and bayonet. Infantry was trained to attack, the bayonet charge being the essence of the assault. Infantrymen were trained to obey orders, not to interpret them or to act on their own initiative, except in a very limited set of circumstances, all of which related to the attack. By 1918, all infantry had been transformed, to a greater or lesser degree, into all-arms soldiers, trained in a range of weapons besides the traditional rifle and bayonet, including the light machine-gun, the hand grenade and the rifle grenade. The infantryman had become a technician who could use his initiative and use the appropriate tools to carry out specific tasks, and did not have to rely on the artillery to provide support. He was now trained to do more than simply engage enemy infantry in open battle. Such changes came about as a direct consequence of the rise of trench warfare on the Western Front. The process was a combination of new technology and new tactics, brought about by new ideas. It was the changing relationship of technology with tactics that held the key, rather than some war-winning new machine.

Unlike any previous war in which entrenchments had become major features of the battlefields, the First World War was the first fully industrialized war in which the economies of the belligerent nations were turned over to the prosecution of the war. Industrialization was not new, of course. The American Civil War was very much an industrialized one, certainly as far as the North was concerned, but the scale of the process during the First World War was unprecedented and this fuelled change. Solutions to problems had to be found much more quickly than in peacetime. What might have taken years to resolve in peacetime had to be done in months. New munitions, which came to be forever associated with trench warfare, had to be invented, developed and manufactured so rapidly that traditional methods did not apply. Both the Mills hand grenade and the Stokes mortar were products of this process. Had not Britain been switching over to full-scale war production across its entire economy in late 1914 and early 1915, neither of these weapons would have existed. Here was a contradiction: less industrialization would have meant that the armaments firms would have taken on the task of inventing and making both hand grenades and trench mortars, but none of them was capable of doing so quickly because the normal process of development took years to complete. New munitions such the Mills and the Stokes were key to the changes that were to take place in infantry combat and the conduct of the fighting on the Western Front.

For all practical purposes, no army went to war in 1914 equipped with grenades and trench mortars, not even the Imperial German Army, although it was better equipped with specialist munitions than the British, French or Belgian armies. While the British had developed a percussion-fused hand grenade from an example of the Japanese grenade brought back from Manchuria, the British possessed so few of the new weapon, about fifty, that it was more of a curiosity than a serious munition. Neither Britain nor France possessed trench mortars but neither Britain nor France anticipated siege warfare to develop. There was no concept of employing what were weapons of siege in open battle. The Germans, on the other hand, had perceived their war-making somewhat differently, if only because they had anticipated fighting two enemies, one in the west, France, and one in the east, Russia. To do this successfully, Germany expected to have to hold the line with one of them until the other was defeated. Hence, there was an inkling that static warfare might become necessary in the short term and, with this in mind, Germany had developed hand grenades and light mortars. However, while the German Army had more grenades than the British, the number it possessed was small as, indeed, was the number of light mortars it had in service in 1914. Germany was no more prepared for static warfare than any other nation.

No army went to war in August 1914 with the intention of engaging in stalemate for even a few days, let alone four years. The Schlieffen Plan, whereby the German Army swept into Belgium and northern France, seemed to have provided the perfect model for outmanoeuvring and outfighting the French and the British. The German advance on Paris seemed unstoppable. The 1914 battles of Mons and Le Cateau were the sort of battles for which the British Army had trained, being fluid and dependent on infantry engaging enemy infantry in firefights, the winner of which was whoever developed the most intense volume of fire at ranges of about 400 and 800 yards. Likewise, the battles of the Sambre, the Marne and the Aisne, which blunted the German advance and turned the German Army aside from it prize of the French capital, were infantry battles in which artillery acted in support rather than as the principal. When the Germans faced the British at Mons, the rapid fire of the British infantry cut them down with such effect and British fire discipline was such that the Germans believed they were being hit by concentrated machine-gun fire. The French, meanwhile, had a 'Schlieffen Plan' of their own, known as Plan 17, which they put into operation as soon as Germany attacked through Belgium. The French hit the region of Alsace and entered German territory but were beaten back with heavy losses.

None of the battles proved to be decisive in that neither the Germans nor the Allies were beaten. The consequence was a series of manoeuvres and battles which turned the Germans from their sweep through northern France to cross above Paris, and engage in further fighting that pushed the Germans northwards. These actions sometimes required the infantry to march 30 miles in a day, then fight intensely for the next two or three days, before disengaging to march yet again, only to fight yet again. The inevitable consequence for British, French and German alike was exhaustion. The armies had to rest and, after the Battle of the Aisne in September 1914, the infantry began to dig in, preparing what they thought were temporary trenches that would offer shelter for no more than a few days, after which time they would move off again to find the enemy. The few days dragged out and became a week while the Allies and the Germans engaged in battles further to the north, the armies trying to outmanoeuvre each other and fight the decisive battle. A series of engagements spread like a rash up from the Aisne northwards towards the Channel coast. The armies fought themselves to a standstill.

While the Germans were content to dig in, sometimes making tactical withdrawals to more advantageous ground before digging in, the British, Belgians and French were anxious to take back every piece of land occupied by the invaders and ended up in far less favourable positions. The Germans were prepared to wait until circumstances improved before continuing their invasion and complete the defeat of France at a time of their choosing. The British, French and Belgians, on the other hand, viewed their positions as no more than temporary while they recuperated from the fighting, re-armed with guns and replenished ammunition and absorbed the rather alarmingly high number of replacements to make up the battle losses, ready to take to the offensive in the spring of 1915. The Allies adopted an aggressive stance, while the Germans, although hardly passive, adopted a holding stance. This difference in approach between the Allies and the Germans was to have profound consequences for the conduct of the war and how the fighting developed along the Western Front. The French and the Belgians, in particular, were not prepared to concede another inch of sovereign territory to the Germans, not even in the interests of tactical advantage. Until the German offensives of 1918, most offensives on the Western Front were Allied operations and most of these had the same object: to crash through the German lines and encircle the German Army in a vast sweep towards the sea.

Between September and December 1914, the armies halted and dug themselves in where they happened to stop, only the contours of the ground, the natural features and obstacles, such as rivers, and the locality of the enemy dictating where they dug. This period, usually referred to as the Race to the Sea because of the general northwards movement of the armies as they tried to outmanoeuvre each other, leading to a series of battles, decided who held which ground. More often than not, the Germans succeeded in holding the higher ground, partly because of the geography of France, which meant that the Allies were usually approaching the German Army from the lower ground. The line of entrenchments eventually stretched almost unbroken from the Swiss border to the North Sea, meandering from mountains in the south and east to the low-lying wetlands of Belgium, and eventually to the sandy dunes near Nieuport, crossing high scarps and undulating chalky plains, divided by the courses of major rivers such as the Somme and the Aisne. This topographically and geographically diverse area, a relatively narrow band no more than a few miles in depth, was to become the principal theatre of operations during the First World War. This was the Western Front. While there were other theatres besides the Western Front, it was here that the main body of the German Army was engaged throughout the course of the war. It was clear to all concerned that the war would be decided on the Western Front, despite those in Britain and France who advocated an alternative approach to attack the soft underbelly of the enemy. This led to operations in the Dardanelles and in Salonika. Palestine and Mesopotamia were also arenas of war as were, of course, the Balkans. The Russian Front was second only to the Western Front and events in the East had a profound effect on what occurred in the West, especially after Soviet Russia made a peace of sorts with the Germans, which enabled Germany to move the bulk of its forces in the East to the Western Front in 1917.

It is important to realize that this line, or band, which came to be known as the Western Front, was neither uniform in composition nor static. While the line did not move much east or west for most of the war, in terms of which side took and held which pieces of ground, nevertheless, the assumption that the Western Front was, therefore, static is a misunderstanding of the nature of trench warfare. Moreover, stalemate did not mean stasis. Between late 1914 and the spring of 1918, the Western Front was transformed from a thin barrier of entrenched men and a few strands of barbed wire, against which essentially nineteenth-century assault tactics were dashed, to a deep zone of flexible strongpoints protected by fields of wire entanglements, the overcoming of which led to the emergence of an entirely new concept of warfare. Had the Western Front been as static as the myths about the First World War would have it, not only would such a radical change in warfare not have occurred but the German Army would not have been defeated militarily on the battlefield in 1918. And let there be no doubting this last fact. Myth upon myth has abounded about how Germany lost the First World War, none of them admitting of military defeat. Yet that is exactly what happened. Had this not been the case, the war would have ended differently, indecisively and unresolved militarily. The changing concept of warfare and Germany's defeat on the battlefield were intimately linked.

Barbed wire became a defining motif of the Western Front. In October 1914, British sappers 'put up three strands of wire' but, by early 1915, belts were being erected in no-man's-land by Allied and German troops that were 16–20 feet wide, forming a wire web between stakes. By 1916, huge rolls of concertina wire and criss-crossing mattresses of wire formed belts 30–60 yards deep, arranged to funnel men into killing zones for machine-guns, mortars and artillery. Such obstacles were impassable and had to be cut to allow men through, not only for raids but especially for major offensives. Much time and effort was devoted to finding ways of destroying wire obstacles. Hand-operated wire-cutters became essential tools for raids and night patrols in no-man's-land. The British tried to use shrapnel fired by 18-pounders in the hope that the balls would cut the strands but it was not very successful. The answer lay in high explosive, although a suitable fuse which detonated the shell immediately it touched the ground, rather than after it had buried itself, had to be developed. Such a fuse, the Newton No. 107 Fuse, was devised well before the opening of the Somme, but its use was restricted before the offensive opened to prevent the Germans learning that the British had a fuse suitable for destroying wire.

The development of trench warfare on the Western Front was a complex process in which no single factor can be said to have been the principal cause of change, except to say that, from the beginning of 1915, the driving force was a need to convert a break-in of the enemy line to a breakthrough, so that mobile open warfare could be resumed. At the same time, the layout of the trench systems and everything related to the defence of the ground they covered, as well as the defence of what lay behind the front line, was a counter-force to tactical development of the break-in. There was, in effect, an arms-and-tactics race between attack and defence. While the tactics of the assault were being developed to overcome existing defences, those same defences evolved to counter any new tactical scheme for the attack. This was very much a dynamic process in which attack sometimes had the lead, while at other times defence was the more advanced. Most of the new weapons, the change in tactics, and the evolution of command and control systems were centred on winning this race. Such a process had not occurred in the American Civil War nor in the Russo-Japanese War. The war on the Western Front was different from preceding wars because of this process of evolution and change.

The trenches dug in 1914 were not very different from those dug in Manchuria a few years earlier or, indeed, those dug in America in the 1860s. Their purpose was the same, protect the occupants from small-arms fire and shrapnel, while offering an obstacle to the enemy should he attack, and sited to provide concealment and a good field of fire, to which end any obstacles, such as trees, buildings and haystacks, were supposed to be removed. According to British pre-war manuals, the field of fire was supposed to be 500 yards, although 300–400 yards was often the best that could be achieved. At this stage of the war, there was still talk of fire superiority; whoever gained this was going to win the fight, irrespective of any entrenchments. The trenches were not intended to provide any sort of permanent defensive position, however, but were a guard against surprise attacks, especially at night. Night attacks had been a feature of the Russo-Japanese War and there was no reason for anyone to assume that hostilities would be suspended on the Western Front merely because darkness fell. With this in mind, it was common practice to stretch a few strands of barbed wire between a row of stakes in front of the trenches, preferably on the flanks as well, and hang empty tin cans or other metal objects from them to provide a crude early warning system. Before the end of the year, tin cans were replaced by an improvised flare alarm. Although, in the BEF, these trenches were dug according to the principals set out in Field Service Regulations, there was a cheerful amateurishness and a sense of improvisation about it all in the early days of trench warfare, which was not shared by either the Germans or the French. They were much more in earnest. This easygoing attitude of the BEF did not last long, however.

Along the line of the Western Front, the British, French and Belgian armies faced the German Army, each side well entrenched and separated by a strip of no-man's-land that varied in depth from a few tens of yards to nearly half a mile. The form of the trenches varied from army to army but the German trenches were mostly well constructed, while those of the French tended to be poorly built and poorly maintained. The quality of the British trenches varied according to which battalion had been responsible for their original construction and the attitude to trench maintenance of those who came afterwards. One aspect that was universal in the early days was uniformity and neatness, much prized initially as evidence of soldierly bearing and professionalism. Uniformity and neatness were soon discovered to be the worst possible qualities in an entrenchment. Indeed, they came to signify inexperience and lack of skill in trench fighting. Such trenches were killers because even the slightest movement or change that broke the neat orderliness was instantly seen; and German snipers soon learned the locations in the Allied trenches where men were careless. Almost from the start of trench warfare, German snipers made British parapets dangerous places for the unwary and they took a steady toll of the incautious. Ideally, trenches not only blended into their surroundings, but the parapet was disordered, uneven and camouflaged, all of this designed to hide the location of the trench and prevent movement in it from being noticed. There are few straight lines of the sort so favoured by peace-time sergeant-majors to be found in nature. Such military orderliness had no place in the trenches of the Western Front.

In the autumn of 1914, some British troops at Ypres adapted Belgian field-boundary ditches by widening and deepening them. By January 1915, many of the trenches in the region of Ypres had flooded and there was no alternative but to abandon them. The new 'trenches' were very shallow indeed because the water table was only a few feet below ground level; dig below it and the trench filled with water. The only way to provide adequate depth of cover was to build a sandbag breastwork 6 feet high and 8 feet thick, a hugely labour-intensive business that took several months to complete, made more difficult by regular shelling. The trenches at Armentières were similarly constructed and, by May 1915, when they were occupied by the Leinsters, Captain Hitchcock noted that they 'were duck-boarded, and the parapets and paradoses were completely revetted with sand-bags. The parapets were 6 feet high, and the wooden fire steps being 1½ feet in height, gave a fire position of 4½ feet. Owing to the low-lying nature of the terrain the trenches were breast-works.'

Clearly, the nature of the ground made a big difference to how the trenches were constructed but the object was always to provide robust trenches with sides revetted with timber, sandbags or corrugated iron to prevent collapse. The trenches dug in the chalk around Arras and in the region of the River Somme were sturdier, drier and less prone to collapse because the ground was firmer than the soil in Flanders. The chalk spoil had to be dispersed much more carefully than Flanders dirt, however, because even a hint of white gave away the presence of a working party, as well as the location of the trench they were digging or repairing. The same problems, of course, beset the Germans and the French. The German trenches at Ypres were just as prone to flooding, just as muddy and just as labour-intensive to build and maintain as any built by the British or the French in that sector of the front, despite the fact that the Germans held the higher ground.

The very first 'trenches' dug by the British were not trenches at all but so-called scrapes, hastily dug hollows in the ground no more than a few inches deep with a low bank of earth thrown up in front. These could only be dug from a prone position, which was no doubt inspired by the Japanese example in the Russo-Japanese War, and they could only be used in the prone position. The intention, of course, was merely to provide cover for riflemen while they engaged enemy infantry. The first 'proper' trenches dug in the autumn of 1914 followed the ideal narrow and shallow ditch principal, with a built-up parapet and a build-up parados, such a trench stretching out in a neat straight line. Those being dug only a few months later were much less in accordance with the peacetime ideals of military precision. Not only were trenches becoming wider and deeper in the last months of 1914 but they were no longer dug in nice straight lines.

Conditions in the first trenches occupied by the British in the Ypres salient in the winter of 1914 were very bad, a situation that did improve but the low-lying land meant that the water and mud were a constant problem. In October, the Royal Welch Fusiliers found that: 'Rain and mud were by now causing a lot of trouble with rifles; and the supply of oil had given out. There was nowhere to lay or clean a rifle without its getting clogged with mud, or a plug in the muzzle, which caused the barrel to bulge or burst when a shot was fired.'

Alf Pollard of the 1st Honourable Artillery Company (HAC), also at Ypres, recalled: 'The trenches in 1914 were terrible. Sanitation was not yet perfected. Corpses, mostly French, were lying about unburied. Dug-outs were mostly unknown. Those that existed consisted of a leaky lean-to against the side of the trench. We privates were exposed to all the elements.' This from a man who was an enthusiast for the war both at the time and subsequently. He praised the comradeship in the trenches and the sense of common suffering which made men selfless in adversity. War brought out 'all the beastliest instincts . . . [but also] the noblest'. It is often hard to appreciate that not everyone who fought in the trenches of the First World War saw only horror or were reluctant participants. Both Pollard and Ernst Jünger, a lieutenant in the 73rd Hanoverian Fusilier Regiment, were enthusiastic soldiers who relished the prospect of hand-to-hand combat. Indeed, Pollard won the VC and Jünger the Iron Cross First Class for taking the fight to the enemy, despite the odds being heavily stacked against them, not because they wanted to make a show of bravery but because neither man could imagine not facing the challenges which the situations presented. Both men, like so many others, were wounded on numerous occasions and both had the opportunity to stay away from the fighting because of their wounds. They always chose to go back to the front because to do otherwise would have been a betrayal of their comrades, their regiments and their countries.

Mud hindered movement and when it rained the trenches became water courses, sometimes knee-deep, while the mud became glutinous. Such conditions rotted feet (trench foot), rusted rifles and jammed everything mechanical. Ankle-deep liquid mud was typical every winter. Heavy shelling made a bad situation worse. Water and mud was no less a problem for the Germans despite being entrenched on higher ground. Rudolf Binding, a German staff officer at Ypres, complained in 1914 that 'hardly a shell bursts on contact, but is imprisoned by the soft, sticky mud.' A year later, the conditions were no better: 'In the trenches and dug-outs the men are literally lying in the water.'

At the same time that the uneven parapet was gaining acceptance, the trace of the trenches now zigzagged or meandered in sweeping curves, dog-legged or formed crenulated patterns. Some trenches were provided with land islands whereby at regular intervals the trench split into two which then rejoined again after about 20 yards. These were instead of traverses. The evenness of parapets began to give way to a disordered jumble of undulations, lumps and bumps, although the uneven parapet did not become universal until well into 1915. The front-line fire trench were now supported by another line several hundred yards to the rear, with a reserve line behind that, all of them interconnected by deep communications trenches. The trench profiles set out in the manuals, which were similar to those of the trenches dug in Manchuria ten years earlier, were not practical as they did not allow for the consequences of constant shelling and regular machine-gun fire that quickly became features of the Western Front. Moreover, the pre-war concerns over the correct sighting of trenches to allow for good fields of fire were abandoned. What mattered now was provision of enough protection from high-explosive shells, avoidance of enfilade fire, especially when it came from a machine-gun, and protection from grenades which had been a nuisance to the British ever since they had first entrenched along the Aisne in the early autumn. Bomb-proof shelters were now being dug, strong enough to be safe against near misses but not yet strong enough to withstand direct hits.

A new factor in the evolution of temporary defensive structures on the Western Front was the introduction of steel-reinforced concrete, a material that had been entirely absent from battlefield structures of the past. While it had been used in more permanent fortifications since the 1870s, which had led to the development of high explosives to combat it, ferroconcrete had not been used in fieldworks before the First World War. Many deep dugouts, reinforced with heavy timbers, were proof against everything but a direct hit by one of the biggest calibre shells, but there were many that were less robust, closer to the surface and less well maintained. These were susceptible to collapse from even near misses during a bombardment. But concrete structures were almost immune to even direct hits from the biggest shells, although the occupants were not – they were often killed by concussion and blast while the structures were left more or less intact. The quality of the concrete was the deciding factor in whether a structure survived shelling. In January 1918, a British howitzer battery commander and two visitors from a medium trench mortar battery sheltered in a pillbox when the position was shelled by the Germans who:

> put down a terrific concentrated bombardment with 8-in. and 5.9-in. howitzers … No sooner had we got inside than the Hun made a direct hit on it with an 8-in. shell. The pill-box was filled with smoke and fumes and fairly shook, but it held together – the only damage was Colonel —'s monocle, which was dislodged from his eye and smashed to pieces.

The Germans began using ferroconcrete in 1915 to build blockhouses and machine-gun posts, known by the British as pillboxes, in the Ypres sector and they continued to build them here for the next few years. These structures were built on the surface rather than below it because of the high water table around Ypres, which made them very conspicuous, although some degree of camouflaging was applied to them. During the Third Battle of Ypres (Passchendaele) which lasted from the end of July to December 1917, these concrete structures were major obstacles to the Allied assault because they had escaped unscathed from the Allied bombardment.

Up and down the length of the Western Front, the Germans poured tens of thousands of tons of concrete into thousands of these formidable obstacles, many of them below ground level and well camouflaged. The best known of these lines, the Hindenburg Line, or *Siegfriedstellung*, to which the Germans made a strategic withdrawal in 1917, was a defensive line unlike any that had been built hitherto on the Western Front. It comprised several lines over a depth of up to 15 miles. From about the autumn of 1915, there was growing controversy in Britain over how Germany was acquiring its cement and aggregate. It led to a diplomatic row with the Netherlands because much of the material was being transported by barge from that country, which was officially neutral. In the latter part of 1916, when work began on the Hindenburg Line, German consumption of cement and aggregate increased nearly six-fold and Britain's relations with Holland worsened. Despite all this, when RFC pilots overflying the construction sites reported the activity below, little notice was taken, despite corroborative intelligence coming in from other sources.

Yet the BEF had already encountered concrete pillboxes during the fighting in the Somme campaign and were well aware of the problems they posed for advancing infantry. When the BEF came to tackle these bunkers and pillboxes, especially those containing machine-guns or field guns, during the Somme battles of 1916 and all the battles of 1917, including Arras, Third Ypres and Vimy Ridge, it was clear that new tactical approaches were necessary. The kind of tactics that had been employed in 1915 and 1916 to capture trenches were ineffectual against concrete structures that were sited to give mutual fire support. Fortunately for the BEF, by 1916, it was acquiring the tools and the experience to engage the pillboxes and neutralize them. Teamwork was the key. Riflemen, rifle-grenadiers, Lewis gunners and Stokes mortar batteries provided the means by which bombers could get close enough to toss grenades through the apertures of the pillboxes and blockhouses to kill or disable the occupants.

The British and Australians also built concrete pillboxes and shelters but they were slower to start than the Germans and, consequently, built fewer. Nevertheless, a great many were built. They also converted many of those they captured. The Allies were less systematic about building than the Germans. British structures tended not to be reinforced, just solid concrete, often built up from concrete blocks, such as the prefabricated Moir pillbox, which housed a Vickers machine-gun. The Moir was built in considerable numbers. The so-called GHQ Line, started in the summer of 1918, made considerable use of concrete structures, set out and arranged with switch lines similar to the Hindenburg Line. It was never completed because the Allies went back on the offensive as the line was started. None of the Allied pillboxes and shelters were really tested in battle until the German spring offensives of 1918 but they proved just as problematical to the Germans as theirs had been to the Allies.

What distinguished the trenches of 1916 and 1917 from those of 1914 and 1915 was not their profile, which remained essentially the same throughout the war, although they became much wider than the early trenches, but how they were built, or rather, how they were given permanence. This was exemplified by the increasing use of concrete. While the German Army always tended to build with the intention of staying put, the British and the French, as already explained, were psychologically disposed to regarding permanence as an admission of defeat, since their avowed intention was to throw the German Army off French and Belgian soil. This had been the case in 1914 and 1915 and it remained so in 1918. The British also believed, wrongly, that if the troops occupying the trenches had a sense of the positions having some permanence, they would lose their offensive spirit. As far as the British and the French were concerned, all operations were geared to the offensive, large and small. In their trenches, they were not on the defensive, merely poised for the next offensive. Permanence implied defence, which ran counter to the Allied aims.

Unfortunately, for the Allied troops, such an approach to the form and structure of the trenches, and especially to the idea of bomb-proof dugouts, only made their lives less comfortable and more dangerous than had a more realistic view been adopted. However, by early 1915, the British had come to acknowledge that breaking through the German lines was not going to happen as easily as they would have liked, so that they were left with no alternative but to make the trenches more robust and, hence, more permanent. To do otherwise left a real risk of too many lives being lost to routine shelling and sniping which, in 1915, was already sapping the strength of the BEF. The French had suffered very high casualties in the battles of 1914 and could no more afford to lose men than could the British. The nature of trench fighting and its principal emphasis altered during 1915 from attacking to containing, shifting the concept of the assault from the élan of the bayonet charge to domination of no-man's-land. Major offensive operations remained at the heart of Allied strategic planning but the day-to-day activity of trench warfare became a different process. In this respect, trench warfare acquired three aspects: battle, small-scale operations and domination of the enemy. A fourth aspect grew in importance during 1915 and into 1916, attrition, whereby the strength and will of the enemy was worn down in relentless but irregular shelling and mortaring.

The importance of dominating no-man's-land and, indeed, the enemy's parapet, became apparent during 1915. Through asserting dominance over the enemy, it was possible to keep the fighting spirit alive by taking the fight to him rather than waiting passively for him to make the first move then reacting to it. Domination was more than mere bullying. It became an essential prerequisite of any operation, large or small, as it laid the foundation for success. An enemy who was dominated was less capable militarily because he became a reactor to circumstances and lost the ability to instigate action. It was the same principal which underlay the pre-war concept of superiority of fire. Domination could be achieved in different ways and ranged from aggressive patrolling in no-man's-land to regular sniping and raiding. One of the ways in which dominance could be measured was by counting the number of intact periscopes that were visible above a parapet. Periscopes were the eyes of the infantry, besides being crucial to the artillery for directing fire and observing fall of shot from the front line. Throughout the war, snipers always targeted periscopes and could hit the smallest target with only a moment's view of it. The poet Robert Graves had a periscope which had a top mirror only an inch square. The first time he used it, a sniper hit it at 400 yards. Thus, the fewer the number of periscopes above a parapet, the more dominant were the enemy. Sniping in active sectors helped create domination. It was common for aggressive battalions to instigate a policy of active sniping in order to deny periscopes to the enemy, harass him and prevent him from doing the same thing back, thereby reducing his ability to interfere with the activities of that battalion.

At first, periscopes were simply poked above the parapet but it quickly become apparent that this invited a sniper to take a shot. While the practice of an individual soldier putting up a periscope to observe a specific target was never stopped, and whenever this was done the periscope was raised very slowly, it became standard practice for the periscope to be permanently fixed to the wall of the trench and camouflaged. Indeed, in some instances a fake tree was erected in place of a real one which was removed during the night, all in a single operation to give the illusion that the same tree was still there. Inside the replicated tree was an observation post or a custom-made periscope.

So important were periscopes to trench warfare that a department was created within the Ministry of Munitions to deal solely with the manufacture, acquisition and supply of periscopes. British infantry often had to make do with second-rate optics because the artillery had priority for the best magnifying periscopes. The Germans had no such problem because the best optical glass had always been made in Germany. Before the war, British makers of optical instruments had imported their glass from Germany. Now, British glass-makers had to learn how to make optical glass to a similar standard as that achieved routinely by the Germans, when they had no expertise in the field; without good glass free of aberrations and other defects, accurate range-finding was impossible and practical observation of the enemy was made very difficult. A periscope was not merely a simple arrangement of mirrors but a precision instrument in which all its optics, mirrors, lenses and prisms had to be optically good to avoid distortions and chromatic effects, as well as clouding. The manufacture of optical glass was a specialist process requiring considerable skill, as well as the right ingredients and the right recipe. Optical artillery gunsights, naval gunsights, telescopic sights for rifles, aircraft gunsights and bomb sights, field glasses, periscopes and cameras were just some of the many instruments which required such glass. To make matters worse, the competition for high-quality optical glass grew with every passing month. And infantry periscopes were not high on the list of priorities.

The earliest periscopes used by the BEF were no more than a single mirror attached at an appropriate angle to a stick, rod or bayonet by which it could be held above the parapet. The observer then had to peer at the mirror. Despite the low utility of such a device, it saw fairly widespread use in the British and French armies in 1914 and 1915 when there was a severe shortage of better periscopes. Versions of it were provided through official supply channels, while Royal Engineers improvised versions of it in workshops; some models could even be bought in department stores in London and Paris. Such was the shortage of periscopes in 1915 that a number of entrepreneurs seized the opportunity to devise, make and sell periscopes, most of which were less than useful, largely because of the poor quality of the glass used in the mirrors. Such periscopes as the Ork-Oie collapsible periscope and the Duerr pantograph periscope, which collapsed to wallet-size and could be slipped into its leather carrying case and popped into a pocket, could be bought in department stores or direct from the makers. These sorts of periscope were of very limited use. Apart from anything else, their mirrors tended to act as heliographs, even when they had a hinged cover, because no one could stand so still when he used one that he could prevent any wobble, which instantly attracted the attention of German snipers. Indeed, the manufacturer of the Ocentric periscope even suggested that an ability to reflect light other than towards to the eye of its user was a desirable characteristic in a periscope, and claimed in an advertisement that 'All military men are demanding a periscope which is no trouble to carry and yet of a size to be thoroughly practical for trench work and scouting', and that it would be 'quite useful for heliograph signalling'. Such was the naivety of those at home to the realities of trench warfare in 1915.

During the war, a wide range of models of periscope were supplied to the BEF by the Ministry of Munitions, some of them simple double-mirror devices, others much more sophisticated with reflecting prisms and lenses to magnify the image. Of the trench periscopes, the No. 9 was perhaps the most widely used by the BEF. The French, Belgian and German armies all had similar models. The No. 9 incorporated design elements derived from accumulated trench experience. It was first issued in about mid-1915 and remained in service throughout the war. The No. 9 was a box periscope, hinged in the middle for storage and transport. It used only two mirrors, set at 45° angles, and had a glass screen with a movable metal shutter in front of the lower mirror to protected the observer's eyes from glass splinters should a sniper hit the top mirror. Experience had shown all too often that glass splinters from the shattered top mirror fell down the shaft of the box and were deflected by the lower mirror so that they hit the user in the face. A foot-long foldable spike attached to its base was used to fix the periscope to the trench wall thereby allowing hands-free use and obviating wobble. By fixing the periscope to the trench, the shaft above the parapet could be camouflaged with sacking so that it did not stand out like a tin duck in a shooting gallery.

A novel device that was first used in late 1914 was the rifle periscope or hyperscope, also referred to as a sniperscope, which enabled a sniper to shoot at the enemy from below the parapet. These weird contraptions, which were fitted to a rifle stock, had the look of Heath Robinson about them but they were widely used by all armies, testimony to their utility, although accurate shooting was hard to achieve at distances greater than about 200–300 yards. While the idea of such a device had been conceived in about 1900, no army had employed one before the emergence of trench warfare on the Western Front. By the spring of 1915, a similar device was being used to fire a machine-gun from below the parapet, to which end a particular design of emplacement had to be built. Although such devices as these were no more than minor innovations, they were born of a desire to overcome the obstacles presented by trench warfare, the same impetus which led to the invention of devices which were to have a profound effect on warfare as a whole, not just trench warfare. Principal among these were the Stokes mortar and the Mills hand grenade, two munitions which were to help change the nature of warfare for ever. These were British inventions, of which only the Stokes saw almost universal adoption by the Allies, but the French and the Germans, and later the Americans, adopted equivalent munitions which had a similar impact on how they engaged in trench warfare. However, of all the grenades devised during the First World War, the Mills saw the widest use by far. Indeed, so effective was this grenade that it became one of the most used grenades in the history of warfare, remaining in production in some countries well into the 1980s.

A great deal of effort went into devising effective body armour that was capable of stopping rifle bullets, especially in Britain. This goal was never achieved although body armour capable of stopping shrapnel was widely adopted during 1916 and 1917. Every army eventually adopted a shrapnel helmet, most in 1915, with helmets becoming commonplace during 1916. They reduced the incidence of head injury from low-velocity and medium-velocity fragments, but none could stop high-velocity projectiles, although there were certainly instances where bullets were deflected. The helmet was the only item of body armour to be worn routinely. They were originally only supplied from trench stores according to need. When the first helmets became available to British troops in 1915, they were only issued to those working at sapheads, to bombers and to those going out on a trench raid. Their limited use was as much to do with a lack of helmets as it was to do with uncertainty about their usefulness. Had they proved to offer no advantage, there is no question that helmets would not have been adopted and standardized, irrespective of manufacturers building the capacity to produce them in their millions.

In December 1914, General Adrian introduced the first 'helmet' of the war, a skullcap worn beneath the French *kepi*; this was an updated version of the *secrèt* from the sixteenth and seventeenth centuries. This steel skullcap weighed a mere 9oz and was hailed as an immediate success, inspiring Adrian to design a helmet. More than 700,000 skullcaps were issued up to March 1915. It was superseded by the Adrian helmet a few months later. Elegant though the Adrian helmet was, it was far from simple to manufacture as it involved more than seventy operations. Nevertheless, it was produced in huge numbers during the war, one manufacturer reputedly making 3,000,000 of them in a little over two years. Versions of the Adrian were used by the Belgians and the Italians. The Adrian was made of mild steel, heat treated to be half-hard; fully hardened steel did not lend itself to the moulding processes. Although it was considerably lighter than the British helmet, the ballistic value of the Adrian was not nearly as high, which was further impaired by the numerous holes punched into it during the complex manufacturing process.

The British helmet, created by an engineer called John Brodie, included an impact-absorbing liner, as described in his patent specification of 1915, so that whereas

> existing steel helmets designed to protect the head against wounds caused
> by the impact of rifle bullets, shrapnel bullets, shell splinters … depend …
> upon the thickness of the metal of which the helmet or head shield is made
> … the method of fitting them on the head has the disadvantage that the
> force of a relatively small impact is transmitted direct to the skull and may
> easily produce concussion of the brain or at any rate a severe bruise.

Removing a damaged helmet from a man with a head wound presented a serious problem as the hole in the helmet was often ragged so that 'the metal gets imbedded in the head'. There was also a potential difficulty with frostbite in cold weather if the helmet metal was in contact with the scalp. Brodie's helmet and liner overcame such problems. Unlike the liner in the Adrian helmet, Brodie's liner held the steel shell of the helmet away from the wearer's head so that head and helmet were never in contact. Indeed, there was a substantial space between head and helmet. The steel shell of the Brodie could be severely dented, even perforated, and the wearer could escape injury. The same degree of damage to the Adrian helmet would almost certainly result in the death of the wearer. Brodie's liner acted

> as a buffer to prevent concussion of the brain by external impact and to prevent injury to the frontal, parietal or occipital bones of the cranium by any indentation or penetration of the helmet. This buffer or anti-concussion lining is by means of studs spaced away from the helmet shell so that a free space or air gap is left between lining and shell, and therefore the helmet may be subjected to a considerable force of impact or even be indented or penetrated without injury to the wearer.

Head, face and brain injuries were potentially fatal but even survivable head injuries often resulted in disfigurement or disability. One of the fields of science which advanced considerably during the First World War was surgery, but head injuries remained the most difficult to treat. Hence, there was a great incentive to devise an effective helmet. However, no helmet was a guarantee of safety. A shell fragment could easily penetrate the metal and enter the brain. No helmet was bulletproof, although it was not unheard of for a bullet to penetrate, follow the curvature of the helmet on the inside and exit on the side opposite the point of entry, without causing serious injury to the wearer. Brodie helmets tended to dent when struck by a bullet that had travelled some distance, was partially spent or impacted at an angle, as Alf Pollard discovered in January 1917 during an attack on the German line at Grandcourt:

> Something hit me in the centre of my forehead and I went down like a log. For a moment I lay stunned ... I ... recovered my steel helmet. There was a dent in the centre of it the size of an orange ... I went back into the road. A shell burst just behind me and a splinter hit me on the back of the head making a second dent.

Months earlier, he had argued with a fellow officer over whether the British helmet would stop a pistol bullet and had taken a shot at a Brodie helmet from 25 yards to make his point. The helmet had been dented but not penetrated.

German helmets tended to be punctured when hit. Often a rifle bullet would penetrate the front and kill the wearer. This weakness led German snipers and sentries to attach an additional brow plate to the front of the helmet, but it was heavy and overbalanced the helmet, making it difficult to wear. Moreover, the additional plate was no guarantee of safety. There are more than enough surviving examples of holed brow plates to testify to how easily they could be penetrated by a well-aimed bullet.

One advantage of the Brodie's bowl shape was that it could be stamped from manganese steel in one operation, which helped to make the Brodie twice as strong as the Adrian, although it was thicker and heavier, weighing around 2lb. The Brodie helmets were not universally liked as they took some getting used to. They gave soldiers a brutal, medieval look, although the British Brodie was less severe in this respect than the German design. The German helmet, with its distinctive coal-scuttle shape, was first used at Verdun in January 1916. Its design was based on a fifteenth-century helmet known as a sallet. It was, perhaps, the most effective design as its shape afforded more protection than any other helmet introduced during the war, providing good protection for the neck and the whole of the head. However, its steel was more brittle than that used to make the Brodie and the helmet was slightly heavier.

While most armies went to war in 1914 equipped with some sort of portable armoured shield for the infantry, such things were impractical and were soon abandoned in favour of fixed trench shields and armoured loopholes, although even these were not necessarily capable of stopping the armour-piercing rounds fired by German snipers. Nevertheless, by mid-1915, no front-line trench was complete without well camouflaged loopholes for snipers and equally well-concealed periscopes with which to observe the enemy. The parapet became the line which was not crossed in daylight. Indeed, anyone looking across no-man's-land towards an enemy trench would have had difficulty spotting it, especially through the long grass that grew in no-man's-land during the spring and summer of 1915. This was particularly true in those regions of the Front that had yet to be subjected to the heavy bombardments which accompanied major offensives and churned up the ground, destroying all the vegetation. A quiet sector of the Front could be recognized by the unspoiled countryside of no-man's-land.

The First World War was a time of considerable innovation, not only in tactics but also in the fields of munitions and techniques such as map-making and communications, as well as in the crucial area of command and control in battle. These facets of the war were all inter-related and developments in one field had an impact in the others. While much attention has always been paid to the perceived war-winning innovations such as the tank, as well as to the more cruel weapons such as gas, neither of which made a significant impact on how the war was fought or, indeed, its outcome, far less attention has been paid to how trench warfare on the Western Front evolved into a new mode of warfare. The process of evolution began in early 1915, but its seeds had been sown almost as soon as war broke out in August 1914.

CHAPTER 8

Grenade Warfare

A weapon closely associated with trench warfare at its most basic level is the hand grenade. During the First World War, and on the Western Front in particular, it had a huge impact on the way the fighting evolved. This was directly related to the grenades themselves, rather to than to mere numbers alone. While the grenades used in Manchuria during the Russo-Japanese War were in the tradition of grenades and grenade warfare as it had been practised for the previous 200 years, the grenades of the First World War were not only entirely different in engineering terms, but they took grenade fighting to an entirely new level. The tactical employment of grenades on the Western Front was derived from how they worked which, in turn, was derived from their engineering. This had a profound effect on trench warfare and, ultimately, contributed to the emergence of an entirely new mode of warfare during 1917 and 1918. The grenades of the First World War permitted the development of sophisticated tactical systems for their use which had not been possible hitherto.

While the German, French and British armies went to war in August 1914 equipped with some sort of grenade, no army had sufficient quantities to sustain the level of usage that developed during the autumn of 1914 and continued to rise throughout 1915. The demand for grenades rose at such a rate that all armies were forced to improvise in much the same way that the Russians and Japanese had extemporized grenades in Manchuria. From September 1914 onwards, Royal Engineers Field Companies improvised all manner of weapons and equipment for trench warfare to meet local demand, including grenades. In November, a large workshop facility was set up in the First Army area. This became known as the Béthune Bomb Factory and was initially run by the 3rd Company Bengal Sappers and Miners to meet the demands of the Indian Corps in the trenches at La Bassée. The Bengal Sappers and Miners had pre-war experience of improvising hand and rifle grenades from which they devised the so-called jam-tin and hairbrush grenades that were widely used by the BEF until the autumn of 1915. The French and the Germans extemporized similar grenades under similar circumstances, but not on the same scale as the British who were rather good at improvisation.

In May 1915, the Second Army Workshops was set up in an abandoned French technical school to devise and manufacture trench warfare stores, including grenades and mortars. The Bomb Factory and the Second Army Workshops both produced thousands of grenades a week as demand continued to rise during 1915. Before the war, there had been no demand for grenades in Britain and there was no intimation that a demand might arise. France was in much the same position, while Germany at least had grenades which could be mass produced. As far as Britain was concerned, a partial solution to the BEF's lack of grenades was to re-engineer the jam-tin and hairbrush types for mass production; the result was the Nos 8 and 9 jam-tin patterns and the No. 12 hairbrush. These stopgaps were intended to make up the shortfall of the No. 5 Mills grenade, invented in January 1915. The manufacture of the No. 5 was initially problematical so that it did not start to become widely available until the latter part of 1915. By the time of the Battle of Loos in September 1915, there were twelve different patterns of hand grenade in British service and few soldiers had mastered them all.

From about July to December 1915, the principal British-made hand grenade was the No. 15 Ball, some 1,670,332 being produced between July and September, with another 4,237,188 being manufactured during the last quarter of 1915. Following the disastrous failure of the Ball grenades at Loos, they were shipped to the Middle East and to Russia. It had rained hard during the fighting at Loos and many Ball grenades failed to light because the rain soaked the fuses. Before Loos, hand grenades were viewed as no more than a 'side-show' but, by the spring of 1916, the attitude to grenades had substantially changed, although grenades and bombing were still neglected in some battalions. When Alf Pollard returned to his battalion, the Honourable Artillery Company, in May 1916, after an enforced absence of some months due to battle injuries, he found that bombs had been completely forgotten. By early 1916, all of the stopgap grenades had been withdrawn from service because they were too dangerous and unreliable. The stopgaps of 1914 and 1915 were unsophisticated and little different from the improvised grenades of the Russo-Japanese War. In the BEF, bombers tended to be pitied by the rest of the infantry because grenades were as likely to kill or injure the bomber as they were to incapacitate the enemy. The Nos 13 and 14 Pitcher grenades were so dangerous that the bombers using them called themselves The Suicide Club.

The shortage of British rifle grenades in 1915 was so severe that each platoon was only issued with six for a tour of between five and ten days in the trenches. By July 1916, however, there was a plentiful supply of rifle grenades, enough for the Royal Welch Fusiliers to fire off thousands in a matter of a few hours during a retaliatory raid by two reinforced companies. Similarly, the Honourable Artillery Company improvised batteries of six rifles and fired off barrages of rifle grenades whenever the Germans mortared them. Each of the three companies was instructed to fire off a minimum of 200 rifle grenades every day. Eventually, such expenditure began to exhaust supplies and it had to be curtailed.

The average monthly supply of hand grenades from Britain in November 1914 was only 280. Sir John French wanted at least 4,000 a month. During the last quarter of 1914, only 2,164 hand and rifle grenades were produced in Britain; most of these were the No. 1 percussion grenade and the No. 3 rifle grenade. During the first six months of 1915, production increased but was still meager; only 65,315 hand and rifle grenades were produced. In early 1915, the War Office placed orders with commercial engineering firms for 5,000,000 No. 5 Mills grenades but, by the end of June, only 16,000 had been delivered because of production problems. It was not until October that the output of the Mills met demand and production now exceeded 300,000 a week. In early 1915, the daily output by the Béthune Bomb Factory of Battye grenades was 1,000–1,500 but it could not cope with demand during the Battle of Festubert in May 1915 and capacity had to be increased; it supplied 80,000 grenades during the Battle of Loos a few months later. By October, grenade production at the Bomb Factory had gone over to rifle grenades; between October 1915 and July 1916, its daily output was 1,000 Newton Pippin rifle grenades. Between July and December 1915, the Second Army Workshops produced approximately 80,000 hand grenades and had a daily output of 5,000 rifle grenades.

The number of hand grenades produced in Britain between June 1915 and the end of the year was 11,698,441. During 1916, the output of hand grenades was 28,956,513, the majority of which were No. 5s. In 1917, production was switched to the improved Mills grenade, the No. 23.

The No. 5 Mills suffered from a number of design faults which led to a rising number of accidents during 1915 and 1916 as the grenade became more plentiful. The accidents had many causes, including premature detonation, early detonation after the pin had been pulled but before the grenade had been released from the thrower's grip, and pins being pulled out accidentally when live grenades were being carried in a canvas bucket, which had been designed specifically for resupplying bombing parties. A major cause of accidents was premature release of the firing pin which required redesign work to rectify it. In essence, the Mills mechanism was a spring-loaded firing pin held in a safe position by a lever which engaged the head of the firing pin. Unfortunately, only a very small amount of movement of the lever could release the firing pin, so small, in fact, that the bomber was usually unaware that the firing pin had been released. Accidents in training schools rose to ten a month in 1916, causing up to thirty casualties. Extensive investigations in Britain and in France led to a number of major changes to the Mills and to changes in handling procedures. Bombers were taught to hold the Mills No. 5 so that the lever was always pressed firmly against the body of the grenade as the safety pin was pulled and to throw the grenade immediately. By the end of 1916, the No. 5 had evolved into a hybrid hand and rifle grenade, the No. 23, for which the SMLE needed a cup attachment. With the improvements to the mechanism, a new pattern appeared in mid-1917, the No. 23 Mk III, but this did not reach the BEF in significant numbers until 1918 because of the huge stocks of the No. 5. The Mk III was safer to handle and far more reliable than earlier Mills grenades.

The rodded rifle grenade was invented in 1908 by an English engineer called Frederick Marten Hale. The Cotton Powder Company, of which he was a director, offered it to the War Office but the Chief Draughtsman at Woolwich dismissed it as 'a crazy and audacious monstrosity' that would burst the rifle barrel. Over the next five years, he pestered the War Office while continuing to improve on his grenade and, in October 1913, the Ordnance Board ordered troop trials. By August 1914, the British Army had an unopened box of fifty rifle grenades, the number ordered from the Cotton Powder Company following the Army's acceptance of the grenade the previous year. Germany also adopted a rodded rifle grenade in 1913 but it was not a copy of the British weapon, although it was clearly inspired by it.

The rifle grenade provided the infantry with a close-support weapon for the first time. It was, however, an imperfect munition. Accuracy decreased with range, while its payload was small, typically 1.5–2.5oz of explosive compared to the 13oz of an 18-pounder HE shell. Whereas the rifle grenade could be fired at local targets of opportunity, the rods were heavy and awkward to carry so that they were a burden for rifle grenadiers. Any rifle used for firing grenades could not then be used to fire ball ammunition so that designated rifles had to be allocated for rifle grenades. Rifle grenadiers needed to be supported by conventionally armed infantrymen. Typically, the maximum range of the No. 3 rifle grenade was 200 yards, while that of the later No. 22 was 350 yards, but range depended on a wide range of factors including obturation, trajectory, 45° giving the greatest range, and weather conditions. Poor obturation and excessive windage could reduce the range by 62 per cent but the aerodynamics of the grenade had little effect.

Grenade fighting became a defining feature of trench warfare. The BEF were on the receiving end of German grenades as soon as stalemate developed along the River Aisne in September 1914. By the beginning of 1916, when grenades had become plentiful for all sides, the daily expenditure was huge, running into tens of thousands a day for each army. In mid-1915, the estimated daily expenditure per division in the BEF was 4,500 rifle grenades and 14,000 hand grenades. While grenades had become more plentiful, however, GHQ began to worry that the BEF was relying on them far too much. It was concerned about the loss of musketry skills and worried that infantrymen would not use their bayonets if they had grenades. However, far from suppressing musketry and bayonet-fighting skills, the hand grenade actually encouraged them because of the way in which bombing was carried out.

Grenade warfare was an integral part of how armies conducted operations on the Western Front. From the outset, GHQ wanted every infantryman to become familiar with grenades. Indeed, General Sir John French, GOC BEF, wanted all infantrymen to be trained as bombers. Yet, GHQ also held that only some infantrymen would 'possess the temperament or the qualifications necessary to make a really efficient grenadier', and expected such men to be an elite within a platoon, chosen from among the best men. Reality was somewhat different from both these ideals. During 1915, it was not uncommon for anyone to be told off as a bomber. Some men volunteered to become bombers, relishing the prospect of getting close to the enemy. A bomber had to be cool under fire. The perception of bombers as hotheads is unfounded. Bombers needed to be fit. They were expected to exercise every day to maintain strength, stamina and suppleness. Clearly, the ideal bomber had the physical attributes of an athlete. Indeed, those who were good at games at school or university were initially considered to be the best candidates.

Although grenades had been used in the eighteenth century and in the Russo-Japanese War, little had changed tactically between 1705 and 1905. In the BEF, the proliferation of grenade types and their short service life in 1915 prevented the development of a tactical system because each type required a different handling procedure. Suitable handling procedures were crucial to the safe and effective use of grenades. They were the foundation on which tactics were built. Despite GHQ's demand for grenades from late 1914 onwards, it viewed the grenade as no more than a 'side-show' until mid-1915. Training in grenade fighting was initially quite ad hoc and it was not until May 1915 that the first specialist bombing schools existed in the BEF. This reflected the poor utility of grenades as well as the lack of training schools in general at this time.

The Germans, on the other hand, were far in advance of the Allies with regard to grenades, tactics and training. But a problem faced by all bombers, irrespective of which side they were on, was the diversity of types with which they had to be familiar. Even at the end of 1917, when the number of patterns had long since been reduced in all armies, the bomber was still faced with having to be familiar with a great many grenades. In the BEF, a bomber had to know three patterns of Mills grenade, the No. 34 egg grenade, three patterns of smoke grenade, the No. 28 gas grenade, five patterns of explosive rifle grenade and three patterns of signal rifle grenade, as well as three patterns of rifle grenade cartridge, various cup attachments for the rifle and the cup discharger for firing the grenades, as well as being familiar with seven patterns of German grenade and two patterns of German bomb-thrower and their bombs. The bomber had to be aware of the lethal radius of all these grenades to avoid injury to himself and friendly troops nearby. The equivalent problem was faced by French and German bombers.

Having more than a passing familiarity with enemy grenades had a practical value, as Pollard discovered at Gavrelle in 1917 when he and his bombing team ran out of Mills grenades. They had to resort to throwing German grenades to prevent a German counter-attack during a bombing attack of their own along a German-held trench. Such a recourse was not at all unusual. It was commonplace for bombers to use enemy grenades if they were available.

During 1915, German grenade tactics were the perhaps most advanced, but every army was having to learn what was, in effect, a new form of fighting. No army had gone to war in 1914 with an established tactical system for employing grenades, largely because the need had not arisen. As grenades became more plentiful and as they became more technically sophisticated and, more importantly,

120

Federal trench at Petersburg, 1865. (*US Library of Congress*)

Federal bunkers at Petersburg. Note the extensive use of timber and sandbags, and the fraise of stakes beyond the positions in the foreground. (*US Library of Congress*)

Japanese trench showing traverses, 1905. (*Taken from* The Russo-Japanese War)

Japanese trenches in Manchuria; left, on 203 Metre Hill at Port Arthur, oblique approach across front on the opposite slope of the valley, about 250 yards from the enemy; right, at the north fort of Teng Chi-kuan Shan, approach round right flank, 40 yards from the enemy. Note the sandbagged parapets and loopholes. (*Taken from* The Russo-Japanese War)

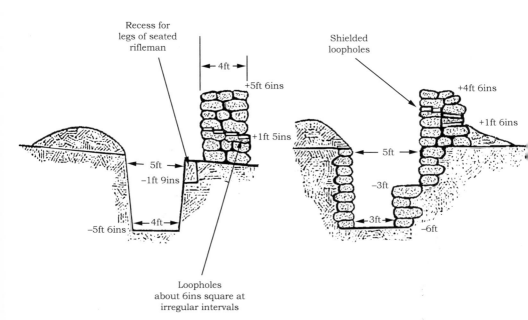

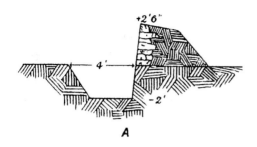

0   5   10 Ft

+2'6"

4'

-2'

A

ORIGINAL TYPE OF TRENCH

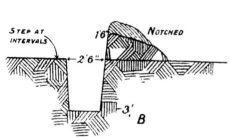

STEP AT INTERVALS

NOTCHED

1'6"

←2'6"→

-3'

B

ON FENG-HUANG RANGE

TAKEN BY SURPRISE 31.7.04.

TRAVERSE EVERY 15'

NOTCHED

-3'6"

C

174 METRE HILL   TAKEN 20.8.04

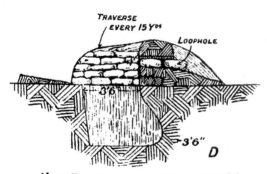

TRAVERSE EVERY 15 Yds

LOOPHOLE

3'6"

-3'6"   **D**

NEAR FORT KUROPATKIN. TAKEN 19.9.04

Russian trenches in Manchuria, taken by the Japanese. Note the use of sandbags, traverses and loopholes and the absence of a firestep. (*Taken from* The Russo-Japanese War)

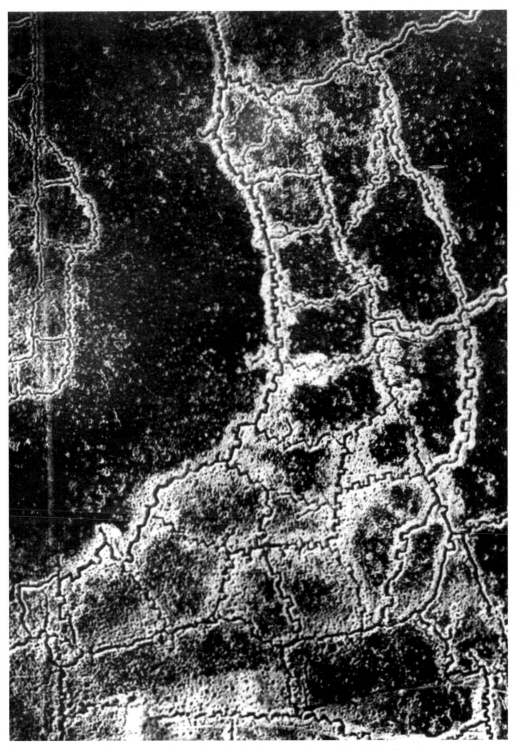

Reconnaissance photograph of trenches in the Loos sector in July 1917, showing no-man's-land. The trace of the network is clearly visible from the air and includes crenulated and zigzag forms. British trenches are at top left. Both British and German trenches have been subjected to bombardments. (*IWM Q45786*)

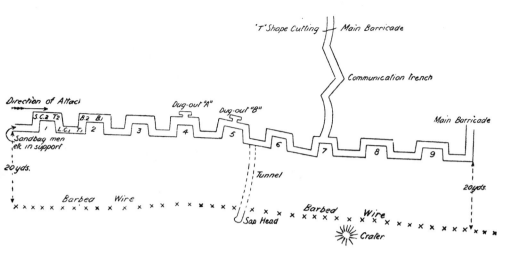

Technique of bombing along a trench employed by the BEF in 1915 and 1916 (Key: B = bayonet man, T = bomb thrower, S = spare man, L = NCO in command). The bayonet men advanced until stopped at which point the throwers tossed grenades into the enemy-held bays. (The Training and Employment of Bombers, March 1916)

Technique employed by bayonet men to advance round bays.
(Instructions on Bombing, Part II, November 1917)

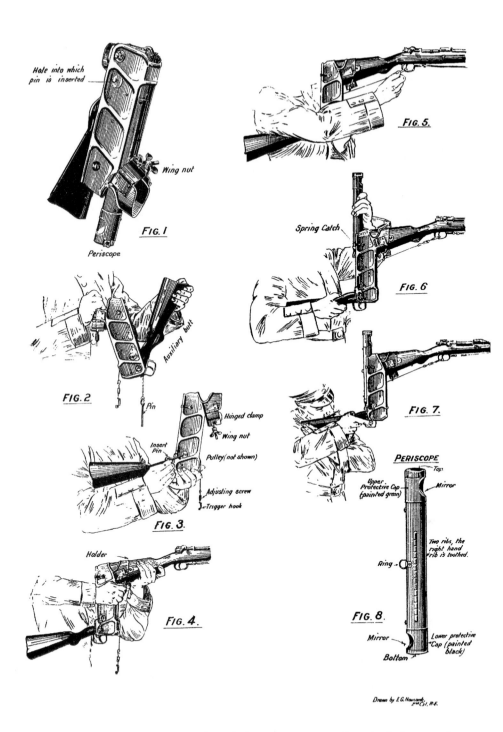

German sniperscope for firing a rifle from below cover, *c.*1917. Note the bolt-operating system and remote trigger. (Royal Engineers Journal)

Water-filled crater from a mine blown in July 1916. (*National Archives of Canada*)

Mills No. 5 hand grenade, introduced in early 1915 but which did not begin to see widespread use for another nine months due to manufacturing problems. More than 75 million Mills grenades were eventually produced during the First World War. (*Author's photo*)

Technique of throwing a grenade at a bomb stop. This block is made up from sandbags. Note the mud and the waterproof leggings, despite the fact that this is a training photograph and is not one taken in the front line. (The Training and Employment of Bombers, March 1916)

The point at which the grenade is released from the hand. (The Training and Employment of Bombers, March 1916)

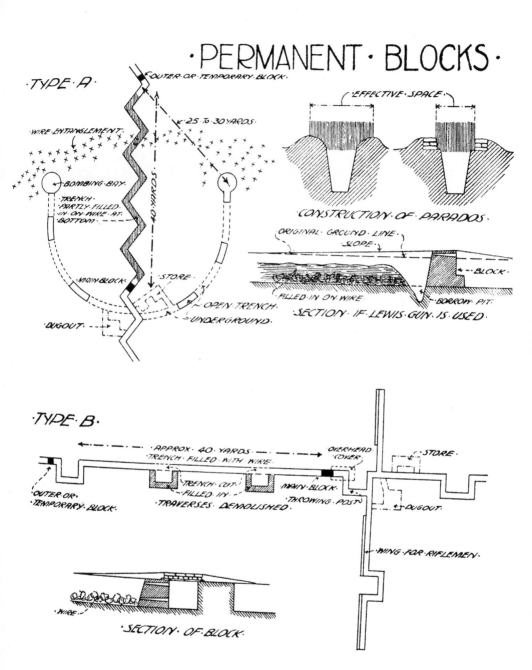

The use of blocks in trenches was widespread. Blocks were meant to prevent the enemy from bombing along a trench as well as to contain an enemy incursion. (*National Archives, WO 142/221*)

A British trench on the Somme, 1916. This is not a front-line fire trench (it has no firestep). Note the trench revetments and the lack of duckboarding. The soldier with the rifle and bayonet is clearly posing for the camera. Note the sleeping men all along the trench. *(IWM, Q3990)*

The GREENWOOD BULLET DEFLECTOR
:—(PATENTED)—:

TO HELP THE TROOPS.

A Shield for the Soldiers.

Interesting Halifax Invention.

Above we give a sketch of an invention by Ex-Hon. Lieutenant and Quartermaster J.H.T. Greenwood, of Halifax. The idea is to protect the soldier with the rifle. The shield placed on the rifle would not weigh more than a couple of pounds, could be carried on the arm, and would be bullet-proof. It is claimed that it would assist in careful and deliberate shooting, and would greatly minimise the danger to troops in the firing line.

Inner View, Showing
: Sighting Aperture :

J. H. T. GREENWOOD, 28, Union Street, Halifax. Tele. 1069.

Patent rifle shield intended to protect the shooter from enemy rifle fire. Although experiments were conducted with shields of this sort, they were far too cumbersome to be useful in the trenches. (*Author*)

TRENCH TO TRENCH ATTACK

PLATOON IN 1st WAVE

MEETING A POINT OF RESISTANCE.

Liaison Patrol

Centre of Resistance

Key :—
- ○ Platoon Commander.
- ⊓ Platoon Sergeant.
- ⊠ Section Commander.
- □ Rifleman.
- ◼ Lewis Gunner.
- ✝ Lewis Gun in Action.
- ○ Bomber.
- ● Rifle Bomber.
- ▲ Mopper Up.
- ⊠ Platoon H.Q.
- ○ Scout.

1ST WAVE to 2nd i.e., Furthest Objective
{ 1st Line
2nd Line
3rd Line (Moppers up for 1st Objective)

2ND WAVE to 1st i.e, nearest Objective
{ 4th Line
5th Line }

15 ft
30
40
100

TRENCH TO TRENCH ATTACK

PLATOON IN 2nd WAVE

MEETING A POINT OF RESISTANCE.

Liaison Patrol

Centre of Resistance

Liaison Patrol

Key :—
- ○ Platoon Commander.
- ⊓ Platoon Sergeant.
- ⊠ Section Commander.
- □ Rifleman.
- ◼ Lewis Gunner.
- ✝ Lewis Gun in Action.
- ○ Bomber.
- ● Rifle Bomber.
- ▲ Mopper Up.
- ⊠ Platoon H.Q.
- ○ Scout.

2ND WAVE to 1st i.e, nearest Objective
{ 4th Line
5th Line }

15 ft
30

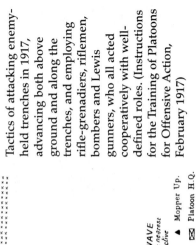

Tactics of attacking enemy-held trenches in 1917, advancing both above ground and along the trenches, and employing rifle-grenadiers, riflemen, bombers and Lewis gunners, who all acted cooperatively with well-defined roles. (Instructions for the Training of Platoons for Offensive Action, February 1917)

Mortar bomb exploding in a barbed-wire entanglement on the Western Front, May 1917. (*National Archives of Canada*)

Westwall bunker in the Hürtgen Forrest, showing a machine-gun embrasure. The design of such bunkers was derived from similar bunkers used in the First World War. *(Markus Schweiss)*

Digging in, March 1945. Private Tom Wyton, 1st Hereford Regiment, 4th Canadian Armored Division, digs a slit trench at Udem, Germany (*National Archives of Canada*)

Captured German trench, 1945. Two soldiers of the Queen's Own Cameron Highlanders of Canada examine a *Panzerschrek*. (*National Archives of Canada*)

more reliable, the need for a coordinated tactical method became apparent to all. Up to the middle of 1915, certainly as far as the BEF was concerned, there were no tactics and grenades were used on an entirely ad hoc basis. Bombing needed to be systemized, if only because the increasing numbers of grenades meant that more were being used. The British took this to heart, transformed the art of bombing and made it into a science. By 1918, they had succeeded in developing the most sophisticated tactical system for the employment of grenades of any army. There is no question that the technical aspects, the engineering, of the grenades were at the heart of this transformation. Had grenades remained like those in use during 1914 and 1915, it is highly unlikely that any tactical system would have been possible simply because of their unreliability. And at the heart of the tactical revolution was training, which itself had to be developed and modified from practical experience at the Front. Thus, the tactics were not devised from theory but from harsh reality.

At the start of trench warfare, bombing was suggested as a way of countering an enemy sap, the idea being that the bombers got as close as they could, then lit and threw their grenades. On the other side of the coin, a few precautions were counselled to counter enemy bombers, such as building trench barriers to prevent grenades landing or rolling into a trench, an idea developed by the French. Because a fairly large number of grenades in use by all armies up to about the end of 1915 were percussion-fused, it was not uncommon for some parts of the front-line trenches to be covered by screens to prevent grenades from hitting the trenches and exploding. Percussion grenades were inherently dangerous because, once armed, they detonated as soon as they struck something. Accidents in the heat of battle were common due to a thrower hitting the grenade against something in the trench while he was still holding it.

The attitude to bombing and training began to change in the spring of 1915. At this point, bombing was more an arcane art than a science, in which enthusiasm and courage were prized as though bombers were an elite warrior caste. While ad hoc training had been carried out since grenades began to be used on the Western Front, what was taught and the thoroughness of the training was unregulated and entirely dependent upon individual battalion bombing instructors. These 'instructors' were, in fact, selected from the ranks and sent on a short bombing course taught by a variety of equally randomly chosen individuals, many of whom were no better acquainted with the grenades than the men they were teaching, although some of these courses were run by Royal Engineers who had experience of grenades. During 1915, the responsibility for training instructors and men in the art of bombing rested with battalion and company commanders. The battalion bombing officer was assisted by an NCO in each company whose job it was to oversee the supply and storage of the grenades. Sometimes, this officer had himself attended a bombing course before he was appointed to the post but it was all a bit hit and miss.

It was not unusual in 1915 for bombs to be dished out to men who had never seen a grenade. Alf Pollard of the HAC was such a man when he was in the Ypres salient in the summer of 1915. He asked if he 'would like some bombs' which he readily accepted because he was keen to 'have a chance to kill some Huns at close quarters'. He was handed

> a sort of waistcoat which I tied on in front of me and a dozen bombs of the type called Mark 6 and 7, light and heavy. One ignited a sort of glorified match by striking it against a brassard like the enlarged side of a matchbox tied to the arm. The match lit a fuse which would burn for five seconds. Having got the fuse under way one threw the bomb into the enemy trench where it either exploded or else it did not. Added to my normal equipment I found the outfit damned heavy and uncomfortable.

The waistcoat had pockets for ten grenades. The Nos 6 and 7 grenades were re-engineered versions of the jam-tin bombs improvised by Royal Engineers in France. Pollard was mistaken about the brassard, however. This was issued for use with the Nos 15 and 16 patterns, the Ball and Oval grenades, which failed so dismally at Loos. The Nos 6 and 7 grenades had looped friction lighters.

Luckily for Pollard and the rest of his section, the attack in which he was to have participated as a bomber was cancelled. Nevertheless, Pollard was not put off bombing. Indeed, after he received some training, he was put in command of the company bombers as he was already a corporal. About a month had passed since his first encounter with a grenade. A month or so later, he attended a two-week course at the Second Army Grenade School at Terdeghen.

The first British bombing manuals did not appear until the autumn of 1915, although rudimentary instructions had been printed as early as late 1914. By March 1916, greater emphasis was being placed on teamwork in which the bombers, rifle grenadiers, and bayonet men within a bombing party and its support troops worked as a coordinated team. Teamwork had been the focus of bombing since the previous autumn but its importance over random bombing by individuals was now strongly emphasized. The rise of teamwork was an indication of the increasing importance of grenades in trench fighting, as well as indicative of the greater reliability of grenades and their wider availability. Without reliable grenades and without large numbers of them, bombing was inevitably going to be haphazard.

The composition of a bombing squad was left to the bombing officer. The number of such squads in a battalion was not made explicit. The number of trained bombers was not supposed to exceed between forty or fifty in a battalion were divided into four squads of eight men which made up the battalion bombing platoon. At this time, March 1916, a squad comprised two throwers, two bayonet men, two carriers of additional grenades and two 'spare' men who also acted as carriers. The squad was led by an NCO. Every man in it was supposed to know how to perform each task so that anyone could take the place of a casualty. Alternatively, a squad could consist of only four men, two acting as throwers, the other two as bayonet men, each thrower carrying a canvas bucket of additional grenades; they were not expected to throw grenades while carrying the buckets. A squad could also include two rifle grenadiers. Finally, in addition to the battalion bombing officer, there was now also a brigade bombing officer who had the task of organizing training. Training was carried out by individual brigades.

Contrary to the popular image of the bomber as a soldier whose sole task was to throw grenades, he was also expected to maintain his musketry skills like any other infantryman in his battalion. In other words, bombers had twice as much to do as riflemen. The trained bombers in a battalion had to practise forming ad hoc bombing parties at a moment's notice so that they could deal with emergencies. Bombers did not remain in the bombing platoon indefinitely but were returned to their usual role as riflemen after a tour of duty. In this way, bombing skills began to be dispersed throughout a battalion. Although this went some way towards making every infantryman familiar with grenades, it is unlikely that many of them retained a high level of proficiency or kept up to date with the latest patterns, simply because they were too busy with other duties. This contrasts starkly with 1915 when men could find themselves using grenades having only watched a demonstration, or even without any training at all.

In September 1916, the British grenade manual was updated to reflect the improvements in grenades and the greater sophistication in tactics. Every infantryman and every machine-gunner was now expected to have thrown at least one live Mills grenade in practice. Yet, even at the end of 1916, some infantrymen still found themselves having to throw grenades in action when they had not thrown a single live one in training. By November 1917, every infantry recruit was expected to have thrown at least three live Mills grenades in practice and 50 per cent of them were now trained as rifle grenadiers. These were all steps towards abandoning the idea of the bomber as a specialist and the development of the infantryman as a technician skilled in a variety of weapons, including the Lewis gun, hand grenade and rifle grenade. No longer was the infantryman solely a rifleman-and-bayonet man.

By the end of 1917, the BEF was a diverse mix of men from a wide range of backgrounds. The pre-war regulars had been greatly reduced in number through attrition and the survivors diluted by the huge influx of citizen soldiers. The pre-war idea that infantrymen were unsuited to learning new skills was laid to rest in the trenches of the Western Front, largely by force of experience. Infantrymen had no choice but to acquire the new skills of trench warfare, such as those of the bomber and the rifle grenadier. GHQ might have taken a little longer to appreciate this reality than brigade and battalion commanders, who were closer to the problems thrown up by trench fighting, but GHQ was certainly not opposed to grenade warfare as an adjunct to more traditional forms of infantry fighting. Nevertheless, GHQ was ambivalent about grenades in 1915 and 1916, largely due to their unreliability and the belief that infantrymen were developing an over-reliance on grenades at the expense of traditional skills such as shooting. By late

1917, however, GHQ had changed its attitude. The grenades of 1917 were superior to the stop-gaps of 1915, handling procedures had been improved and the usefulness of grenades was well proven. Hence, the perception of grenades was different in 1917 from what it had been in 1915. There was also a better understanding of German grenade tactics: the March 1916 issue of the bombing manual had included two pages on German bombing tactics while the September 1916 issue included twelve pages on the subject. Unfortunately, such information was out of date by more than six months when the manuals were printed.

Major Beddoes of the Gloucesters formed the first bombing school, at Clapham, in the spring of 1915. From the beginning of 1916, each command in Britain and each of the five Armies in France had its own bombing school, their activities being coordinated by Major Beddoes. Every month, an officer from each of the eight Home Command schools was sent out to France, while officers from the schools in France or from the line were sent to the Home Command schools. This allowed the latter to keep up to date with the latest bombing tactics in France. The main purpose of the schools was to train instructors but they also trained bombers in order to replace casualties. Brigades still held bombing classes – as opposed to schools – to train instructors. A school was larger than a class, permanent and established by GHQ, Army or Corps, while a class was set up by divisional or brigade commanders at their discretion. A combined Bombing and Light Mortar School was affiliated to each Corps Infantry School and each battalion was now supposed to have one sergeant instructor who had been trained at this school. By late 1917, bombing classes at divisional, brigade and battalion levels were commonplace. The art of bombing was by now much more a science with well-established practices. Bombing had long since ceased to be an ad hoc free-for-all.

A distinction was always made between offensive and defensive bombing operations, although in practical terms the main difference was the amount of preparation that was possible, such as reconnaissance and stores of grenades in the trenches. In any operation, it was essential to scout the ground, study aerial photographs, understand the objective, and organize the supply and replenishment of grenades. The preparation and storage of the grenades was crucial to any operation. Out of the line, grenades were kept in an unarmed state in a bomb store and were armed when they were moved into the line so that they were ready for use. Unlike the stopgaps of 1915, Mills grenades were easy to arm and safe when armed. Armed grenades were kept in bomb stores in the support or reserve line near junctions with communication trenches, in clearly marked boxes. Bomb stores were some of the most important positions in any trench system. Typically, by 1916, a store for a two-battalion brigade held 3,000 grenades, each battalion's store held 1,000 and the company stores held another 1,000 grenades between them, making a total of 6,000 grenades for the brigade. The stores had to be well sited, bomb-proof and clearly identified so that there was no question about what they contained, namely armed grenades.

Bombing parties were dispersed along the front in the support trenches, close enough to communication trenches to enable them to counter-attack should the Germans make an incursion of the British line. Bombing posts were also set up in mine craters and at sapheads. Sapheads was covered in such a way that allowed British bombers to throw grenades from the saphead but prevented the Germans from bombing the British fire trench from the same position should they capture it. Bombing trenches were dug behind the fire trench and within throwing distance of it to deal with any German incursion into the fire trench. Defensive blocks in trenches had been used since 1914. During 1915, short dead-end trenches dug round a blocked sap that extended into no-man's-land were developed as a way for bombers to break up enemy encroachments into the British line. In a counter-attack, the bombers would have to go both left and right along a fire trench as they emerged from a communication trench, so it was essential that everyone knew beforehand which way they were going.

A bombing party had to rehearse counter-attacking so that it became second nature and could be executed at a moment's notice. The rest of the platoon supported the counter-attack, which was supposed to develop from the support line. By the end of 1917, rifle grenadiers were added to the section, although they had begun to feature in defensive tactics a year earlier. From a carefully chosen reserve position, the rifle grenadiers fired ranging shots with dummy grenades into the British front line; in the event of German troops making an incursion in that section of the front, rifle grenades were immediately fired on them.

The standard bombing party of eight men led by an NCO went through a gradual transformation during the war. By spring 1916, each platoon had its own bombing squad led by a sergeant, with only one spare man who acted as an extra carrier, while the eighth was now a rifle grenadier. Six months later, the spare man became a sniper or an additional rifle grenadier, while the carriers were now reserve throwers as well as carriers. Although everyone in a squad was still expected to be able to act in whatever capacity was required according to the situation, the sheer attrition on members of bombing squads meant that the carriers were now reserve throwers. By the autumn of 1917, bombing squads became sections, with each four-section platoon having a section of hand bombers and a section of rifle grenadiers.

As the war progressed, there was a gradual change in emphasis on the purpose of bombing, progressing from a caveat that grenades were short-range weapons for trench fighting and for tossing into dugouts, to a definite statement that bombing operations rarely succeeded without the support of riflemen and Lewis gunners. Initially, bombing had been an end in itself and there had been every expectation that it could achieve specific objectives, which went against some of the lessons of the Russo-Japanese War. Even in 1915, bombers were expected to act in cooperation with riflemen rather than independently, because lone bombers and bombing parties were vulnerable. By 1917, the object of a bombing operation was to force enemy troops out of their trenches and dugouts into the open, where rifle fire and machine-gun fire could deal with them. The change in objective from killing the enemy with grenades to forcing him into the killing zone of other weapons shows how grenade warfare had become more sophisticated than merely trying to outbomb the enemy, which had been the main purpose of bombing up to about the middle of 1915.

This change in purpose of bombing affected how bombers were used tactically in major offensives. In 1915, bombers were supposed to position themselves in front of the main infantry attack so that they could 'cover the bayonet assault with a shower of grenades'. The optimism of this somewhat unrealistic scenario did not escape the author of the manual, however, and he conceded that the bombers would be better advised to mop up after the main assault. Nevertheless, it was noted in June 1915 that bombers throwing grenades into an enemy fire trench could effectively suppress enemy riflemen which would allow infantrymen to cut intact barbed wire by hand, an unfortunate necessity due to the great difficulties in cutting wire with artillery at that time. When the bombers reached an enemy trench, they worked along it for at least 50 yards to clear it, then built bomb-stops to prevent enemy bombers from getting within range of the captured part of the trench. As an alternative to this, the bombers kept on working outwards from the point at which they penetrated the German line until they made contact with adjacent battalions taking part in the attack. Parties of bombers guarded trench junctions, where communication trenches joined the fire trenches, to prevent enemy reinforcements from getting into the trenches that had been captured, and to break up counter-attacks. Clearly, being a bomber was a very high risk job.

A bombing squad learned to work up the traverses of a trench in a set routine, moving in single file, the two bayonet men leading. Then came the first thrower, the first carrier, the commander, the second thrower, the second carrier and the two spare men at the back. In this formation, the squad occupied three traverses, arranged two, three or four men to a traverse. The remainder of the platoon followed them. The job of the bayonet men was to protect the rest of the squad. On entering an enemy trench, the first thrower tossed several grenades as quickly as possible into the two traverses beyond the bayonet men. Then, the first bayonet man went forward to check if the bombed traverses were clear. If they were, the whole squad advanced to the furthermost of the bombed traverses and the process was repeated. By spreading the squad between three traverses, the effects of enemy action were minimized. The bayonet men had to be skilled at snap shooting as well as being proficient with the bayonet. Their job was not only to protect the rest of the squad and the lightly armed throwers, but also to prevent a grenade duel from developing. Indeed, the bayonet men had to actively pursue the enemy and prevent him from taking up a new position further along the trench. While this was the formation and procedure set out in the manuals, it was not necessarily followed. Pollard, for example, believed the formation to be flawed and changed it while on a bombing operation. This was how bombing tactics evolved.

On the afternoon of 30 September 1915, Pollard, by now promoted sergeant, and his bombing squad counter-attacked German troops who had fought for and captured the crater of a mine they had blown that morning under the British line at Sanctuary Wood, about 2 miles to the east of Ypres. When the covering barrage opened at 3.00 pm, he recalled that they:

> moved forward in the correct formation … Fifty yards from where we started the trench was blocked with a barricade which brought the leading bayonet man up short … The first bomb thrower pulled the safety pin out of the bomb he was holding [possibly a No. 5 Mills], swung his arm, a long throw – a pause – bang! … For three minutes or so we had it all our own way … A thing like a jam tin on the end of a stick came hurtling through the air; landed on our parapet … followed by another. Then another and another.

The trench barricade prevented both Pollard's men and the Germans from moving and it became a contest to try and outbomb the enemy. Pollard realized that as leader he should be at the front not near the back of the party, as he had been taught, for the simple reason that men follow a resolute leader. And he could not envisage urging his men to go over or round the barricade with an active enemy on the other side while he was near the back. He decided to lead from the front. Under a barrage of grenades thrown by his squad he 'climbed out of the trench closely followed by half a dozen men'. Exposed to enfilade fire, four of them were immediately shot down. He and the two survivors jumped into the trench the other side of the barricade and were nearly killed by an exploding German grenade. Pollard was blown backwards and peppered with splinters. He ordered the two men to the next traverse to keep guard while he and the rest of the squad dismantled the barricade. As they renewed the bombing, they were fired on by snipers in nearby trees. The squad bombed its way along the trench until they reached another barricade which was overcome in a similar fashion. Pollard was severely wounded again as he picked up a bag of grenades, this time more seriously, hit by a sniper's bullet that had killed the man in front of him. Of the twenty-two men involved in the operation, including Pollard, only seven emerged from it unscathed, a testimony to just how dangerous bombing operations were. The attrition of trained bombers was high. He was awarded the Distinguished Conduct Medal for the action.

During the early summer of 1916, the emphasis in bombing changed from the bomb to the bayonet; grenades were now only to be thrown when the bayonet men were unable to deal with the enemy in the traverses by themselves. The NCO controlled the progress of the team, while the carriers ensured that their respective throwers did not run out of grenades. The spare man, acting as a carrier, resupplied these carriers. When the spare had none left, he had to find the nearest bomb store for a resupply. The job of the rifle grenadier was to suppress enemy bombers or prevent enemy reinforcements from interfering with the operation. For any bombing operation to succeed in its objective, teamwork was essential. Bombers could not work alone and hope to survive, let alone achieve much of consequence. It was essential for everyone involved to avoid crowding in the traverses. Preferably, each man stood at a corner of a traverse so that he could retreat behind it should an enemy grenade land in front of him.

This process of bombing remained the standard tactic for advancing along an enemy trench, although some refinements were introduced when the composition of the bombing squad changed in 1916. The presence of two rifle grenadiers altered the arrangement of men behind the NCO so that he was now followed by the first rifle grenadier, the second thrower, the second carrier and, finally, the second rifle grenadier. Each rifle grenadier had to carry his own stock of rods, grenades and cartridges. In addition to the standard explosive grenades, smoke grenades were also carried to toss into dugouts and force out their occupants. Two were recommended for each dugout. The composition of a squad was varied according to the requirements of each operation. It was crucial that everyone in the squad, whatever its composition, knew the objective of the operation, understood his own task in it and worked in a disciplined manner. During 1916, Lewis gunners and Stokes mortars began to be part of a support team for a bombing squad, especially when the objective was the destruction of an enemy machine-gun post. The support could even include 4-inch Stokes mortars, operated by the Special Brigade, Royal Engineers, which provided a smokescreen, particularly when attacking a machine-gun or to cover the return of a bombing party from a trench raid.

And yet, the practicalities of warfare and the needs of the moment often meant that deviations from standard procedure were inevitable. Nevertheless, the key to effective bombing was good training and familiarity with grenades, which provided a foundation for making informed on-the-spot decisions. After all, success on the battlefield, and in trench warfare in particular, required flexible responses of the men on the spot according to the circumstances in which they found themselves. This was especially true for bombing squads that were under strength or which suffered casualties in the course of an operation. At the same time, of course, individual courage and determination played a significant role as well.

The question of how bombers should be armed was the subject of correspondence in *The Times* in late 1915 and early 1916. By September 1916, the manuals made it clear that a thrower was expected to be lightly armed with a revolver, knife or knobkerrie instead of his rifle. The knobkerrie, also known as a mace or a club, could take many forms but their heads were often studded with hobnails or other pieces of metal. The Royal Engineers even cast a flanged mace head which could be fitted to the entrenching tool handle instead of the usual spade or pickhead. Such medieval weapons were used by all armies. A bombing operation was all about close combat in which hand-to-hand fighting often took place. Bombers had to be able to throw grenades with their 'rifle slung over their left shoulder'. By mid-1916, they were expected to wear the steel helmet which had become standard equipment during the spring, which hindered them further. Bombers had to be able to throw grenades irrespective of how they were encumbered at the time. Being weighed down or inconvenienced by equipment was seen as typical of trench fighting. They had to be able to work in a gas mask or wearing the box respirator, introduced in about mid-1916. To these ends, bombers had to practice under a range of conditions so that they could cope with any situation in which they might find themselves.

A bombing squad could expect to take part in a lot of raids and small enterprises, working in cooperation with riflemen to take a limited objective, such as a crater or a trench. Every man on a raid carried two grenades for the bombers. This practice was later extended to any size of operation as there was often a problem getting enough grenades across no-man's-land to resupply the bombers, especially on big operations. These grenades were supposed to be dumped at a collection point but reality did not always match expectation. Company-sized operations placed a bombing squad at the point of the attack, with another one in support to replace the inevitable casualties and to deal with dugouts after the point had moved on. There were also side parties whose job was to block communications trenches to prevent counter-attacks. Supporting riflemen and Lewis gunners could block trenches as well until a side party could take over. Bombers at the point did not remain there throughout the operation and those relieved from the point joined the main body of the attacking force. Success depended on momentum. Whenever possible, two or three throwers threw their grenades simultaneously, the man with the shortest range throwing to the nearest traverse, the man with the longest throwing to the furthest. Rifle grenadiers supported the point using No. 23 Mills grenades.

Rifle grenadiers usually worked in pairs in an eight-man section. One man in each pair observed the fall of shot, loaded the rifle with the No. 23 and took out the pin. The shooter then loaded the cartridge. Volley, rapid or individual fire was adopted according to circumstances. Individual fire involved firing one grenade per pair. Rapid fire required each pair to load and fire as quickly as possible until a specified number of grenades had been fired. Volley fire required rifle grenadiers to fire simultaneously. The NCO in command specified the target and its range.

In any large-scale attack, the role of the bomber was slightly different. The principal tasks were to clear trenches that the assaulting infantry had gone beyond and to protect the flanks of their respective companies once the objective had been taken. They also countered enemy bombers who had been overtaken in the attack. During the opening battles of the Somme offensive in 1916, bombers helped to support the infantry assaulting across open ground by bombing up the same trench being assaulted, provided the infantry assault was preceded by 'adequate preparation'. Ironically, GHQ now complained that bombers threw too many grenades, which exhausted the bombers and wasted grenades. It blamed poor throwing discipline. A bombing squad was armed with up to 120 grenades. One of the most important tasks for rifle grenadiers was suppression of enemy machine-guns and strongpoints during the attack to enable bombers to get close enough to deal with them. Hand grenades were often more effective than shellfire when it came to silencing the occupants of pillboxes. A Mills tossed through an aperture killed or wounded those inside, whereas shells often only chipped at the concrete. The bombers had to dig a sap towards the pillbox with the rifleman, Lewis gunners and rifle grenadiers providing covering fire to allow the bombers to reach the pillbox. The alternative to sapping was a process of encirclement to enable bombers to approach the pillbox from the flanks or rear.

Although Rifle grenades had been used to suppress enemy machine-guns as early as 1915, this was a rather ad hoc business until 1916 when the fire-suppression role of rifle grenades became much more important. Now, the rifle grenadier section put down a barrage of grenades 30–40 yards ahead of the bombing section. The role of mopping up by bombing sections, a role that is often associated with bombers, was a distinct operation with very specific goals and procedures. The mopping-up team now included a couple of riflemen and often a Lewis gunner. Coordination and organization was the key to ensuring that all captured trenches and dugouts were dealt with in a methodical way so that nothing was overlooked or left to chance. But the employment of grenades to repel a counter-attack was now very much discouraged as it had proved to be wholly ineffective. This was a reversal of the tactics used in 1915.

A significant development during 1917 was the use of bombers above ground in coordination with those working along a trench. The idea was to throw grenades into a trench simultaneously from both sides whenever possible. Those working above ground had a better view of enemy movements than those in the confines of the trench. The team of bombers and their support now totalled more than thirty personnel, most of whom were above ground. Only four of the team advanced along the trench: a bayonet man, followed by a thrower and his carrier, followed by a rifle grenadier. The speed of advance was determined by the speed of the bombing group above ground. This group included a thrower and his carrier, with two bayonet men or one bayonet man and a rifle grenadier on the flank to give covering fire when needed. The thrower above ground threw a grenade into the trench and took cover – the Mills grenade produced a great many lethal fragments which travelled well beyond the distance someone could throw a grenade. His carrier ran several yards beyond him, before he also took cover. The process was repeated until the trench was cleared. Such tactics mostly applied to large-scale attacks in which the assault infantry had already passed beyond the first line of German trenches; this was mopping up.

Now, when working inside a trench, no grenades were thrown until the bayonet men were stopped by the enemy. The technique of attacking round a traverse with a bayonet was highly skilled work and essential to successful bombing operations. Far from rendering the fixed bayonet redundant or shooting skills unnecessary, the grenade made them more important than ever. For bombing to be effective, the skills of the bayonet men were crucial. Bombing alone could not clear a trench of the enemy. In 1915, there had been doubts about whether the traditional rifle and bayonet could be used in the confined space of a trench and there was much talk about knives, clubs and pistols, even suggestions that men had resorted to their fists and their boots. But the skills developed by the bayonet men in a bombing section proved otherwise.

The specialist bomber was phased out during 1917 and every rifleman became a bomber. Bombing was becoming a universal skill rather than one that was invested in only a few. A platoon consisted of between twenty-four and forty men, divided into four sections, plus a headquarters. By the end of the year, the bombing sections had lost their role descriptions and had become merely numbers; the hand grenade section became No. 2 Section, while the rifle grenadiers became No. 3. In 1918, the infantry platoon was an all-weapons unit in which everyone in it was familiar with rifle, bayonet, hand and rifle grenades, and Lewis gun. There were three rifle sections and one Lewis gun section. There was no longer a separate bombing section, although one of the rifle sections could be trained as a bombing team. Each member of this team carried up to seven grenades, while the carriers had up to fourteen, making a maximum of eighty-four for a ten-man section, which was a 30 per cent reduction on an eight-man bombing squad of mid-1916. The nine-man squad of mid-1917 had carried ninety grenades, five by the throwers and at least ten by everyone else in the section. The same team could act as rifle grenadiers, in which case, they each carried seven grenades including some smoke grenades for providing cover.

The rifle grenade was described as 'the "howitzer" of the platoon', which provided fire support at up to 100 yards to allow riflemen to get to close quarters with the enemy, and often fired in cooperation with a Lewis gun team. Barrages of rifle grenades were fired on machine-guns and points of resistance. By 1918, the idea of mopping up had been abandoned and each section in the platoon was given an objective which it had to take, so that no pockets of resistance or enemy-held areas were left in the rear of the advancing infantry. The whole approach to trench warfare as carried out in 1915 and 1916 had completely changed by 1918. Now, a bombing team only worked up a trench when there was no other means of clearing the enemy, and only with the support of riflemen and Lewis gunners above ground.

The biggest problem with grenade fighting was its pace. It was very slow and exhausting. Moreover, as soon as bombing became necessary in an assault, the advance effectively ended because bombing did not move along the line of attack but spread out sideways along trenches which faced it. To engage the enemy, the bombers had no choice but to move along the trenches. Even when bombing involved teams above ground, the same problem remained. And there was much the same problem when a strongpoint was the focus of a bombing attack. The inability to maintain momentum was one reason for GHQ's concern about infantrymen abandoning the rifle and bayonet in favour of grenades. It also helps to explain why the bombers ceased to be specialists and why bombing ceased to be a set-piece operation.

Bombing had been rather haphazard in 1915 due to the severe shortage of grenades. With the sudden brief gluts of new but dangerous stopgaps, followed by the novelty of having an abundance of reliable and effective grenades in the form of the No. 5 Mills, it was inevitable that bombing then became indiscriminate. The increasing use of grenades, however, led to the fear that they might supersede the rifle and bayonet as the infantryman's weapon of choice. In June 1915, General French wrote to the War Office about the higher than anticipated expenditure of hand grenades in recent heavy fighting, which he blamed on the inability of the infantry to use the rifle and bayonet in the trenches, resulting in a profligate use of grenades. This showed just how little anyone in the BEF knew about grenades and trench fighting at that time, which in turn meant that there was no tactical method for bombing, made worse by a lack of training and reliable grenades. The notion that the rifle and bayonet could not be used in the confined space of a trench was subsequently proved to be quite false and the so-called 'cult of the bomb' was no more than an irrational fear. The bomb never ousted the rifle or the bayonet.

In the same way that shooting and bayonet fighting were skilled jobs which had to be learned and practised, the skills and technical expertise in handling grenades had to be learned. Bombing was no less of a skill and there was no reason for infantrymen to favour grenades. The idea that men lurked fearfully behind traverses with grenades rather than advance with their rifles is a misunderstanding of grenades and how they could be used. Although during the first half of 1915, some men used grenades without proper training, this ceased to be the norm during the second half of the year. With better throwing discipline, aided by safer and more reliable grenades, the numbers of grenades carried and used on a bombing operation decreased in 1917 and 1918. The real problem with bombing operations was that they tended to move sideways rather than forwards.

The tactics of the rifle grenade were essentially fire support and suppression. In 1917, GHQ complained that more practice firing rifle grenades was needed because accuracy was poor. However, this was as much a technical deficiency as it was one caused by absence of skill. Rifle grenades were inherently inaccurate because of their poor flight characteristics. Consequently, rifle grenades were often fired in barrages to ensure that enough of them landed close enough to the target to achieve the desired effect, namely, to force the enemy into the open where they could be engaged with rifle fire and Lewis guns. There tended to be fewer rifle grenades taken on an operation than hand grenades because of their weight. It was not surprising, then, that their effect was limited in comparison to the Lewis gun which was used in a similar way for fire support. The Lewis gun was more flexible because of the comparative ease of providing Lewis guns with plenty of ammunition, although that is not to suggest that supplying plenty of drums during an advance was not without problem.

Grenade fighting went through three phases on the Western Front. Initially, grenade fighting was an ad hoc affair in which the object was merely to outbomb the enemy bombers. The problems were those of supplying enough grenades to do this and the unreliability of the grenades. As they became more plentiful and more reliable, a systemized method of fighting was developed involving specialists in bombing who had to be trained, to which end Bombing Schools were set up. While these specialists were expected to maintain their musketry skills, the level of technical expertise and tactical skill required of the bombers meant that they were formed into separate sections which only engaged in bombing. Finally, bombing was absorbed into standard infantry tactics. Bombing was no longer a specialism but an adjunct to the traditional skills of the infantryman. At the same time, he became familiar with rifle grenades and the Lewis gun, which transformed him into a technician proficient in a range of weapons and accustomed to teamwork. By 1918, he only used a hand grenade when it was the appropriate tool for the job.

German tactics had always differed from those of the British. Indeed, in 1915, German grenades and tactics had generally been superior to British grenades and tactics. Like the British and the French, they liked their bombers to be 'courageous and expert hand grenade throwers'. The big difference, however, was that all German troops were trained to throw grenades and the bombing section was made up of the best in the platoon. A typical German bombing squad comprised six men, including its leader, and was located in the centre of the platoon when they were in the trenches. Significantly, if the British or French made an incursion into their line, any of the riflemen could throw grenades while the specialist squad only counter-attacked if the other members of the platoon were unable to dislodge the invaders. German bombers always carried 'their rifles slung, bayonets fixed and daggers ready, with the exception of the two leaders who do not carry rifles'. Trench clubs or sharpened spades were also carried. The two leading men in the squad carried as many grenades as they could manage and were armed with pistols. Likewise, the commander was armed with a pistol. The men were spread in threes with the second three in the next traverse back. The two leading men advanced at the crouch so that the commander who followed immediately behind could shoot over them. Squads in the support and reserve lines were positioned near communication trenches, much like the British practice. By early 1916, the number of grenades each man carried was reduced to six but the size of the team had grown to nine, including the leader, two of whom were spares. In an emergency, bombers were expected to carry as many as twenty grenades each. Half of the team carried twenty-five empty sandbags each so that bomb-stops could be erected when necessary to prevent British or French bombers ejecting them.

As with British grenade tactics, German tactics evolved from experience but also from pre-war theory and it is significant that the Germans ended the war with the same hand grenade, only slightly modified, as the one with which they began the war. This was the time-fused 'potato-masher' stick grenade, which was essentially a cylinder of explosive containing a detonator and fuse, attached to a wooden handle containing a friction lighter, lit by pulling a wire through the base of the handle. Although a percussion-fuse version was produced, it was not as widely used as the time-fused version. The Germans introduced a lighter egg grenade in 1916, in response to which the British developed an egg grenade of their own, the No. 34. These lighter grenades could be thrown further than their bigger cousins, but they packed a smaller lethal punch.

While British bombers were always taught to throw a grenade immediately after lighting it, irrespective of the type of grenade, German bombers were initially taught quite the reverse. The Germans feared there was time to avoid a time-fused grenade that was thrown too soon after it was lit. There were instances where British bombers had scooped up the grenade before it exploded and had thrown it back, a highly dangerous, not to say foolhardy, act since the fuses in German grenades burned no longer than those in British grenades. This instruction was rescinded during 1917 so that German bombers threw their grenades immediately in the same way that their British and French counterparts did.

German stick grenades could often be thrown further than the Mills because the handle allowed more momentum to be imparted to the grenade. The Mills was heavier and thrown in a bowling action similar to delivering a cricket ball. The Mills was far more lethal because of the large number of fragments it produced when it exploded, in excess of 700, far more than the stick grenade which relied more on blast than fragmentation for effect. The stick grenade tended to produce a louder bang than the Mills so tended to have a greater moral effect. The moral effect was no less important than the lethal one since, by 1917, the purpose of bombing had become more a matter of forcing the enemy into the lethal zone of small arms and machine-guns than it was about killing the enemy with the grenades themselves.

CHAPTER 9

New Weapons and New Warfare

In the years between the end of the Russo-Japanese War and the start of the First World War, the German Army developed small mortars for engaging entrenched defenders. These early trench mortars were effectively scaled-down artillery pieces with rifled barrels and came in light, medium and heavy categories. The German Army was the only one in 1914 to be equipped with such weapons, but it possessed only 160 mortars all told. Britain and France had none at all, not because of incompetence but because no demand for such weapons was predicted by the sort of war which Britain and France anticipated fighting in Europe. Neither Britain nor France had been sufficiently impressed with the crude 'bomb-throwers' used in Manchuria to consider such things worth the bother. However, as soon as the German Army began using its mortars in the trenches in the autumn of 1914, it became apparent to everyone that the only way to deal with them was to reply in kind. So mortars had to be improvised and invented. The trench mortar, together with the grenade, came to symbolize trench fighting on the Western Front.

Such were the straits in which the BEF found itself that, until the end of 1915, bomb-throwers powered by springs or rubber had to make up for the lack of mortars, although the French gave the BEF some 1840s Coehorns. By mid-1915, the BEF had about 750 catapults and bomb-throwers in service. Principal among the British catapults was the Leach or Gamage catapult but its range was poor, its accuracy worse, 75–100 yards being typical. The Germans and the French also made use of catapults, many of which were locally made improvisations. The British had a mechanical bomb-thrower, the West Spring Gun, named after its inventor, Captain West. About the same number of Spring Guns saw service in France as Leach catapults. The Spring Gun worked under the combined action of twenty-four springs, distributed in banks of equal size and, as Guy Chapman of the 15th Royal Fusiliers observed:

> was supposed to hurl a hand grenade with much force and accuracy into the enemy's lines. In practice, it was much more apt to shoot the missile straight up into the air to return on the marksman's head, supposing he still possessed one; for the machine was also calculated to decapitate the engineer if he was clumsy enough to stand in front of its whirling arm.

Whereas the Leach catapult could be propped up against the trench parapet, the Spring Gun needed to be set in an emplacement 8–9 feet square. Its long cocking lever was often visible above the parapet. The gun could be traversed slightly by slewing it round on its bed, which required the securing bolts to be slackened off, but traverse was limited to 15 yards in 100 yards. Setting up the gun was something of a rigmarole, as described in a 1919 history of trench warfare:

> The ground had to be as level as possible. Then by means of carrying rods, the gun was carried into position. The sandbag boards were then unstrapped and fixed in position on each side, 13 or 14 sandbags being placed upon each of them. The throwing arms were then put in with the straight side up. It is advisable not to tighten the holding shoes till the bomb cup is affixed.

The BEF first encountered German trench mortars, *minenwerfer* or 'minnies', at the end of October 1914 when the Connaught Rangers near Ypres 'complained of "a sort of howitzer" which was dropping shells on them from the enemy's trench 300 yards in front of their right'. According to the Official History a field gun was run up 'by hand behind a hedge and with the first shot ... knocked the weapon out and killed a number of the enemy who showed signs of attacking'. This was also one of the earliest instances of an 18-pounder firing an HE shell in the war. Such action by British gunners would not be possible once the trenches had become established. German trench mortars were loathed right from the start, although because the bombs travelled at subsonic speeds, it was easy to spot them in flight. The same was true of rifle grenades but mortar bombs were especially disliked. The bombs described a high arc and it was possible to predict where they would fall so that single bombs could be dodged. Alf Pollard noted that in the Honourable Artillery Company, a warning system was introduced in 1916 whereby

> each Company posted a sentry provided with a whistle. Three blasts meant that the danger was to the right; two blasts to the left; one, that it was coming straight over. When the warning sounded the troops moved along the trench to another traverse. In this way we suffered very few casualties.

The biggest German bomb, the 260mm weighing in at 200lb, about half of which was explosive, arced almost inaudibly across the sky, like a black dustbin, until it descended, making a humming noise as it tumbled out of the sky. One of these could clear an area 33 feet in diameter in a barbed-wire entanglement. Single fragments from these large projectiles could travel up to 440 yards and cut a man in half. The delayed-action fused projectiles could penetrate the 23–30 feet of earth cover of a dugout and destroy it, forming craters 16–20 feet deep and 26–33 feet in diameter. This mortar, a relatively simple piece of ordnance, could throw a heavyweight bomb more than 500 yards in 1915. By 1917, the 260mm mortar could throw one 1,000 yards. They had a slow rate of fire, managing only twenty rounds an hour. The small trench mortars fired a 10lb bomb up to 1,000 yards and could sustain twenty rounds a minute for a brief period. The 170mm medium mortar had a rate of fire of thirty-five rounds an hour, firing a 110lb bomb out to a maximum range of 1,000 yards. In 1915, the British had nothing to compare with these German weapons.

Nevertheless, British trench mortars were as unnerving for the Germans as theirs were for the British. Lieutenant Ernst Jünger described the noise of a bomb as it descended as a 'whistling, whispering noise'. Once, when he was preparing for a raid

> I was scared out of my wits by a terrific crash close to the dugout. The Englishmen were sending 'toffee-apples' over which, in spite of the moderate report they made when fired off, were of such weight that the splinters from them smashed the stout tree-trunk posts of the revetment clean through.

Clambering out of the dugout he saw 'one of these black fellows describe his circular course through the air'. Retaliation was swift and 'for every toffee-apple that came over we returned a Lanz'. The Lanz was a stopgap type of light mortar, produced in 1915 and 1916, smooth-bored with a calibre of 91mm. It fired a 9lb bomb to a range of about 350 yards. The so-called toffee-apple mortar was the British 2-inch medium, the bombs for which were spherical casings fitted with a detachable 11.3-inch tail or stem so that they resembled toffee apples. The tail fitted inside the mortar barrel. The spherical casings were also known by the British as footballs or plum puddings. These mortars were never popular with the British infantry because the steel tail was projected back at the British line when the bomb exploded. It caused friendly casualties while contributing nothing to the destructive effect of the bomb. It was also a waste of steel, a material which the British could ill afford to waste.

In 1917, the 2-inch mortar, which had been designed by Woolwich, was replaced by the 6-inch Newton, invented by Captain Henry Newton, formerly in command of the Second Army Workshops, latterly in the Trench Warfare Department of the Ministry of Munitions. The Newton worked on the Stokes principal and had a higher rate of fire and a longer range than the Woolwich mortar. The Stokes mortar had a fixed firing pin in the breech, while the bombs held a propellant cartridge in the tail. When the bomb was dropped down the barrel, the cartridge hit the pin and ignited the propellant. The Stokes, invented in late 1914, could fire as fast as a man could load it, but only for short periods. Henry Newton invented the incremental ring charge to supplement the cartridge and extend the range by a known amount. Up to three or four rings could be fitted round the tail of the Stokes bomb. It saw widespread use from about late-1916 onwards.

There were a lot of British duds, or blinds, in the early years of the war due to the fuses malfunctioning. Jünger recounted an incident when a NCO attempted to take off the fuse of a dud toffee-apple 'and observing that the powder was smouldering he put the end of his cigarette into the opening'. The toffee-apple exploded and killed him. A fellow lieutenant stored a collection of duds in a dugout, which everyone else was very careful to avoid. He spent his spare time unscrewing the fuses and examining them. This dangerous fascination was not confined to the Germans, of course, and collecting fuses was a pastime practised by the foolhardy in all armies, often with predictable results. Short rounds were also common, due to the propellant not burning fully. These could either fall in no-man's-land or on friendly troops in the front line. The infantry always regarded shorts as bad gunnery by the mortar crews concerned, whereas the fault was often technical rather than human. The other serious problem was premature explosion of the bomb, either while it was still in the barrel or just as it left the muzzle. Then there was the problem of misfires when the propellant failed to ignite, leaving a fused bomb in the barrel. Mortar crews had to learn the drills for dealing with these sorts of situation. Such hazards were a good reason for firing mortars from behind cover by means of a lanyard. Few mortars could be fired safely any other way, the main exceptions being the Stokes and the Newton, although all mortars became much safer to operate during 1916.

The first British mortars were improvised by the Indian Corps in 1914 but they were little better than the drainpipes they resembled. They had a range of about 150 yards, which was barely enough to reach the German trenches, and they were very inaccurate. The mortars were slow to load and fire. The jam-tin bombs they fired were little more than a nuisance to the Germans. The 3.7-inch and the 4-inch mortars sent out from Britain in late 1914 and early 1915, themselves improvised, were little better than the mortars cobbled together in France. The Royal Engineers continued to improvise mortars well into 1915 and the Second Army Workshops produced mortars cast from the brass of spent cartridge cases to make up the shortfall of what was coming from Britain. The latter included a mortar designed by Vickers that was similar to the 2-inch mortar designed by Woolwich. As far as GHQ was concerned, the trench mortar was still little more than a cheap substitute for the howitzer, a weapon the BEF also lacked in sufficient numbers. At the beginning of 1916, the BEF had eight patterns of mortar, not including the Coehorns. This caused huge logistical problems, so the number was reduced to three by May 1916. The 3-inch Stokes light mortar, 2-inch medium mortar and the 9.45-inch heavy mortar (based on a French design and built in Britain under licence) became the mainstays of the BEF's mortar establishment for the next eighteen months. Advances in mortar technology, propellants and ammunition, gained through the practical experience of fighting on the Western Front during eighteen months of trench warfare, all contributed to the BEF's rising expertise with mortars. There were persistent problems, however, which were difficult to resolve.

Two of the biggest of these were noise and flash when a mortar was fired. They were the tell-tale signatures of a trench mortar which, once detected, prompted a retaliatory bombardment from enemy artillery, mortars or rifle grenades. Inventors experimented with attachments to suppress muzzle flash, smoke and noise, one of which, the Temple silencer, was adopted by the British. This was invented for the 2-inch medium mortar which was particularly loud and produced a considerable muzzle flash. A limited number of silencers were available from about the spring of 1916. Silenced mortars were mostly used for night firings when muzzle flash was very noticeable. The problem with the silencer was that it made the barrel very hot so that it had to be cooled after a few rounds. A hot barrel was a leading cause of prematures with the bombs.

Light mortars were primarily anti-personnel weapons. Medium mortars could be used to destroy barbed-wire entanglements or to destroy dugouts and trenches. The bomb fired by the 2-inch mortar was not really suited to demolition work as it did not bury itself before detonating because of its spherical body. The problem for the British was that until mid-1916, no fuse existed which would allow mortar bombs or artillery shells to destroy wire entanglements without cratering the ground in the process, thereby substituting one obstacle to the infantry with another. The sole purpose of heavy mortars was the demolition of enemy trenches and dugouts.

The short range of British trench mortars restricted the sort of targets they could engage. When no-man's-land was wider than the effective range of the mortars, a situation that was worsened by the development of defences in depth from late 1915 onwards, the mortar was useless. In early 1915, ranges were typically in order of 100–250 yards. Range had been increased to 300–500 yards by mid-1916. By about mid-1917, ranges had been further extended to 800–1,200 yards. The maximum range was to about 1,500–2,500 yards, depending on the type of mortar, in 1918. The range of the 9.45-inch was increased from 1,100 yards in 1916 to 2,400 yards in 1917, whereas the 8-inch howitzer had a range of 10,500 yards in 1916. A Mk1 18-pounder of 1914 had a range of 6,500 yards while the Mk4 of 1918 had a range of 9,300 yards. The 3-inch Stokes mortar, the calibre of which was comparable with the 18-pounder, had a range of 750 yards in 1917 thanks to the incremental ring charge.

British mortars were organized into batteries of four but, by 1917, Stokes batteries had been doubled in size to include eight in two half-batteries of four. It was common for a battery to be set up in one location to fire on a target, then relocate to somewhere else. As soon as a battery opened fire, it gave away its position, which usually resulted in retaliation by enemy artillery, mortars or rifle grenades. Thus, mortar crews tended to be unpopular with the infantry who bore the brunt of the retaliation. To a large extent, the location of a battery was determined by the range of its mortars since they had to be able to hit the target. The emplacements of a battery were dispersed behind the front-line trenches over a distance of a few hundred yards to avoid presenting a single target to enemy gunners or rifle grenadiers. If the battery was intended to protect the British line, the battery location was chosen so that it could provide enfilade fire and crossfire in the event of an enemy break-in. Irrespective of whether the battery was intended for attack or defence, the important aspect of any emplacement was the arc of fire.

Each emplacement was connected to a communication trench, rather than from a fire trench or a support trench.

All emplacements had to be camouflaged to conceal them from enemy reconnaissance aircraft and the crew shelter had to be bomb-proof to protect it from shelling; ideally, the roof of a permanent emplacement was reinforced concrete. British engineers worked on the principal that 2.7–3 feet of concrete, or 24 feet of earth or clay, was required to make a dugout bomb-proof. However, a variety of materials, depending on what was available in the locality, were employed for making a roof bomb-proof, including timber beams, steel girders, rails, fascines, bricks and stone, all in combination with earth and concrete, so that the thickness of the resulting roof might be anything between 3 feet and 24 feet. By 1916, a 'bursting course' of hard material, such as concrete, stone, bricks or pavé blocks, was put on the top so that the percussion fuse of the shell was activated, thereby detonating the shell, before the projectile could penetrate the roof. Beneath this layer was a shock-absorbing or 'distributing' course of timber, fascines or rails, all of which had to be laid so that the components were in close contact with each other. These layers were supported on stout uprights of timber or steel, locked together by struts, ties and dogs to form a strong framework. Inside this structure was a second one of corrugated steel formed into a half-cylinder. Preformed, these corrugated structures were known as elephant shelters; small ones were called baby elephants. Sometimes, only a layer of sandbags was placed on the shelter, which only provided minimal protection from shrapnel and shell fragments. To be proof against a 5.9-inch high-explosive shell, there were several options, including at least 6 inches of earth and 6 inches of bricks. Alternatively, 2 feet of sandbagged earth on top of a layer of rails or 10-inch timbers would provide the same level of protection.

Not all dugouts had to be cut into the earth and constructed in this way. Where the ground was chalk, such as in the region of the Somme, deep dugouts could be excavated with considerable ease, and both the BEF and the German Army took full advantage. Indeed, when the British troops came upon some of the German dugouts in the Somme area, they were surprised by their depth which made them proof against even the largest-calibre shells. As part of the preparations for the Somme offensive, Royal Engineers constructed shallow tunnels, Russian saps, under no-man's-land. Some of these tunnels were subsequently converted into trenches by removing the top layer of chalk and earth, while others became mortar emplacements and machine-gun positions.

By 1917, the emplacements for medium and heavy mortars were often below ground level, with only an opening to fire through. In 1916, a permanent emplacement for a 2-inch mortar consisted of a mortar pit, with two trenches connecting it to the magazine, so that the two were separated by an island. The mortar was fired by a lanyard in case of a premature. Double emplacements were sometimes used with the mediums but neat geometrical patterns were avoided as they were a dead giveaway. The 9.45-inch mortar had an L-shaped emplacement, the mortar pit being at the right-angled junction of the two arms. The long arm of the L was 30 feet, while the shorter arm was 24 feet and the mortar chamber was 8 feet square. The crew dugout, at the end of the long arm, was 10 feet by 6 feet. The magazine, at the end of the short arm, was 12 feet by 6 feet. The whole emplacement was 6 feet below the surface and reinforced with timber pit props and beams, as well as corrugated-iron sheets. The mortar could be rotated on its traversing ring to allow the barrel to point towards the magazine for loading. This facility for rotating the mortar for loading determined the shape of the emplacement. The mediums, on the other hand, needed space at the front of the pit for loading.

In 1916, Stokes mortars were often temporarily sited in a fire trench; alternatively, a small recess was cut in the back of the trench for the mortar. An emplacement could be dug behind the parados or the mortar could be set up in a large crater in no-man's-land, especially in preparation for an attack, a sap being dug out from the front line to the crater. The Stokes could be set up almost anywhere. However, it suffered from the same problem that beset all mortars when kept in one location for any length of time, namely, a propensity to sink into the ground after prolonged firing. Like all mortars, the Stokes needed a wooden bed to provide it with a firm firing platform. By 1918, pairs of Stokes mortars were put into permanent emplacements dug in a disused trench. An emplacement for two mortars could also be built in the cellar of a damaged house. The magazine in a permanent emplacement held 200 rounds for each Stokes in the pair.

Various methods of fire were possible with all mortars: battery fire, section fire and so-called gun fire. Battery fire involved all the mortars firing right to left in sequence, with a specified time interval between each shot, typically ten seconds. With section fire, only specified mortars fired, again at specified intervals. Gun fire was independent fire. Rapid fire was only possible with some German light mortars and the Stokes mortar. The number of rounds to be fired could be specified, or the mortars might fire until ordered to stop. Another option was salvo fire in which all the mortars in the battery, or specified sections, fired simultaneously. It had the advantage of putting several bombs into the air at the same time which meant that the enemy was less able to dodge them. Salvos had the advantage of making it difficult for the enemy to locate the battery.

In 1916, mortars had to fire registration rounds in the same way as artillery, preferably during an artillery shoot on nearby targets or under cover of a shrapnel barrage to prevent the enemy from seeing the mortars. It was all too easy to identify the location of a mortar from its muzzle flash and the noise it made, as well as from the trajectory of its bomb. Registration for mortars and artillery was only valid for the day on which it was done because weather conditions affected trajectories and, of course, temperature and wind speed and direction changed from day to day. On the day the mortars were scheduled to fire on a target, several rounds had to be fired on to a specified point, which had already been carefully registered, to determine the appropriate corrections for the weather. This was known as the 'error of the day'. This technique was developed by British artillery and refined as the war progressed. By 1918, the error of the day was sometimes changed several times in a matter of hours because of changing weather conditions. Nevertheless, there was a persistent problem with accuracy with medium and heavy mortars.

Effective gunnery depended on good communications between the battery and the forward observer, who was usually the artillery's forward observer. These observers were in the front-line trenches and used magnifying periscopes of far better optical quality than any periscope provided to the infantry. The observer communicated with the battery commander by telephone but the cables were often cut by enemy shellfire, so runners had the unenviable task of keeping contact active between observer and commander. Communication between the mortars, the battery commander, the brigade commander and the advancing infantry were likely to be fragmentary, so it was essential that the mortars and the infantry had pre-arranged SOS signals to call for assistance.

Light mortar batteries were part of an infantry brigade, whereas medium and heavy mortars were part of the divisional artillery. Sometimes, the mediums and heavies were attached to infantry brigades, in which case command passed temporarily to the infantry brigadiers concerned. Heavy mortars were preferably located near roads or railways for ease of transporting the mortars and their ammunition. Heavy mortars were used to destroy dugouts, trenches and strongpoints in the enemy's first line, allowing howitzers to shoot at targets that were out of the mortars' range. Mediums were sometimes used to do the same thing. From the end of 1915, the mediums were also used to destroy barbed-wire entanglements. Light mortars lacked the power to penetrate dugouts but were easier to transport than mediums or heavies. Neither 9.45-inch nor 3-inch bombs were fitted with fuses that would enable them to destroy barbed wire without cratering the ground. Similarly, the 9.45-inch bomb was unsuited to the infantry support role because the magnitude of the explosion made it dangerous to friendly troops. Heavies and mediums added to an artillery bombardment that preceded an operation, large or small, especially targeting strongpoints. When a bombardment extended over several days, the mediums and heavies did not open fire until the last day to avoid their being discovered and hit by a counter-bombardment.

In the spring of 1916, there was still much to be learned about such tactical uses of mortars. The light mortars in service with the BEF at that time included the highly unreliable 3.7-inch and 4-inch patterns. In theory, these could be moved forward in an attack to support the infantry, but it was not until the widespread use of the Stokes mortar that this was feasible. The rapid fire of a Stokes mortar had a significant effect on enemy troop concentrations prior to a counter-attack, especially when such concentrations were in the open. By the beginning of 1917, emphasis was placed on all mortars being part of the overall artillery fire plan, with clear zones and specific tasks allocated to the batteries. The rapid fire of the Stokes mortar was now used to harass the enemy during the final stages of a preliminary bombardment, supplementing shrapnel fired by 18-pounders. Stokes batteries, located in the fire trenches or in no-man's-land, fired a barrage beyond the objective of the infantry assault to prevent the enemy from bringing up reinforcements or organizing a counter-attack. The Stokes was also used in cooperation with Lewis guns and bombing teams. Barrages in support of the infantry and in support of bombing parties were very effective.

Stokes mortars were used for interdiction in support of a raid. In 1916, this meant that the target had to be registered before the operation without revealing that the target was about to be hit by a raid. By 1917, the Stokes was typically used to provide tactical support to bombers on a raid by firing over their heads. Providing suppressing fire on the flanks of an attack along a trench was standard practice in 1918. Although the 2-inch mortar was far less mobile than the Stokes, two medium mortars were sometimes formed into an ad hoc section which went forward to support the infantry, but the crew needed a GS wagon or a couple of pack animals to do this. The idea was that mediums could deal with concrete pillboxes and wire obstacles should they be encountered by the infantry. Unlike Stokes detachments who could count on carrying parties to take their ammunition forward, medium mortar detachments could only rely on themselves. For the most part, once the infantry assault had begun, the mediums and heavies stayed silent as they were more of a hindrance than a help. Mortars often fired to cover the withdrawal of the raiding party.

The raid became the symbol of aggressive defence on the Western Front as far as the BEF was concerned. The first raids were carried out in early November 1914 by troops from the Garwhal Rifles of the Indian Corps. In February 1915, Sir John French gave his official sanction for 'local attacks on a small scale'. GHQ stated that raiding was important because:

We are for the moment acting on the defensive ... but this should not preclude the planning and making of local attacks on a comparatively small scale, with a view to gaining ground and of taking full advantage of any tactical or numerical inferiority on the part of the enemy. Such enterprises ... should receive every encouragement, since they relieve monotony and improve the morale of our troops, while they have a corresponding detrimental effect on the morale of the enemy's troops ... enterprises of this nature constitute the most effective form of defence ... [but] ... these minor operations should, of course, not be of an aimless character but should be based on a specific object.

All armies on the Western Front took up raiding which went on throughout the war. Raids were a constant nuisance. Troops manning fire trenches had to be alert during the hours of darkness, sentries especially. Raiders might approach in complete silence, before killing the unfortunate guard with a knife. While raids could provide valuable intelligence when prisoners were taken, they were often wasteful of lives, especially in the early days, because of their lack of planning and the lack of experience of the participants. Initially, raids were more about bravado than they were about military objectives, and a raiding party might be no more than a handful of enthusiastic volunteers who wanted to get to grips with the enemy. Even in early 1918, there was sometimes a sporting-like approach to raids when some battalions competed with each other for a monthly cup based on a marking system: one point for an identification of a killed enemy, two for a prisoner taken, three for a mortar or a machine-gun. Nevertheless, raids acquired greater purpose during 1915 and by 1916 they had become small enterprises with clear objectives which could involve as few as ten men or as many as 200 but sometimes upwards of 400 men – at least two companies – complete with artillery bombardment with a pre-arranged fire plan and timetable. They were, in many ways, the ideal training for bigger offensive operations as they tested how well artillery and infantry worked together. The point of a raid, as set out by GHQ, remained the same throughout the war, namely, to

> enter the enemy's trenches by surprise, kill as many of his men as possible, and return before counter-measures can be taken. Special tasks may be added, such as obtaining prisoners for 'identification', damaging mine shafts, destroying a length of trench or post which is giving particular trouble.

The levels of raiding fluctuated between great intensity and periods of relative calm. Between 19 December 1915 and 30 May 1916, the BEF carried out sixty-three raids, the parties ranging in size from ten men to 200. Of these, forty-seven were successful. During the same period, the Germans mounted thirty-three raids on British trenches, twenty of which were successful. During nights of the week immediately preceding the start of the Somme offensive in 1916, many raids were carried out by the flanking armies to mask the efforts of the Fourth Army which was about to mount the assault on 1 July. The First Army launched fourteen, the Second Army mounted seventeen, seven of which were carried out by troops from I Anzac Corps, while the Third Army mounted twelve. Just how successful these raids were is debatable since many lives were lost and, while the Germans were left in some doubt about the precise location of the coming offensive, they knew one was about to be launched. During the same period, the Germans mounted only six raids over the entire frontage of the three armies. Over the period of July to the middle of November 1916, the period of the Allied Somme campaign, the three armies stepped up their raiding and hit the Germans 310 times. The raiders ranged from two platoons to two companies, with accompanying engineers who carried out demolitions of the German trenches. Of these raids, 204 were deemed to have been successful. The Germans responded with a mere sixty-five raids of which twenty-two were reckoned to have been successful.

These compare with the nineteen British raids mounted by IX Corps between 16 May and 7 June 1917, as a prelude to the Battle of Messines. The raiders numbered from a mere twelve to 300. While 171 prisoners were taken, a number of Germans were killed and British casualties amounted to 172. Clearly, raiding took a steady toll on both the raiders and the enemy. In mid-November, about 300 soldiers from the German 184th Regiment raided troops of the British 55th Division who suffered ninety-four casualties, more than half of them taken prisoner. However, during the winter of 1917/18, the BEF severely cut back on raiding while it recovered from the bloody fighting that had gone on at Passchendaele. Now the Germans stepped up their raiding and between 8 December 1917 and 21 March 1918, they mounted about 225 on the Ypres salient, but only sixty-two were deemed by the British to have been successful in that they managed to identify the British troops they raided.

Sometimes several raids on successive nights were carried out simply to secure prisoners. This occurred in August 1916 when the Highland Light Infantry were raided three times by German troops, twice on the same night and once more the next night. On the first occasion, the Germans crawled forward through the long grass in no-man's-land, then dropped into the British trenches undetected. They tried to take two prisoners who, in resisting capture, were stabbed with *Nahkampfmesser*, trench knives. The Germans tried again a few hours later and once more failed to take a prisoner. The following night, they bombed their way into the British trenches but again failed, this time losing two dead for their efforts. As they retreated to their own line, they were mortared by 2-inch mediums.

Although most raids were carried out at night, some small-scale actions mounted during the daytime were also raids, although here the objective was often to take a small section of the enemy position and hold it. One of the main reasons for this sort of operation was to put a stop to German activity in that area because it was proving troublesome. Typical of such minor operations was the action to capture Infantry Hill on 14 June 1917. This tactical feature had been assaulted unsuccessfully on three previous occasions, although the British line had been taken closer to it each time. The three previous assaults had all been preceded by an artillery bombardment which had provoked a prompt German response targetting the British parapets with shellfire and machine-gun fire. As described in the Official History, the fourth attempt was approached differently and for five days the enemy trenches were subjected to 'a slow continuous bombardment by all calibres … increasing in intensity each night … assisted by frequent bursts of machine and Lewis-gun fire … to cease from 5 to 9 a.m. daily'. The assault was carried out by the 2nd Suffolks and 1st Gordon Highlanders, with 8th King's Own Royal Regiment and 10th Royal Welch Fusiliers following on. The troops trained and practised on a simulation of the actual ground for three days, followed by two rehearsals, in between which the five-day bombardment began. At 7.20 am on the morning the bombardment ended, the two assaulting battalions of which 'a proportion of [the] men were … "skirmishers," i.e., good sprinters carrying only rifle, bayonet, 2 bombs and 20 rounds', took the enemy completely by surprise.

145

British 60-pounders broke up a disorganized two-battalion counter-attack and the British held the ground they had taken.

There then followed a day and a half of sporadic German shelling before the whole captured area was subjected to *Trommelfeuer* followed by a German attack in battalion strength which pushed the Highlanders out. Three bombing assaults to retake the lost ground failed but 'a fourth made under a shower of rifle grenades succeeded'. Similar actions took place over the next two days with the British managing to hold on to the ground despite being attacked by '1000 men of 3 different battalions. During the day the Trench mortars did excellent work, "putting up" enemy out of shell-holes to be dealt with by small-arms fire'. The British took 201 prisoners and held the ground. This episode illustrated how well the different arms were beginning to work together.

Novel tactics were devised by Stokes crews during the fighting on the Somme in July 1916, none of which was feasible with any other mortar in British service. The high rate of fire of the Stokes, the speed with which it could be brought to bear on new targets and its portability, all encouraged crews to find ways of using these advantages. At the start of the Somme, the Manchesters set up Stokes mortars at the head of several Russian saps which had been dug into no-man's-land before 1 July. These mortars put down a barrage on the German trenches a few minutes before the Manchesters went over the top. The result was that the Manchesters suffered few casualties as they crossed no-man's-land. Commanders of Stokes batteries were expected to use their initiative when targets presented themselves, rather than seek permission from higher authority before engaging them. By 1918, however, independent action by a Stokes battery without regard to friendly troops in the area was discouraged, as this could cause more trouble to them than to the enemy. The battery commander now needed specific orders from brigade to ensure that the mortars were used in the most effective way. Each division drew up a list of suitable targets for harassing fire, an indication of the level of cooperation that had developed between infantry and artillery involved in an operation.

A 4-minute barrage from a Stokes battery before a brigade assault in the spring of 1917 neutralized five enemy machine-guns at a range of 550 yards. The barrage was in accordance with the methods developed over the previous twelve months for dealing with enemy machine-guns which had escaped the preliminary artillery bombardment. Cooperation between riflemen, Lewis gunners, bombers, rifle grenadiers, Vickers gunners and Stokes mortar crews was well rehearsed and understood in 1918. A barrage from a Stokes mortar allowed rifle grenadiers to get close enough to engage a target, at which point, the mortars ceased firing. The Stokes battery then put down a barrage to interdict forming-up areas to prevent a counter-attack. Sometimes only a few rounds were needed to force the enemy to surrender. All in all, this required good communications between batteries, infantry commanders and brigade, a long way from the vagaries of 1915 and the uncertainties of 1916.

Wilfrid Stokes always intended that his mortar should be easily transportable, which was why he designed it to have a modular construction. The Stokes mortar of 1918 weighed 113lb: the base plate weighed 29lb, the barrel weighed 49lb and the mounting weighed 35lb. One man carried one component. By the end of 1917, Stokes batteries were divided into those which would go forward with advancing infantry and the reserve, which remained in the British line. The reserve mortars engaged machine-gun positions, trench junctions, shell craters in front of the German trenches and other choke points during the final stages of the preliminary artillery bombardment. The Stokes mortars which went forward did not participate in the preliminary bombardment. In addition to engaging similar targets that had escaped the bombardment as they were encountered by the advancing infantry, the accompanying mortars also fired on snipers and local pockets of resistance. These mortars crossed no-man's-land with the second wave of infantry, preferably before the Germans could fire a counter-bombardment although it was also possible to cross during the counter-bombardment once its weak spots had been identified. Spotting the deficiencies of the German barrage was a technique that was developed during 1917. By identifying them, casualties among the second and third waves were greatly reduced.

At Arras, a single mortar fired twenty rounds on a group of Germans who had become isolated in a trench, forcing them to retreat, but they were contained by several more rounds from the same mortar whose crew lengthened the range to fire over their heads. Some seventy-two of the enemy, including two officers, were taken prisoner. A similar thing happened when a mortar fired over the heads of a party of Germans working in no-man's-land. The range was gradually decreased so that the Germans were forced towards the British front line with the result that they were taken prisoner. These examples show the flexibility and precision with which the Stokes could be used, a unique quality of the Stokes mortar. The accuracy of the Stokes was superior to that of other mortars in British service. On one occasion in 1917, a mortar crew targetted their Stokes on their German counterparts, who were trying to set up a light mortar of their own. The second round from the Stokes made the Germans scatter, leaving their mortar exposed. A brief barrage then scored three direct hits on the mortar. The ease with which the Stokes could be adjusted for elevation, its accuracy and its high rate of fire meant that it could be used to search dead ground, including mine craters, sunken roads and even sap heads.

The Stokes mortar was often used for retaliatory fire, a role for which it was well suited because of the weight of fire which could be put on to a target in a short time. The intention was not neutralization but destruction of the source of hostile fire. Retaliatory barrages were similar to shooting on SOS lines and required registration shots and calculations for the error of the day. Surprise was a key element and night shooting on known targets was highly effective in this respect.

To sustain the high rate of fire that was possible with the Stokes, a lot of ammunition was needed. If the mortar was taken forward to support an infantry assault, it was not realistic to assume that a large number of rounds would also be taken forward. In addition, firing off thirty or forty rounds a minute could only be sustained for two or three minutes because the barrel became too hot to shoot for any longer. One mortar firing thirty rounds a minute for three minutes expended ninety bombs which, if the mortar was responding to an SOS, was highly effective. SOS ammunition had to be kept fused and ready for immediate use but it could not be kept stored in this state for very long because it deteriorated, so it had to be fired off and replaced regularly. The customary rate of fire of six rounds a minute could be sustained for long periods, however, provided the ammunition was available. During the fighting for High Wood on the Somme in July 1916, the Stokes mortars of the 140th Trench Mortar Battery fired 750 bombs in 15 minutes, successfully breaking German resistance in the area.

Supplying enough ammunition to feed any mortar battery was always a problem and it made itself especially felt on the Somme in July 1916 for the Stokes mortars that were taken forward in the advance. Four members of a Stokes mortar crew had to carry ammunition. They wore vests which held four rounds, a load of 44lb. They also had to carry a box of three rounds in each hand, a further 66lb, making a total of 110lb. Some infantrymen were detailed to carry a bomb each in addition to their normal fighting kit but it was not always successful since the bombs sometimes got 'lost' along the way. In 1917, carrying parties of ten or more infantrymen were detailed for each mortar section in an assaulting battalion. A rifleman was expected to carry four rounds although, if he left his rifle behind, he was expected to carry six or even eight rounds. The carriers had to bring ammunition up to the site of the Stokes battery before an advance to form a forward dump. From there, ammunition was taken forward to an agreed rendezvous point, located at least 300 yards from the objective but inside captured territory. This became the No. 1 dump. The battery crews rendezvoused here. The idea was to maintain a continuous supply of ammunition from the brigade store behind the British lines to the forward dump in the old front line and, thence, to the No. 1 dump, so that the mortars could maintain fire at the rate demanded by circumstances. In 1918, the load for carriers was somewhat more realistic than in 1917. One man might carry four rounds in a sandbag, six rounds in a Yukon pack or six rounds with tump lines. A party of ten men could carry between forty and sixty rounds. As many as forty carriers might be involved in supplying a forward battery.

By mid-1918, the mobility of the Stokes allowed batteries to move to any part of the battlefield where the infantry required fire support. Up-to-date range tables for determining the appropriate propellant charge and the correct elevation to shoot to a precise range, along with improvements in gunnery, meant that mortar crews could engage targets accurately and quickly. Engaging a target was now a mathematical calculation. Contrary to the fears of the Master General of Ordnance in 1915, infantrymen proved to be just as capable of handling mortars as gunners.

The tactical employment of the Stokes mortar had become a science which allowed a target to be fired on quickly and with a high degree of accuracy.

Bombing might have been something of an art but by 1918 mortaring was cold science. While mortar crews were still infantrymen who were required to maintain their musketry skills, their specialization, unlike bombing, was not absorbed into the general training of the infantry. Mortar crews were sometimes forced to rely on their rifles. During the fighting at Arras, a Stokes crew fired 200 bombs on two German counter-attacks, then had to defend themselves with their rifles, showing just how close to fighting mortars tended to get when they advanced with the infantry.

Although, by 1918, registration was still taught to mortar detachments, the use of reliable maps, prepared by the surveying section of the Royal Engineers, enabled Stokes crews to use predicted fire employing the same techniques as the artillery. To shoot by the map, accurate compass bearings had to be taken and this presented a problem peculiar to mortar batteries in emplacements reinforced with corrugated iron because the metal could affect the needle and give a false reading. As with conventional artillery, barrel wear was now taken into account as well as weather conditions and the weight of each bomb. Each mortar was calibrated in much the same way in which a field gun or howitzer was calibrated by measuring the muzzle velocity of each mortar in the battery so that their accuracy could be compared with each other and the map. A correction table was then drawn up for each mortar so that they could all be adjusted to shoot to the same range. However, the process was less reliable with mortars than it was with rifled artillery because of the low pressures in mortar barrels compared to those in the rifled barrels of artillery pieces.

Mortars were often fired to harass and disrupt the activities of the enemy rather than for a specific objective in support of an operation. The mediums of X and W batteries of the 32nd Division 'strafed' the Germans about once a day during October 1916; the Germans sometimes responded in kind so that a form of duel between the British and German mortars often ensued. The commander of X and W batteries had

> to sit in the dug-out adjoining this emplacement for over half an hour one day while the candle was blown out nine times by the explosions of enemy 'minnies' which had got the range of this position very accurately … 7.30 p.m. Our trench mortars retaliated … 9.50 p.m. More retaliation necessary.

Four days later, at 11.00 am, the batteries:

> Fired 200 bombs on the enemy support line. The Huns retaliated and hit No. 15 emplacement, filling it in and badly shaking the detachment without casualties. The emplacement was restored in two hours. The mortar was none the worse – it was marvelous that no bombs had detonated as there were several fuzed … and the force of the falling earth and other material ought to have set them off. Trench mortar bombs were peculiar things – in fact, quite incomprehensible to us at times.

Three days later, the two batteries fired another 300 rounds at the German trench mortar positions, augmented by fire from the heavies.

Between 1915 and 1918, mortaring was transformed from a rather amateur pastime for annoying the enemy in 1914 into a decisive instrument of battle capable of inflicting considerable damage on the enemy and reducing his ability to fight. The trench mortar was very much a child of trench warfare and quite unrelated to the siege mortar. Moreover, from the light trench mortar emerged the infantry mortar that was capable of providing the infantry with tactical support. This had a profound effect on infantry warfare on the Western Front and helped to transform the way in which the infantry fought. On the other hand, medium and heavy mortars were made instantly redundant when open mobile warfare reasserted itself during 1918. No one had much expectation of mortars when they appeared in 1914 and, even in 1915, their tactical value was limited. As mortars became technically more sophisticated and more reliable, their tactical roles were developed beyond mere tit-for-tat retaliation. The heavies and the mediums freed conventional artillery to engage other targets which might not otherwise have been hit. Before the end of 1916, light, medium and heavy mortars had clear tactical roles. The development of tactics was a process of fluid change, driven by practical experience. An ambivalence remained among the infantry who had to tolerate the retaliation that mortar shoots exacted but they also had to get used to the retaliation that followed barrages of rifle grenades.

Three tactical roles evolved for the Stokes mortar. Firstly, after the artillery barrage had lifted, the Stokes provided fire suppression during the assault, particularly targetting machine-gun posts and strongpoints. The mortars were often supplemented by 18-pounders firing shrapnel. These mortars stayed in the British line and were a part of the artillery fire plan. Secondly, the Stokes was used in a mobile role, moving forward with the infantry during an assault to provide fire support to the infantry and dealing with whatever obstacles they confronted during their advance. In this role, close cooperation between the infantry and mortar crews was essential, fostered by constant practice behind the lines before the assault. Finally, the Stokes was employed in the interdiction role to prevent counter-attacks. The supply of ammunition was fundamental to success and this was down to good planning, clear organization and cooperation between all the elements involved in the assault. By the end of 1917, the Stokes mortar had become an integral part of an infantry brigade.

At the start of the First World War, the BEF had no infantry support weapons other than Vickers and Maxim machine-guns, neither of them in very large numbers. This led to the BEF adopting the Lewis gun in 1915. All armies engaged on the Western Front adopted a light machine-gun for the same reasons as the British adopted the Lewis, namely flexible firepower that could accompany the infantry and which could be brought to bear on targets of opportunity and for fire suppression. The French adopted the Chauchat while the Germans adopted the *Maschinengewehr* 08/15, the so-called Light Maxim. The Chauchat was disliked by everyone. It had been hastily conceived in 1914 and was built from cheap materials using stamping instead of machining wherever possible. It jammed far too often and vibrated far too much when it was fired on fully automatic so that it was grossly inaccurate. The Chauchat was the epitome of what a light machine-gun should not be. The Light Maxim was more reliable than the Chauchat but it was less manageable than the Lewis gun, weighing 39lb compared to the Lewis gun's 27lb. Moreover, the Light Maxim had the disadvantage of being water-cooled like the M08 Maxim from which it was derived, whereas the Lewis and the Chauchat were both air-cooled. The Chauchat and the Lewis were both drum-fed. The Light Maxim was belt-fed but the ammunition was housed in a box fixed to the side of the machine-gun.

The question of increasing the firepower of the infantry led France to adopt an automatic rifle in 1918 and Germany to develop an entirely new weapon, the submachine-gun. Neither had a significant impact on the fighting, although both the automatic rifle and the submachine-gun would lead to major changes in infantry warfare after the end of the First World War. Unlike the Chauchat which was a hastily cobbled together compromise, what would become the French M1917 automatic rifle, also known as the RSC (from the initials of the designers, Ribeyrolle, Sutter and Chauchat, who were also responsible for the Chauchat machine-gun), had been under development since the turn of the century. Nevertheless, it was less than ideal. It tended to jam and was cumbersome. About 86,000 M1917s were produced but far fewer actually found their way into the hands of front-line troops. Britain would have adopted the Farquhar-Hill automatic rifle but the time between setting up a factory to produce them and when they would have arrived in quantity in France was too long for it to be a practical proposition. The war would have ended before a significant number of the rifles reached the BEF, so the plan to manufacture them was dropped. The French experience of automatic rifles was not very good as the weapons tended to be heavy and were often unreliable in action. In 1918, the American Expeditionary Force (AEF) was armed with the Browning Automatic Rifle (BAR), although this was more a light machine-gun than a rifle. Before production started in 1918, the AEF was stuck with the awful Chauchat which the Americans had bought from the French.

By 1918, the infantry in all armies could call on a range of support weapons without recourse to artillery, including the light machine-gun, the rifle grenade and the light mortar. In the BEF, the Mills grenade, the rifle grenade, the Stokes mortar and the Lewis gun began to change the nature of infantry warfare. While the infantry platoon of 1914 was trained in musketry and bayonet work for the purpose of engaging enemy infantry, to which end the artillery provided support, the infantry platoon of 1918 was an all-weapons unit. Everyone in the platoon of 1918 was trained in musketry, bayonet fighting and bombing, while experience of the light machine-gun was widespread among the infantry, especially so for the Lewis gun in the BEF. Tactically, the infantry platoon of 1918 was much more flexible than the infantry platoon of 1914.

In the BEF, the tactics of the light mortar were the tactics of the Stokes mortar. It was portable, easy to set up and accurate, with a high rate of sustained fire and, for short spells, a very high rate of rapid fire. Crucial to the development of light mortar tactics was the incremental ring charge, invented in 1916. This allowed targets to be engaged in depth as well as laterally, giving the Stokes a larger zone of fire than was possible with any other mortar. The speed with which new targets could be engaged meant that targets of opportunity could be fired on. The Stokes was very versatile. Its capabilities allowed the development of an entirely novel form of infantry warfare.

The search for weapons which would act as a force multiplier, to use the modern term, and thereby enable the deadlock of trench warfare to be overcome not only led to the battlefield experiments with automatic rifles but to experiments with flamethrowers, the rise of chemical weapons and the development of the tank. The flamethrower was not, in fact, a new weapon, having been invented some years before the outbreak of war. The Germans used flamethrowers on the Western Front against a French position north of Verdun at the end of February 1915, before turning them on the British 8th Rifle Brigade at Hooge on 30 July 1915, eleven days after the Germans had blown a mine under the British line. The British subsequently experimented with them on the Somme in 1916. In no instance were they a success, although they were very frightening. Indeed, the moral effect on the troops which faced the liquid fire was out of proportion to the actual danger. The German flamethrower was operated by two men, one to carry the fuel tanks, the other to aim the hose. During the fighting at Hooge, the Leinsters were 'instructed to aim at those who carried the flame-spraying device, who made a good target'. The fuel tank of one German operator was hit during the attack and it 'blew up with a colossal burst'.

The flamethrower was a very inefficient weapon largely because too much of the fuel was consumed as it was projected with the result that comparatively little of it arrived at the target. When flamethrowers were again used in the Second World War, the use of thickened fuels turned them into highly effective weapons for dealing with bunkers. Thickening agents such as napalm turned the fuel into a gel which could be projected further than unthickened fuels and without being consumed before reaching the target. Moreover, gels tended to stick to the target. Napalm, a derivative of naphthenic acid and palmitic acid, was not developed until the 1940s but, had anyone realized it at the time, natural rubber could have been used to thicken the fuel in the First World War.

Of all the weapons to emerge during the First World War, chemical weapons were, perhaps, the deadliest of them, although they had the considerable disadvantage of unpredictability because of the effect of the weather. Like incendiary weapons, chemical weapons were not new to warfare but, unlike incendiaries, the poison gas used in the First World War had the potential to decide battles and, indeed, was decisive in several instances. It was delivered in many ways, including cylinder release, artillery shells, mortar bombs and the Livens projector, as well as in hand grenades. The whole purpose of gas was to break the trench deadlock and the fact that it failed to do so highlights the conflict between weapons and tactics in achieving a military goal. The tank was also devised to break the deadlock on the Western Front but again it failed to do so, largely because, unlike poison gas, it was technically flawed; so much so, in fact, that more tanks were disabled by mechanical failure than were destroyed in battle. However, unlike gas, the tank had a future in warfare and it went on to play a significant role in preventing the sort of deadlock that had arisen in 1914. However, again, this was more to do with tactical change than it was to do with mechanical improvement, although the latter was essential to the former.

Gas warfare was a complex business which required a mix of technical skill, scientific knowledge and tactical ability, as well as favourable weather conditions for operations to be successful. Gas was first used by the Germans on the Eastern Front, then against the French at Ypres where it caused panic. The widespread use of gas led to the development of gas masks which became as essential to the soldier as his helmet and his rifle. Millions of gas shells were fired throughout the war, many of which failed to explode in the soft mud, as did so many high-explosive shells. Even now, hundreds of unexploded shells are dug up by French and Belgian farmers, road workers, utilities engineers and construction workers every week, testimony to the huge amount of ordnance that was fired during the war.

The Germans first released chlorine from 5,700 cylinders opposite the Allied line running from Langemark to Poelkapelle, in the northern part of the Ypres salient on 22 April 1915, during the Second Battle of Ypres. The dense cloud of yellow-green gas dissipated as it drifted across no-man's-land to become a bluish-white mist as it entered the trenches of the 45th Algerian and 87th French Territorial Divisions. The shocked troops fled, leaving a gap of about 5 miles in the line. Failure of the Germans to exploit this fully allowed the British Second Army to counter-attack and push the Germans back. The following day, the Germans released more chlorine, this time opposite the Canadians and, again, the Germans made huge gains only to be pushed back by counter-attacks. A Canadian medical officer identified the gas as chlorine and recommended that the troops wear cotton gauze soaked in water or urine; the latter contains urea which reacts with the chlorine. Because chlorine is water soluble even wet gauze could neutralize the gas. The Germans released chorine twice more during the battle, on both occasions against the British part of the line, the last of them against Hill 60 on 5 May, causing ninety immediate deaths, followed by another forty-three soon afterwards and another twelve sometime after that, a total of 145. There is a perception that gas attacks accounted for a high number of deaths during the First World War but, as already pointed out, this was an artillery war and approximately 60 per cent of casualties were caused by high explosive. In fact, gas only accounted for about 4 per cent of fatal casualties.

For the next three years, chemical warfare become the focus of much attention, both in terms of developing better and more efficient delivery systems and in terms of counter-measures, especially gas masks and respirators. Indeed, the British became some of the most dedicated users of gas warfare of all the combatants and set up a dedicated gas warfare section of the Royal Engineers, the Special Brigade, which developed perhaps the most devastating of delivery system of all, the Livens projector. The advantage of gas was that it was heavier than air and drifted over a wide area, flowed into trenches and seeped into dugouts. Its disadvantage was its dependence on favourable weather conditions. The air temperature, wind speed and its direction were critical to the effectiveness of gas. While cylinder release methods were used throughout the war by all sides, artillery shells and mortar bombs were commonly used later in the war as they increased the chances of the cloud drifting on to the intended target. In each case, however, early warning of a gas attack allowed the men in the trenches to don their gas masks and the occupants of dugouts to drop the heavy anti-gas curtain at the entrances. Such measures were highly effective at minimizing casualties.

Chlorine, although poisonous, is not the most effective toxic gas for military purposes, partly because it is easy to see and counter-measures such as gas masks are very effective. Thus, it was inevitable that experimentation would lead to the introduction of other, more poisonous gases. Principal among these were phosgene, first used by the French in 1915, the Germans in December of the same year and by the British in June 1916; and mustard gas, first used by the Germans against the British at Ypres in July 1917. It was not used by the French until June 1918 or by the British until September 1918 because of difficulties in manufacturing the gas, although the British fired captured stocks of German mustard gas shells, from German artillery, in November 1917 during the Battle of Cambrai. Mustard gas, dichloroethyl sulphide, was less lethal than both phosgene and chlorine. Indeed, the mortality rate was only about 2.5 per cent, while about 94 per cent of mustard gas casualties made a full recovery. At the time, however, the horrific injuries caused by mustard gas led the press to express the view that the reverse was the case. Mustard gas is a vesicant; in other words, it blisters the skin, and causes temporary blindness and vomiting, attacking the mucous membranes of the bronchia, making breathing very difficult. The injuries are extremely painful. Like the other toxic gases used on the battlefield, mustard gas is heavier than air. It tended to settle as an oily liquid on the ground, contaminating the earth for weeks or even months, depending on the weather conditions. As an incapacitating agent and as an area-denial weapon, mustard gas was very effective but phosgene and chlorine were more effective killers.

Phosgene is less easy to detect than chlorine because it is colourless and has very little odour but is about sixteen times more toxic. However, phosgene was difficult to deliver as it is much denser than chlorine, which meant that it did not drift so easily and tended to collect in hollows without travelling very far. To overcome the delivery problems, phosgene was often mixed with chlorine in equal proportions; the chlorine acted as a carrier gas and helped the phosgene to travel. The release of 88 tons of phosgene by the Germans in December 1915 caused

1,069 British casualties, of which sixty-nine were fatal. The disadvantage to phosgene was that it did not always incapacitate its victims straight away so that attacking infantry following a gas cloud could face serious opposition. However, there was a delayed effect and those who had been in its path and had apparently escaped unscathed usually developed symptoms of gas poisoning within the next 24 hours.

The British introduced the H gas helmet to counter chlorine gas. This was a flannel sack that covered the entire head, impregnated with sodium hyposulphite, or 'hypo' – hence the term H helmet. The hypo completely neutralized the chlorine but had no effect on phosgene so that the P helmet was developed, first used operationally at Loos. The fabric was also soaked in sodium phenolate, or phenate, which neutralized phosgene. A mouthpiece was subsequently incorporated so that carbon dioxide did not accumulate in the helmet. Nevertheless, wearing one for a prolonged period was hard to bear as breathing became increasingly difficult. The P helmet was superseded in January 1916 by the PH gas helmet in which the fabric was also impregnated with hexamethylenetetramine. These helmets were fitted with eyepieces to enable the wearer to see out but after a relatively short time the wearer's body heat and his breath made them mist up. Goggles were subsequently fitted in the PHG helmet.

They were all superseded by the box respirator which first appeared in February 1916. By 1918, all British troops were trained to fight while wearing the small box respirator. The box was a metal casing containing charcoal and layers of granulated permanganate. The charcoal absorbed the gases while the permanganate neutralized them before the cleaned air was inhaled via a short rubber hose connected to the face mask of rubberized canvas. At the end of the hose was a metal pipe with a mouthpiece that was held between the teeth. A clip went over the nose to ensure that the wearer inhaled and exhaled through the mouthpiece. Exhaled air passed through a valve back into the atmosphere. The masks had two large round eyepieces. This form of respirator remained in service, although improved upon over time, until the end of the Second World War.

The French used half-face masks in combination with separate goggles but, by the beginning of 1916, they had adopted the M2 face mask which, with some modifications, remained in service until almost the end of the war. This incorporated a face pad soaked in a neutralizing chemical. Despite being uncomfortable to wear for long periods, it could provide protection from high concentrations of phosgene for up to 5 hours. The M2 had eyepieces similar to the British gas helmets and, like them, were prone to misting with prolonged use. The M2 was superseded in 1917 by the *Appareil Respiratoire Spécial* (ARS) which incorporated a filter similar to the British small box respirator but was fixed directly to the front of the mask without a connecting hose, giving it the look of a pig's snout.

The first German gas masks were impregnated pads similar to those worn by British and French troops but these were quickly superseded by filter masks. The

GM15 *Gummischutzmaske* first appeared in 1915. This had a rubberized fabric mask but the model that superseded it in 1917, the GM17 *Lederschutzmaske*, was made from leather, not because leather was superior but due to the severe shortage of rubber in Germany, who had no access to the natural rubber plantations owned by the British and the French. Indeed, this was why German chemists developed synthetic rubbers or elastomers. The last model, the GM18, appeared towards the end of the war and incorporated a valve to expel the exhaled air into the atmosphere. The valve had been fitted to later models of the GM17. The improved models were each successively more effective than their predecessors.

Besides toxic gas, the Germans favoured lachrymatory compounds and fired millions of tear-gas shells at the Allies from about 1916 onwards. The effect on the fighting capabilities of the troops was only slight, although the gas was very unpleasant and forced them to don their gas masks. The British and the French also used irritant gases in shells as well as in grenades to clear dugouts.

A gas-attack warning was often given by someone ringing a bell that was hung up specifically for the purpose and were often improvised from shell casings. The British also introduced the strombus horn which was worked by compressed air and could be heard up to 9 miles away. Drills for dealing with gas attacks were regularly practised by troops on both sides. For gas to be truly effective, it needed to be delivered to a specific area in a high concentration. Gas released from cylinders, no matter how many cylinders were used and irrespective of the weather conditions, always dissipated as it drifted towards the target so that a very high concentration could never be achieved. Similarly, gas delivered by shells or by mortar bombs could not form a high concentration. Moreover, there was often sufficient warning for troops to put on gas masks, a drill which was rehearsed time and again so that at the first hint of gas, troops were into their masks in a matter of seconds. If, however, a sufficiently high concentration of gas could be delivered at the target in a very short space of time, the enemy would be denied the opportunity to don their masks. Indeed, if the concentration were high enough, the masks would provide no protection at all. This only became possible with a device invented by Captain Livens who was serving in the Special Brigade. In essence, he devised a one-shot mortar that fired a drum of 30–40lb of gas. What made his weapon especially deadly was the manner in which the projectors were used. Rather than fire them in the same way as the 4-inch Stokes mortar, which was operated by the Special Brigade to deliver gas and smoke, large numbers of projectors were fired simultaneously so that all the drums arrived at the target at the same time.

The first troop trial of the gas projector occurred during the capture of Thiepval in September 1916, followed by a second operation during the capture of Beaumont Hamel in November. During the Thiepval attack, about 1,100lb of gas was fired into a frontage of only 80 yards. A 'gas lake' flooded the cellars of the ruined Thiepval Chateau, occupied by the German commander of the Thiepval garrison. He, along with at least 130 other German soldiers, were killed by the gas. On the day after the gas attack on Beaumont Hamel, the infantry took what remained of the village and Livens discovered a deep German dugout untouched by 'our heaviest shelling with twelve inch howitzers'. It contained fifteen Germans, five rats and a cat, all dead. The troops had died as they tried to escape. Here was the evidence that there was no protection against very high concentrations of gas. Livens recorded that:

> This dug-out was in the track of a cloud containing nearly a ton of gas, and the number of seconds in which these men were killed could be gauged almost exactly, because the three furthest from the entrance down which the gas had come, had had time to put their gas-masks on before they died, the fourth man had his mask half on, and the fifth had it to his face, the sixth out of the box, the seventh had opened the box, and completing the series, the eight[h] had his hand on the lid, while those in front were killed so quickly they had not had time even to think about their masks.

The well-trained German soldier could don his gas mask in less then 6 seconds. What made the scene all the more remarkable was the fact that the centre of the beaten zone was some 300 yards away and the nearest drum had landed 280 yards from the dugout entrance. The main target, the deep bomb-proof dugouts used by the German garrison, were found to contain approximately 300 dead, all of whom had been killed by the gas. This was why the attacking British infantry had suffered so few casualties when they crossed no-man's-land.

The first operational use of the Livens projector was at Arras on 9 April 1917 when thirty-one targets along the German front were subjected to a gas attack unlike any other before it. Major General Foulkes, commander of the Special Brigade, observed the operation from St Eloi. The projectors were fired almost simultaneously so that

> a dull red flash seemed to flicker all along the front as far as the eye could reach, and there was a slight ground tremor, followed a little later by a muffled roar, as 2340 of these sinister projectiles hurtled through space, turning clumsily over and over, and some of them, no doubt, colliding with each other in their flight. About twenty seconds later they landed in masses in the German positions, and after a brief pause the steel cases were burst open by the explosive charges inside, and nearly fifty tons of liquid phosgene were liberated which vaporised instantaneously and formed a [dense] cloud.

The projectors were also used to fire drums of ammonal and on 12 May 1917, seventy projectors fired ammonal on a German strongpoint. The ton of high explosive contained in the drums detonated more or less simultaneously. The resulting explosion was 'appalling'. Drums of incendiaries were also fired on German positions. The projector was first used operationally to fire incendiaries against machine-gun positions at La Boiselle on the night of 25/26 July 1916 when the Australians attacked Pozières. Reconnaissance had revealed three strongpoints which included 'ring trenches at the junction of other trenches'. These 'ring trenches' held machine-gun positions with good fields of fire over that part of no-man's-land the attacking Australians would have to cross the next day. The projectors were fired at 12.30 pm 'and the bursting cans made a fine splash of flame all over the German machine gun posts'.

The biggest such operation took place on 3 June 1917 when 1,500 oil drums were fired into Bois de Wytschaete, Grand Bois and Unnamed Wood, together with a thousand 4-inch Stokes rounds as part of the Messines Ridge operation. Many more gas drums were fired than incendiary or ammonal drums, however. The largest gas projector operation was at Lens on 21 March 1918 when 3,750 projectors were fired simultaneously. Firing large numbers of projectors was achieved electrically, the wiring being joined together through many junction boxes. Two days earlier, 2,960 drums were fired at St Quentin. The Special Brigade carried out 768 gas operations between June 1915 and November 1918, releasing gas from 88,000 cylinders and firing 178,000 4-inch Stokes bombs and 197,000 Livens drums. This amounted to 5,700 tons of gas. During the same period, the German Army suffered 200,000 gas casualties of which 9,000 were fatal, although this includes those from all theatres, while the BEF suffered 180,539 gas casualties of which 5,981 were fatal. France had 190,000 casualties of which 8,000 were fatal. Less than 3 per cent of British gas casualties died in 1915, but a year later this had risen to 17 per cent. However, fatalities had dropped below 3 per cent by 1918 despite the fact there were nine times as many gas casualties than in 1915, testimony to the effectiveness of the later respirator gas masks and to improved medical treatment.

CHAPTER 10

Destruction and Deep Battle

About 2 miles east of Ypres, along the Menin Road, lies the village of Hooge. Between 1914 and 1917, this was the scene of fierce fighting. Hooge was obliterated as the village passed from Allied hands to the Germans, then back again. In May 1915, the British retook Hooge and set about mining the German trenches. It took just over five weeks for the 175th Tunnelling Company Royal Engineers to dig a 190-foot tunnel under no-man's-land to two concrete pillboxes. The charge of 3,500lb of ammonal was placed in a chamber above the gallery which had 6 inches of water in it. German mining in the area had been halted because of the water problem. This was one of the first occasions that ammonal used. Ammonal was a commercial explosive adopted by the Royal Engineers because of the shortage of conventional military high explosives which were needed for artillery shells. The mine, largest of the war thus far, was fired at 7.00 pm on 19 July 1915. The lip of the resulting crater was 15 feet above ground level, while the crater was 120 feet across and 20 feet deep. The crater was immediately occupied by two companies of the 4th Middlesex. The troops had awaited the detonation in saps that had been dug into no-man's-land in preparation; ten men were killed by falling debris when the mine exploded because they were too close. Several hundred German troops died in the explosion. The Germans counter-attacked but were fought off by bombing parties from the 4th Middlesex and the 1st Gordon Highlanders. Unfortunately, they ran out of grenades and lacked artillery support because they were too far forward, so two-thirds of the trenches that had been captured from the German 126th Regiment were taken back by them.

The Germans initiated mining operations on the Western Front when, on 20 December 1914, they exploded ten mines under British positions at Givenchy. In early 1915, they blew numerous mines, large and small, under the Allied lines. Some of the smallest contained no more than 100lb of explosive. The BEF had no specialist mining unit within the Royal Engineers at the start of the war. It was evident that such a unit was urgently needed. In the meantime, the Royal Engineers did the best they could with the personnel available. Prior to the creation of the tunnelling companies, the Royal Engineer siege companies attached to individual regiments performed most of the mining tasks but there were not enough of them to carry out all the mining operations that were needed. Not only mining but counter-mining work became increasingly important to operations on the Western Front. Digging counter-mines was the only effective way of dealing with German attempts to put mines under Allied trenches.

Eight tunnelling companies were formed in February 1915 from men with civilian mining experience and especially clay-kickers who knew about tunnelling in clay. Another twelve companies were formed later in the year with another added in 1916. In addition to these companies, the Canadian Army formed one in France in December 1915; another two were formed in Canada and arrived in March 1916. A New Zealand tunnelling company arrived in France in March 1916 and three Australian tunnelling companies arrived in May of the same year. By June of that year, the BEF had twenty-five companies and an additional seven from overseas, all actively engaged in mining operations. These operations involved approximately 25,000 men.

Mining operations were a major aspect of the fighting on the Western Front throughout the war. While mines in siege warfare had a long history, the scale of the mining operations carried out on the Western Front was unprecedented. Indeed, mining became a quite distinct form of warfare in itself in which, whenever the two sides met face to face, it was always underground. The fighting under such circumstances was very close and savage. This occurred because each side dug counter-mines and listening parties eavesdropped on the enemy. Counter-mining inevitably led to break-ins on enemy mine shafts, either deliberately or accidentally, although when the break-in was deliberate, the attackers were not usually the miners but infantry brought down the gallery for the job. Battles underground were especially vicious affairs in which pistols, maces, daggers and spades were the principal tools but sometimes even poison gas was pumped in. Miners always tried to work quietly to minimize the risk of detection; sometimes it was necessary for them to remain still and silent for long periods. Mining was not only physically demanding but it was high-risk work. Apart from detection by the enemy there was always the risk of collapses. If a mine was discovered, it was often blown by the men who had dug it in the hope of destroying the counter-mine at the same time. Then it could become a race to see who fired their mine first. The subterranean war on the Western Front was initially fought almost independently of what occurred above ground in the trenches. For the most part, the first the men in the trenches knew of a mine, friendly or hostile, was when it exploded. This had a detrimental effect on nerves since everyone feared being buried alive.

In every major offensive operation on the Western Front, several mines were detonated and it was not unusual for some of these to be big mines. They were also fired in many small-scale operations to straighten out the line, capture a strongpoint, dislodge snipers or destroy machine-gun positions. In every instance, companies of friendly troops were tasked with capturing the resulting crater. The race for the crater rim was as crucial as blowing the mine in the first place. This race could not begin until time had been allowed for the debris to fall back to earth, which could take 20–30 seconds, although troops did not always wait that long because getting to the crater before the enemy was paramount. The rim was usually far higher than ground level so that whoever held it dominated the surrounding area by means of snipers, machine-guns and, of course, observation posts. Trenches were dug along the rim and dugouts could be built into the side of the crater. The crater bottom tended to fill with water, forming greasy, stagnant, gas-contaminated pools.

British tunnellers became very good at mining and counter-mining, so much so that they established a dominance over their German counterparts during the first half of 1916, a dominance which they maintained throughout the rest of the war, especially after Messines in 1917. There were a large number of mine craters in the British-held part of the line around Loos in early 1916, most of them from mines blown by the Germans under the ground captured by the British in the battle the previous September and October. In the Hohenzollern sector, so called because of the German Hohenzollern Redoubt which the British had failed to capture in the fighting at Loos, there were nine craters from mines blown by the Germans when they recaptured some of the ground they had lost. Most of these craters were then taken by the British in the fighting of 2 March 1916, following the blowing of three more mines of 8,000lb, 10,055lb and 7,000lb, running north–south along the German front line.

Many of the early British mining operations were relatively small scale, partly through lack of time to dig the galleries and partly through lack of explosives. Some of them were merely to dig underground listening posts intended to detect German miners but even those that were offensive, rather than passive, often were dug too hastily. This was entirely due to lack of organization and no defined tactical scheme for such operations. The idea developed that quickly dug small mines, blown all along German positions in random locations opposite the British line, would keep the Germans wrong-footed. However, the lack of coordination of mining with operations above ground merely squandered resources and achieved very little. Yet sections of the front line at Givenchy and Hill 60, the Bluff and St Eloi in the Ypres salient became the scenes of almost continuous mining and counter-mining. At St Eloi, the British fired thirteen mines and twenty-nine camouflets in 1915, while over the same period the Germans blew twenty mines and two camouflets. A camouflet was a small charge set to blow up the gallery of a hostile mining operation. At the end of March 1916, as part of an operation to capture the small German salient at St Eloi, the BEF fired six mines under the German positions which ranged in size from a mere 600lb of ammonal to 31,000lb, completely wrecking the German trenches. There then followed intense fighting to take and hold possession of the craters which continued for the next three weeks. In the end, the Germans occupied four of them.

By the time of the opening of the Somme in July 1916, the BEF was actively mining in twenty-eight sections of the British-held front line, between Hooge in the north and Mametz in the south. The most active sections were between Givenchy and Arras, which made the First and Third Armies the most active of the four British armies in France at that time.

The French were also very active with mining and counter-mining. French miners dug some of the longest galleries of any army. They tended to favour small charges, partly because they needed less time to set up than larger charges, but a lot of small charges in the same area tended to make the ground more difficult for the infantry to cross without doing significant damage the German line. When the British took over some of the sectors previously held by the French, they found numerous galleries of unfinished mining operations, some of which the British proceeded to complete. The Germans undermined all the French and British trenches with a very large number of shallow galleries which meant British tunnelling operations had to start further back behind the line and the miners had to dig to a greater depth to ensure that their galleries passed undetected beneath the German works. The absence of cooperation between the infantry and the tunnellers led to uncompleted British galleries being abandoned because newly arrived battalions chose to dig new trenches in fresh ground, sometimes over German mines which were subsequently blown. To make matters worse, miners began to encounter mine gas and carbon monoxide, which led to accidents. These in turn led to the formation of mine rescue teams which worked in the same way as rescue teams in civilian collieries. Poison gas sometimes seeped into the galleries from above.

With the growing number of tunnelling companies and the BEF taking more frontage from the French, it became clear in late 1915 that a proper organizational framework to coordinate and manage mining operations needed to be established. Hitherto, all mining operations had been controlled by Armies without any overall control by GHQ. In December 1915, such an organization was set up, headed by an Inspector of Mines who reported to the General Staff. Henceforth, tactics, listening and rescue became systemized with properly formulated training schemes to enable the miners in each army to follow standardized procedures. The first mining school was set up by the First Army in June 1916 and soon afterwards the Second and Third Armies set up their own schools.

One of the remarkable successes in mining operations was the development of effective listening techniques which were aided by the invention of the geophone, designed to detect sound pulses in the ground. Using several of these instruments, each at a different location, listeners were able to pinpoint individual miners by triangulation, although this was not achievable until the end of 1917; the instrument nevertheless proved invaluable long before that level of skill was achieved. Neither the French nor the Germans were any better equipped for any aspect of mining than the British at the start of the war, although the British and the French could at least share expertise and experience as they gained more knowledge. The French tended to dig narrower galleries than the British, who were less than enthusiastic about taking them over when they acquired new sections of the line as the BEF grew in size during 1915. The Germans were active miners up to the Battle of Messines in June 1917 when the BEF detonated nineteen big mines and effectively annihilated the German mining force. All mines had to be dug by hand using hand tools to avoid making undue amounts of noise, although the British did have the advantage of the clay-kickers who could dig tunnels much faster in clay than men working with hand tools.

At the beginning of March 1916, the BEF took over 20 miles of the front formerly occupied by the French Tenth Army, running from Loos in the north to Ransart in the south. This included the ridge known as Vimy Ridge that ran south-east from Souchez for 9 miles. The region had been fought over by the French since September in three major battles, the Battles of Artois, and while the French had made some territorial gains, Vimy Ridge had remained in German hands. This dominant position allowed the Germans to observe whatever the French and, subsequently, the British were doing, pick targets and shell them. The problem for the British when they took over this section of the line was compounded by the poor state of the trenches previously occupied by the French. By this time, the defences consisted of three lines of trenches connected by communication trenches, part of a process of evolution that had begun following the Battle of Loos the previous September, whereby defence in depth became the standard. The Germans had initiated the process as a counter to a break-in by assault troops. Hitherto, a single line of defences could be penetrated by attacking troops and if follow-up forces were fed into the penetration, break-in could be converted into breakthrough, allowing the attacker to get into the open country behind the defensive line. By developing a defence in depth, a break-in could be contained by a second line of defences that mirrored those which the attackers had just broken through.

One reason why penetration had not become breakthrough at Loos was a problem with command and control of a fluid battle, not one of poor generalship or lack of fighting spirit. The truth was that there was no reliable means by which a commander could maintain control of a battle in 1915 nor, for that matter, in 1916. This was not a matter of inadequacy on the part of individual generals but rather a practical problem. Information that reached commanders was already many hours old whereas battlefield decisions needed to be taken straight away to respond appropriately to the situation on the ground. However, artillery timetables in particular did not allow for changes to the plan once the battle had started. There was no simple or reliable means by which the artillery fire could be redirected. Nor, indeed, was there a quick means by which reinforcements could be directed to the right place at the right time. These were problems of command and control which were very much on the minds of commanders and had to be resolved if the deadlock on the Western Front was to be broken.

The principal means by which commanders were kept informed about the progress of a battle were telephone and runner. Alternatively, pigeons or dogs could carry messages and there was visual signalling with rockets and flags. None was ideal. By the time runners reached the intended recipient – provided they managed to survive and many didn't – the battle had moved on and the information they carried was out of date. Pigeons and dogs ran much the same risks as runners. Visual signals were often useless in the smoke of battle and while rockets were visible at night, the correct colours of the day had to be used. The telephone overcame the delay problem but, even when lines were buried the regulation 6 feet below ground, an instruction which dated from April 1916, the lines were still vulnerable to shellfire. Six feet of earth was supposed to be enough to prevent a 5.9-inch shell from damaging the line but repeated shelling reduced the depth of earth and made the line vulnerable. Breaks had to be found and repaired, a Sisyphean task. As part of the many preparations for the Somme offensive in July 1916, an unprecedented amount of line laying was carried out. In all, 7,000 miles of cable were laid for this one offensive alone. This was but a fraction of the total distance of telephone line that was set up for the coming battle. Another 43,000 miles of line was set up between poles, well behind the front, as well as the countless miles that were simply laid on the surface.

In the past, generals had commanded from the front but armies were too big and spread over too large an area for that to be a realistic way to control the flow of battle by the time of the First World War. Indeed, no one individual man could control a battle because of the many different elements involved. Staffs were needed to gather and process information. Generals and staff officers knew that the only sure of way of finding out what was happening was to go and look for themselves. Many did and many died in the front line as a result – sniped, shelled or killed by any of the many ways a man could die on the Western Front. Fifty-eight British generals were killed in action or died of wounds on the Western Front. Most were brigade commanders but a significant number were divisional commanders. In all, ten divisional commanders became fatal casualties, three of them at Loos. A further 117 British generals were wounded on the Western Front, eight of whom were gassed, while another four became prisoners of war.

While new methods of command and control were developed, and as new fighting tactics were devised from experience, the defensive lines became ever more complex. By 1917, German defences along the Hindenburg Line were up to 15 miles deep, with three defensive lines, each one a formidable obstacle. This was a far cry from the single and discontinuous trench line protected by a few strands of barbed wire of 1914.

In early 1916, neither the British nor the French had developed defences in depth. Some defensive lines, in fact, were little better than those dug in 1914. Those in front of Vimy Ridge were in dire need of improvement as far as the British were concerned. In March, the ground was a quagmire of deep mud. There were no continuous trenches, merely a collection of shell holes and craters hastily joined up. By May, the ground was bone hard but the conditions were otherwise atrocious, with few of the usual trenches of any kind and, according to the Official History:

all were undrained and utterly unsanitary. Dead bodies, months old, still lay unburied, and a vast amount of débris and rubbish covered the whole area. The wire, where any existed, was 'thin and weak', or 'in bad condition'; the positions for machine guns were 'very poor'. The dug-outs, except those some distance from the front, were 'small, damp and bad'.

In addition to which, the parapets were not bulletproof. When the British took over, they spent a week digging and building frantically, always under the gaze of the Germans on the Ridge above them. Apart from the parlous trenches, the French had left the British an extensive network of underground galleries, incomplete and not very suitable for future mining operations. Moreover, the Germans were also actively mining, their galleries going deeper and further than those left by the French. The sensible decision would have been to withdraw to the old French line of a year earlier but this was not an option so the British had to make the best of it. The British chose to take the mining fight to the Germans and, over the next three months, ten BEF tunnelling companies and five French companies were engaged in mining operations here. The British fired four mines on 3 May 1916 and another five on the 15th. The detonating of so many mines played on the minds of the Germans manning the Vimy Ridge trenches. The 163rd Regiment reported that:

> These continual mine explosions in the end got on the nerves of the men. The posts in the front trenches and the garrisons of the dug-outs were always in danger of being buried alive. Even in the quietest night there was the dreadful feeling that in the next moment one might die a horrible and cruel death. One stood in the front line defenceless and powerless against these fearful mine explosions. Against all the other fighting methods there was some protection – against this kind of warfare, valour was of no avail, not even the greatest foresight. Running back, retirement, were useless: like lightning from the clear heavens, like the sudden occurrence of some catastrophe of nature, these mine explosions took place.

And the 86th Reserve Regiment stated that:

> Our companies had suffered heavy losses through the British mine explosions. It was accepted that other large parts of our trench system were undermined and might fly into the air at any moment, and that some counter-measures must be devised. We could not fight the enemy any longer with his own weapons, for he was superior to us in men and material.

The Germans lost the battle of the mines but dominated the British above ground by constantly shelling and mortaring the mine craters held by them. Eventually, the Germans were left with no choice but to mount a major assault to capture the craters and the mine shafts, which they did on 21 May. The British were forced back, losing over 2,000 men in the fighting. Whether the constant mining in the region and, indeed, elsewhere, proved to be productive or counter-productive is open to question. Certainly, as far as the Germans on Vimy Ridge were concerned, the mining forced them into mounting an attack above ground so that the British lost men, material and ground to no real purpose.

Considering the importance placed on mining by the British, it is hardly surprising that mines should play a significant role in the opening of the Somme offensive on 1 July 1916. Here the ground was chalk rather than clay or earth in which it was easier to tunnel but to avoid making unnecessary noise push-picks were used. When the tunnellers got close to the German line, they used carpenters' augers to bore holes in the chalk into which vinegar was poured to soften the chalk, making its removal much easier. Eleven small mines and eight big mines were prepared in the weeks preceding 1 July. These were distributed along the front line from Beaumont Hamel in the north, where one of the large mines was set, to Mametz in the south, where two large mines and nine small ones were distributed along a relatively short frontage. Three large mines of 9,000lb, 15,000lb and 25,000lb were set under a German salient, the Tambour, opposite Fricourt, by the 178th Tunnelling Company. Two large mines and two smaller ones were also prepared at La Boisselle. Had more manpower been available, many more mines would have been dug along the entire frontage of the Fourth Army. The Tambour area had been a very active mining area when it had been held by the French and subsequently; there were already eight large craters. All but one of the British mines were fired at 7.28 am on 1 July.

The galleries for the two mines at La Boisselle had been dug with infinite care to avoid making any noise whatsoever. The area had been mined many times since 1915 when the French held this part of the line. There were many galleries dug by both sides and craters. The British tunnellers worked in bare feet while the floor of the gallery was covered with sandbags to muffle sound. Each piece of chalk was carefully prised out of the chalk face with a bayonet held in one hand, the other hand catching the piece of chalk or flint before it hit the floor. Working in this way, the men of the 179th Tunnelling Company managed to advance about 18 inches every 24 hours in tunnels that were only 4.5 feet by 2.5 feet. A charge of 60,000lb of ammonal was place in a chamber under the Schwaben Höhe Redoubt, while a charge of 40,600lb was placed under Y Sap at the end of a tunnel 1,030 feet long, the longest dug in chalk during the war. When the Lochnager mine under the Schwaben Höhe Redoubt was fired, the German strongpoint was obliterated, leaving a massive crater 70 feet deep and 270 feet across. The lip of the crater was 15 feet high. Second Lieutenant Cecil Lewis RFC, who was flying an SE5a above the battlefield when the mines were fired, estimated that the debris rose to nearly 5,000 feet. The detonation not only destroyed the redoubt but collapsed dugouts in nearby trenches.

The 10th Lincolns, the battalion assigned to attack opposite the mines, waited 5 minutes before leaving their trenches, a fatal error of judgement. The Germans were ready for them and cut them down in an intense artillery barrage and with enfilading machine-gun fire. Moreover, the Germans had discovered the Y Sap mine and, not surprisingly, evacuated the garrison above the mine before it was detonated. However, these mines were not merely intended to kill the German garrisons. The principle aim was for the lips of the craters to obscure the view to the flanks and thereby prevent the Germans enfilading the attacking infantry. In this, the British were not entirely successful.

All but one of the mines along the frontage held by the Fourth Army were fired 2 minutes before the infantry were due to climb out of their trenches – go over the top. The mine under the Hawthorn Redoubt at Beaumont Hamel, containing 40,000lb of ammonal, was detonated 10 minutes before zero. The early firing of this mine was a serious error of judgement by the Inspector of Mines, GHQ and Lieutenant General Hunter-Weston, GOC of VIII Corps which faced the Germans on this section of the front line. It represented a compromise between all parties but it was the worst of all possibilities rather than the most logical choice. Hunter-Weston had wanted to detonate the mine 4 hours before zero to allow time for the British to take the rim and hold it. The action would be over and German alarm would have subsided long before 7.30 am. However, the plan was vetoed by the Inspector of Mines on the grounds that, in all likelihood, the Germans would take possession of the crater, not the British, because the Germans were better at doing this than the British. Nevertheless, firing the mine 10 minutes before zero not only alerted the Germans but the artillery fire plan had to be altered to lift the barrage from the Hawthorn 10 minutes before everywhere else to avoid shelling the attackers, which gave the advantage to the German defenders unaffected by the mine. According to the account by the 119th Reserve Regiment which held the German line at the Hawthorn:

a terrific explosion ... completely drowned the thunder of the artillery. A great cloud of smoke rose up from the trenches of No. 9 Company, followed by a tremendous shower of stones, which seemed to fall from the sky over all our position. More than three sections of No. 9 Company, were blown into the air, and the neighbouring dug-outs were broken in and blocked. The ground all round was white with the debris of chalk as if it had been snowing, and a gigantic crater ... [130 feet in diameter and 58 feet deep] gaped ... This explosion was a signal ... and everyone got ready and stood on the lower steps of the dug-outs, rifles in hand, waiting for the bombardment to lift.

Clearly, the British infantry stood little chance of getting across no-man's-land unscathed. Almost as soon as the mine was fired, two platoons of 2nd Royal Fusiliers, with four machine-guns and four Stokes mortars, ran for the near lip of the crater which they reached, but the Germans reached the far lip first and brought the Royal Fusiliers under intense fire. Not only did they suffer but so did the attacking infantry a few minutes later when they climbed out of their trenches. The far lip gave the Germans a better field of fire than had they remained in their trenches. Ironically, the explosion of the Hawthorn Redoubt mine is probably one of the best known, certainly the most recognized, due to the fact that it was filmed from a mile behind the British lines. Tons of earth and chalk rushing upwards is still an awesome sight.

While the mines detonated at the opening of the Somme may not have achieved what was intended, British mine warfare went on unabated. The greatest success occurred in June 1917 at Messines Ridge when nineteen large mines were detonated prior to an assault on the Ridge. There is no doubt that this was the most ambitious and the most intensive mining operation of the war. While mining had been carried out in the area since 1915, the galleries had been dug at a depth of 15 feet; the galleries of the mines blown in 1917, on the other hand, were 60–90 feet below the surface and had taken eighteen months to construct. Some had been started as early as August 1915. It was for the work on these mines that the clay-kickers were employed to deal with the blue clay of the area. The galleries were started 300–400 yards behind the British line and extended for up 720 yards under the Ridge so that the explosive chambers were 80–120 feet below the German trenches. One of the biggest problems was disposal of the spoil which had to be concealed from German reconnaissance aircraft. To this end, it was hidden in 'distant woods or buried under sandbag parapets'. The Germans never suspected the British were mining under the Ridge. The operation was far from easy as the diggers had to deal with treacherous slurry, a water-saturated mixture of clay and sand which lay between two seams of clay. The whole process of mining at Messines, from surveying and geological analysis of the strata to the employment of silent air pumps, was carried out much more scientifically than any previous mining operation on the Western Front.

In all, twenty-four mines were prepared, but three were not fired and one had been abandoned in August 1916 when the Germans discovered it and blew a camouflet that demolished a great length of the gallery. The usual night-time shelling of the German trenches ceased half an hour before dawn. In the meantime, the assault divisions had assembled and fixed bayonets silently. When the shelling stopped, the quiet was 'so marked that from the front line nightingales could be heard singing in the distant woods'. Then, at 3.10 am, the British detonated the mines, not quite simultaneously; from first to last, the detonations were spread over 19 seconds. The eruptions of fire, smoke and debris were volcanic. According to one eyewitness, the explosions 'stood like great pillars towering into the sky'. It was a spectacle in which

> roses with carmine petals, or as enormous mushrooms … rose up slowly and majestically out of the ground and then split into pieces with a mighty roar, sending up multi-coloured columns of flame mixed with a mass of earth and splinters high into the sky.

Tremors from the explosions could be felt in London. The report compiled by the German 204th Division, which was holding the line near Hill 60, described how the ground trembled as in a natural earthquake, heavy concrete shelters rocked, a hurricane of hot air from the explosions swept back for many kilometres, dropping fragments of wood, iron and earth; and gigantic black clouds of smoke and dust spread over the country. The effect on the troops was overpowering and crushing.

The timing of the explosions was especially cruel for the Germans as they were in the middle of a relief, so that both the relieving troops and those being relieved were caught in the blasts. Although the exact number of German casualties is uncertain, in the region of 10,000 died. Most of the trench line was obliterated. When the British, New Zealand and Australian troops crossed no-man's-land, they met no opposition and took their objectives with hardly a casualty. Those Germans who had survived the mines now surrendered meekly, such was the shock of what had happened. Elsewhere along the front, the Germans were completely demoralized by the scale of the explosions and by the fact that they were not simultaneous which created the fear there were yet more to come.

Not all the mines fired on 7 June detonated. Two failed to explode. The British lost their locations and the mines remained undetected when the war ended. Thirty-seven years later, on 17 July 1955, one of them finally exploded when it was struck by lightning. Fortunately, the only casualty was a cow. The other mine is still where it was laid in 1916 and no one is certain of its precise location. This is the mine abandoned by the British after its discovery by the Germans. The Battle of Messines Ridge, a success of limited scale because the objectives were limited in scope and was well planned and executed, was a preliminary operation to the Third Battle of Ypres which went awry almost from the outset and descended into a bloody slugging match of attrition.

The effects of the mines undoubtedly were a significant factor in the British success at Messines. However, several other factors, arguably of greater importance than the mines, lay at the root of the success; these related to the changing tactical approach to major offensive operations on the Western Front that had been going on for the past eighteen months. Indeed, rather than tactics remaining fixed and unchanging, they were constantly changing and evolving. However, the conclusions drawn from successes, when they came, were not always the right ones and tactical errors were inevitable. Trench warfare had two distinct but intimately related elements, namely small-unit combat, that is, fighting at the section, platoon and company levels; and large-scale combat at divisional, corps and army levels. The tactics of hand grenade and rifle grenade warfare were the tactics of small units. As the platoon was transformed from a rifle-and-bayonet unit to an all-arms one, so the principals of cooperative interaction between the different weapon groups within the platoon reinforced the small unit as a fighting entity, capable of engaging a range of targets which, prior to 1915, were outside the scope of the infantry. These were the means by which infantry engaged and overwhelmed similarly equipped and organized enemies. These were the building blocks from which the tactics of big offensives were formed.

The Messines Mines

Mine	Started	Finished	Depth (ft)	Charge (lb)	Crater dimensions			Gallery length (ft)
					Diameter (ft)	Depth (ft)	Diameter of complete obliteration (ft)	
HILL 60								
A Left	22.8.15	1.8.16	90	45,700 A 7800 GC	191	33	285	Branch 240
B Caterpillar		18.10.16	100	70,000 A	260	51	380	1380
ST ELOI	16.8.16	28.5.17	125	95,000 A	176	17	330	1340 300
HOLLANDSCHESCHUUR								
No. 1		20.6.16	60	30,000 A 42,000 B	183	29	343	825
No. 2	18.12.15	11.7.16	55	12,500 A 2400 B	105	14	215	Branch 45
No. 3		20.8.16	55	15,000 A 3500 B	141	25	201	Branch 395
PETIT BOIS								
No. 2 Left	16.12.15	15.8.16	57	21,000 A 9000 B	217	46	417	Branch 210
No. 1 Right		30.7.16	70	21,000 A 9000 B	175	49	375	2070
MAEDELSTEDE FARM	3.9.16	2.6.17	100	30,000 A 4000 GC	205	23	585	1610
PECKHAM	20.12.15	19.7.16	70	65,000 A 18,000 B 7000 GC	240	46	330	1145
SPANBROEKMOLEN	1.1.16	26.6.16 (recovered 6.6.17)	88	91,000 A	250	40	430	1710
KRUISSTRAAT								
No. 1		5.7.16	57	30,000 A	Flooded Feb 1917			
No. 4	2.1.16	11.4.17	57	18,500 A 1000 GC	235	34	395	-
No. 2		12.7.16	62	30,000 A	217	40	367	Branch 170
No. 3		28.8.16	50	30,000 A	202	30	332	2160
ONTARIO FARM	28.1.17	6.6.17	103	60,000 A	200	0	220	1290
TRENCH 127								
No. 7 Left	28.12.15	20.4.16	75	36,000 A	181	10	232	Branch 250
No. 8 Right		9.5.16	76	50,000 A	210	16	342	1355
TRENCH 122								
No. 5 Left	15.2.16	14.5.16	60	20,000 A	195	22	323	Branch 440
No. 6 Right		11.6.16	75	40,000 A	228	28	356	970

A – ammonal B – blastine GC – guncotton

Tactical change was driven by the conflict between firepower and mobility, principally the firepower of artillery and the mobility of infantry. While the firepower of artillery had contributed to the stalemate of 1915, it was not the cause of the protracted mutual siege that began in the autumn of 1914. Indeed, immobility in late 1914 had been a consequence of many factors, including exhaustion of the armies, the unwillingness of France and Britain to concede a foot of territory to the Germans under any circumstances, and lack of weapons and ammunition to continue fighting. The entrenching of the armies in 1914 was intended to be no more than a pause in offensive operations which would resume in the spring of 1915. The trenches were not continuous. They lacked strength in both form and structure. The line of defences lacked depth. Indeed, the Western Front was a discontinuous line of poorly made entrenchments with a few strands of barbed wire stretched out in no-man's-land. The puzzle, then, is why this weak defensive line could not be penetrated.

At the start of 1915, the French mounted several unsuccessful offensive operations in the Artois and Champagne, while, at the beginning of March, the BEF launched an offensive at Neuve Chapelle. The significance of Neuve Chapelle was not that it failed but that it very nearly succeeded. The problem for the BEF was converting the break-in into a breakthrough. The German defensive line consisted of only one trench line and lacked support and reserve lines, although it did include several strongpoints 1,000 yards behind the trench line. There was some wire in no-man's-land. After an intense bombardment by 354 British guns lasting only 35 minutes, targetting the trenches, four divisions of 40,000 men from the First Army attacked along a 3,280-yard front. The artillery was supported by eighty-five Royal Flying Corps aircraft which acted as aerial spotters. This was not an innovation as aerial spotting of this kind had been tried during the Balkan Wars a few years earlier. The field guns successfully destroyed the wire but the howitzers, which were supposed to destroy the trenches and the strongpoints, failed to do any significant damage.

Taken by surprise, the Germans were overrun and, in a matter of a few hours, the British had advanced beyond the German line of strongpoints. A rigid timetable and an inflexible plan, made worse by poor communications between the advancing troops and First Army HQ, all contributed to poor control of the battle and prevented the near breakthough from being developed further. After the success of the first few hours, the advantage had been lost by the afternoon. German troops were quick to counter-attack and, within two days, the status quo had more or less been restored, the Germans having lost very little ground.

Sir John French, blamed the failure at Neuve Chapelle on the severe shortage of high-explosive shells. This shortage not only afflicted British artillery at Neuve Chapelle but the whole of the BEF during the first six or seven months of 1915, and became a national scandal when it was made public. The Shell Scandal brought down the Liberal government and led to the creation of the Ministry of Munitions in June 1915, which took over all aspects of munitions production in

171

Britain. The shortage of shells had undoubtedly been a significant hindrance at Neuve Chapelle as the guns had been restricted to 200–400 rounds apiece, a paltry figure when later bombardments lasted for days and weeks of sustained firing. The problem highlighted the importance of artillery in deciding the outcome of battles on the Western Front. Without enough guns and without enough shells, no army could attack and expect to win. Moreover, and just as important, no army could properly defend itself or, in this case, deal effectively with counter-attacks. The intensity – although not by later standards – and the brevity of the preliminary bombardment at Neuve Chapelle wrong-footed the Germans, however, who had already come to expect a longer bombardment to precede an infantry assault. Without question the short, heavy bombardment of the trenches and line of strongpoints had been a major factor in the initial success but the fixed barrages on a strict timetable had been unhelpful. However, at that time, there was no means by which the schedule could be amended once the fire plan had been set in motion.

Despite the shortage of shells, the bombardment neutralized the Germans, thereby allowing the British infantry to seize their objectives. However, because the howitzers failed to destroy the German defences, which allowed German infantry firepower to recover from the initial shock, the British drew the conclusion that more intense and longer bombardments were necessary to secure success. The conclusion that neutralization of enemy firepower rather than destruction of his defences was the key to success was not apparent to anybody at that time. Neuve Chapelle led to an expansion of the artillery so that it became the dominant force on the battlefields of the Western Front. It was evident from French and German experience earlier in 1915 that a preliminary bombardment was essential to success. The question was whether it should be short and intense, or carried out over several days, choices that tended to made according to the number and calibre of guns available. After Neuve Chapelle, a doctrine of destruction of the enemy was adopted by the British in the belief that, not only was complete destruction possible, but the inevitable loss of surprise that came with long intense bombardments did not matter as there would be no enemy left to be surprised.

At the Battle of Festubert in May of the same year, the British adopted a policy of destruction with a bombardment that went on for two days. The loss of surprise cost the British 24,000 casualties, although the failure at Festubert was attributed to insufficient destruction of the German defences. When the British launched an offensive at Loos in September, the barrage lasted for four days but its effects were diminished by the fact that the gun density was only one every 30 yards of front engaged, whereas at Neuve Chapelle it had been one gun for every 5.5 yards. This compromise had been necessary because of the shortage of ammunition which did not allow a heavier bombardment. The ideal level of destruction of the enemy defences was not achieved. The bombardment at the start of the Somme offensive, nine months later, lasted a week and included a hitherto unprecedented number of heavy guns, as well as trench mortars. The number of guns per yard during the preliminary bombardment on the Somme was approximately twice that at Loos, while the frontage was twice as long, 25,000 yards compared with 11,200 yards. Unlike at Loos, there was no shortage of ammunition. The prolonged bombardment and the greater gun density on the Somme was intended to obliterate the wire and German resistance, and especially to destroy German machine-guns, before the infantry assault on 1 July.

At Messines, in June 1917, the preliminary bombardment lasted seventeen days as the doctrine of destruction reached its zenith. The mines fired at Messines were in accordance with this doctrine. The gun density was such that, yard for yard, there were twice as many field guns at Messines than for the preliminary bombardment on the Somme and three times as many heavy guns. On the Somme, there was one field gun for every 21 yards and one heavy for every 57 yards, whereas at Messines, there was one field gun every 10 yards and one heavy every 20 yards. Between 3 June and 10 June, the guns fired 3,258,000 rounds, nearly twice the quantity fired during the first eight days of the Somme (1,732,873 rounds). The mortars at Messines fired 800,000 rounds.

At the same time that the number of guns and quantities of ammunition were increasing in order to bring about the realization of the ideal of complete destruction of the enemy, the manner in which the bombardments were conducted and the targets engaged by the guns went through a series of fundamental changes. Such changes were driven by a need to overcome the enemy and his trench systems. The nature of defence also changed. The concept of defence in depth was created after Neuve Chapelle so that by the time of Loos, the Germans had more than one line of trenches. Had not the nature of defence changed, the search for ever greater firepower to destroy the enemy's defences would have lacked impetus. At the same time, the increases in firepower and the increases in defensive depth drove a change in infantry tactics. By the beginning of 1916, the power of artillery was such that infantry were at its mercy, while the firepower of the infantry in defence had also increased so that attackers stood little chance if they were caught in the open, especially en masse. The purpose of the attackers' artillery was to destroy the defenders, to enable the infantry to take their objectives. To complicate matters, the enemy artillery attempted to destroy the attacking infantry and the attackers' artillery. While counter-battery fire had been employed before the Russo-Japanese War, it now came into its own. This was not merely a question of shooting first since weight of fire and accuracy were crucial. Accuracy was not simply making sure that the shells landed where they were intended, but it was imperative to know the location of the enemy batteries. Thus, aerial photography and mapping became essential to gunnery. Then there was the question of how the infantry should work with the artillery. This was the nature of the struggle which attackers and defenders both faced in 1915–17.

While the French and the British both concluded from the battles of 1915 that the way forward was to increase the firepower of their artillery and lengthen the preliminary bombardment phase of an offensive, the Germans took a somewhat different lesson from these battles. On the one hand, the growing power of artillery seemed to offer the German Army a way to defeat France, which ultimately led to the epic struggle at Verdun that began at the end of February 1916 and continued for ten months; while on the other, the Germans realized that a single line of trenches was not sufficient to prevent a determined Allied assault from breaking through, sweeping all before them. The solution to this problem was to build a second line of defence, similar to the first, which would contain any break-in and prevent a breakthrough. By the time the British launched their offensive at Loos in September 1915, the Germans were in the process of building this second line. And by the time of the Somme offensive in the summer of 1916, the Germans had developed their defence in depth to include a third line. When in 1917, they built the Hindenburg Line, the defensive zone was up to 15 miles deep and included five lines.

To make matters more difficult, the Germans stopped manning their front-line trenches in strength, but withdrew the bulk of their troops to what was, in effect, the second line, with only about a quarter of the infantry being located in the first two trench lines immediately facing no-man's-land. Thus, at the start of the Somme in 1916 the German trenches closest to no-man's-land were held very thinly and, once the preliminary bombardment started, the troops in them sheltered in deep bomb-proof dugouts, leaving very few troops to man the trenches. By 1917, the German front line was no more than a series of outposts, thinly held, located hundreds of yards in front of the main line of defence. At the same time, the development of strongpoints with all round defence began to replace linear defensive lines of continuous trenches, a process of change that led to the construction of the Hindenburg Line. Here, the defensive lines were more in the nature of zones than linear trench lines of the sort commonly employed in 1915. In conjunction with the dissolving of rigid lines of defence, the Germans adopted an elastic defence in which the immediate counter-attack to retake any ground lost played a major role.

The tactics employed by the infantry went through a similar process of change. While the infantry tactics of the assault employed in the early battles of 1915 tended to be based on pre-war tactics, so that infantry engaged infantry and artillery provided support, this was soon found to be costly and ineffective. Nevertheless, the notion of attacking in lines or waves persisted well into 1916, largely because of the relationship between the infantry and artillery, whereby the artillery timetable dictated how the infantry attacked. The growing dominance of artillery placed restraints on the infantry because of the nature of artillery barrages. The barrage was intended to support the infantry by preventing the enemy from engaging the assault troops as they approached. However, it forced a rigid timetable on the infantry and took no account of obstacles that might have to be overcome which slowed the advance. Equally, the assault troops had to contend with enemy fire and as his firepower increased so the likelihood of their crossing no-man's-land unscathed to engage the enemy on his territory diminished. Thus, while linear tactics favoured reasonable coordination between the attackers' artillery and their assault troops, it also favoured the enemy as linear waves presented unmissable targets, especially when the enemy was able to enfilade the attacking waves. Far from being a straightforward problem that might offer a straightforward solution, a quite different approach to infantry assaults was required.

The idea of doing away with rigid linear tactics and adopting a more flexible approach was considered as early as May 1915, when Captain André Laffargue devised tactics of infiltration which avoided the massed frontal assault. These were derived from his own experience and were a variation on the wave theme. No one took much notice of his theories. At much the same time, and quite independently, Major Wilhelm Rohr, who commanded the German Army's Assault Detachment, also devised tactics of infiltration. The purpose of the Detachment was to develop new tactics for offensive operations. Rohr and his unit tried the new tactics against the French in the Vogues before using them at Verdun. Rohr and the Assault Detachment, renamed Assault Battalion Rohr in April 1916, were the first Stormtroopers.

The artillery barrage, as distinct from the bombardment that preceded an infantry assault, was intended to help the assault by preventing the enemy infantry from bringing their weapons to bear on the attackers. Counter-battery fire, on the other hand, was purely a duel between the guns, a duel which the Germans increasingly lost from about 1917 because the Allies, and the British in particular, could bring a heavier weight of fire to bear. It was clear from early 1916 that artillery had become the dominant force on the battlefield, and battles were won or lost according to how the artillery was used, or, at least, the casualty level was decided on how well the artillery could deal with the enemy. Indeed, when the Australians attacked Pozières during the Somme campaign and did so without a preliminary bombardment, they suffered very high casualties and failed to take their objectives because of German firepower, both from infantry in the trenches and from artillery. The protective barrage in support of an assault was not an alternative to a preliminary bombardment, of course. The problem was how to hit the enemy trenches while the infantry advanced without causing friendly casualties in the process.

The first barrages were no more than lines of bombardment across the width of the battlefield, targeting the front-line trenches. After a fixed time interval, it moved on a somewhat arbitrary distance to lay down another line of shelling beyond the advancing infantry but not necessarily on the next line of trenches. The straight barrage was of very limited help to the infantry who were often left behind by the advancing barrage. The next development was the lifting barrage, first used by the French in early 1915 in the battles in the Artois and Champagne. The barrage still advanced in the same way as the straight barrage but it hit trenches each time it lifted to the next target. By now, the infantry were accompanied by Forward Observation Officers whose job it was to direct the artillery to improve its shooting. In both cases, the artillery employed indirect fire and one of the problems this highlighted was the difficulty of accurately locating the targets due to a lack of reliable maps. Shooting by the map with accuracy was more of an aspiration than an achievable goal before the middle of 1916. Unfortunately for the infantry, the lifting barrage was no easier to follow than the straight barrage. The added disadvantage was the necessity for the guns to fire registration rounds beforehand to ensure that they had the range of the target. In registering the guns, the enemy was, of course, alerted to the targets that were about to be hit and, indeed, to the fact that an offensive was likely in the near future. Suspicions were increased if a lot of guns were firing registration shots. They were easy to identity because of their apparent randomness, although they bracketed what was clearly a target. It was because of this easy identification of registrations that trench mortars hid theirs during an artillery bombardment.

Although the preliminary bombardment also gave away the fact that an offensive was starting, prior registration of the guns was insignificant to overall lack of surprise. Any bombardment that lasted more than a few hours gave the enemy time to move his infantry and his guns. By 1917, greater effort was made to conceal registration shots so that the targets were less likely to be identified by the enemy. With this in mind, every effort was made to conceal the location of gun batteries to avoid counter-battery fire. They were sited on reverse slopes and some batteries remained inactive so that they remained hidden until the moment they opened fire for the offensive.

In 1916, the so-called piled-up barrage was introduced to satisfy the infantry's need for a barrage that focused on the trace of the enemy trenches. Whereas the earlier barrages moved forward in lines parallel with the gun line and passed over the enemy trenches in the same straight line irrespective of the trace of those trenches, the piled-up barrage concentrated or piled up as it hit the enemy trenches, until the rest of the barrage had caught up, thereby concentrating the fire on the trenches. This ensured that the entire trace was hit simultaneously, which had not been possible with straight-line barrages. Both the straight and lifting barrages had allowed the enemy in those parts of the trench that were ahead of the advancing barrage line to enfilade the infantry to their left or right. The piled-up barrage overcame this problem. However, to be effective, the full extent of the enemy disposition needed to be identified beforehand. Trench raiding and patrolling helped in this respect but there was no foolproof way to locate all the enemy's trenches or to determine the strength with which he held the various sections. There was also the disadvantage that the attacking infantry had to assault the trenches simultaneously, irrespective of the location of the trenches. In practical terms, this meant that those troops which had the furthest to go to hit the enemy trench allocated to them had to leave their own trenches before those troops which had a short distance to cover. This made them vulnerable to enemy fire.

The creeping barrage was a solution to the problems posed by the piled-up barrage. Now, instead of the barrage moving forward parallel with the gun line, it was parallel with the enemy trench line. For the first time, it was possible for the assaulting infantry to hit the enemy trenches immediately after the barrage had passed over these trenches. To achieve this, the infantry still had to leave their trenches according to their distance from the enemy so that they all hit the enemy, irrespective of the trace of his trenches, at the same time. Unlike with the piled-up barrage, the infantry did not have to wait until the entire enemy line was under the barrage before leaving their trenches, although in practice they had left their trenches before then, but had to slow their advance or speed it up according to the distance between them and their targets. Good planning and execution were necessary with every type of barrage. And in every instance, the infantry had to advance as close to the exploding shells as they could safely get. Hence, rehearsals on ground that replicated the enemy line were carried out before the offensive, although this was not done with live shells.

Until about the middle of 1916, the infantry assault was a linear operation in that it consisted of lines, or waves, of men with specified time intervals between each line, each of which was straight irrespective of the trace of the enemy trenches. The first day of the Battle of the Somme has been made infamous by the fact that the British troops approached the German trenches in straight-line waves. While the idea of infiltrating groups of men was considered, the plan was not taken up. It has passed into folk lore that the reason for this was the lack of faith of the generals in the troops of the New Armies to execute anything but simple manoeuvres on the battlefield, with infiltration and group tactics being considered too sophisticated for their abilities. However, not only is this view of the relationship between British generals and the New Armies quite unfounded, but the reason for using linear wave tactics had nothing to do with any supposed lack of ability on the part of the citizen soldier of Britain's New Armies. The linear nature of artillery tactics at that time precluded an alternative to linear infantry tactics. To have attempted to employ non-linear infantry tactics would have required a highly complex artillery plan. Moreover, there was a real fear among the planners of the Somme offensive that localizing concentrations of artillery firepower, which non-linear infantry tactics would require, could lead to sections of the German trenches, and machine-guns in particular, being missed by the barrage. One advantage of the linear barrage was that the whole of the hostile territory was eventually swept by fire so that everything was subjected to shelling before the infantry reached the trenches. To this end, there was one 18-pounder for every 25–30 yards and one howitzer or heavy gun for every 65 yards.

The infantry wave tactic would have been successful had the artillery been able to destroy or neutralize all the enemy machine-guns, some of which were positioned in shell holes in no-man's-land, as well as between the trench lines, but the artillery had been unable to do this. So long as the waves moved forward according to the timetable in the plan, they could keep up with the barrage. In some areas of the front, the lifts were short enough for a creeping barrage to be created. This was as much a function of the accuracy and precision of the guns as it was a deliberate intention to creep the barrage forwards. But as soon as the leading wave was held up by more resistance than anticipated, such as machine-guns or surviving enemy infantry, the whole assault scheme ran the risk of descending into chaos as each successive wave ran into the back of the preceding wave. For the plan to function smoothly, the timetable had to be followed, which was governed by the artillery lifts and the resistance of the enemy. Had the artillery had the technical sophistication to achieve a precise piled-up barrage rather than an imprecise approximation of one, the effect on the German trenches would have been much more destructive. To achieve a precise piled-up barrage, precise gunnery was needed but, at the time of the Somme, such precision was not technically feasible.

The rise in importance of counter-battery fire meant that more heavy guns were allocated to this role than to infantry support, which hindered the weight of fire in the preliminary bombardment and in the supporting barrages. The Germans discovered in 1915 from their experience on the Eastern Front that surprise and weight of fire were more important to success than bombardments which might last for up to a week. Indeed, contrary to the Allied practice of prolonging bombardments and increasing the weight of fire, the Germans increased their weight of fire but decreased the duration of the bombardment. Whereas the Allies bombarded the Germans on the Somme for a week and the British shelled the Germans at Messines in 1917 for a week, the Germans fired a preliminary bombardment on the French at Verdun for only 10 hours. On 21 March 1918, at the start of the German Michael offensive, the assault was preceded by a bombardment of only 5 hours in which 6,473 guns and 3,532 trench mortars fired millions of shells, including more than 2 million gas shells. German artillery outnumbered British guns by more than 2.5 to 1.

This highlighted the different philosophies of destruction and neutralization. While the Allies had gone down the total destruction road, the Germans had opted for neutralization and had developed their infantry assault tactics accordingly. At the same time, they adapted their defensive policy to reflect the same principals. As the Allies tried ever harder to destroy the German lines before an assault in 1917, so the Germans withdrew the bulk of their infantry and artillery from the forward zones at the start of an Allied offensive, shelled the British trenches when they calculated the assault was about to start, withdrew again and shelled their former positions when the Allies were in possession. Reserves were kept out of artillery range, approximately 5.5 miles to the rear but still within the defence zone. By extending their defence zone the Germans diluted the effect of Allied destruction tactics. They developed island strongpoints each of which was located to take advantage of local topography and road links and sited so that each strongpoint could act cooperatively with its neighbours, thereby creating lethal zones through which attacking infantry would have to pass. And always the Germans used the immediate counter-attack, with ad hoc formations of troops when necessary, to deal with any loss of ground. The notion of linear assault tactics and barrages were made redundant by such defensive measures.

Destruction tactics were applied by the British with ever greater intensity at Vimy Ridge, Messines and Passchendaele. While Vimy and Messines were both limited actions, Third Ypres was a major offensive and, while the limited actions achieved limited successes, Third Ypres became a costly battle of attrition in atrocious conditions which, in terms of its original objectives, was far from a success. At Passchendaele, the tactic of destruction was at last shown to be counter-productive.

The last British offensive of 1917, Cambrai, marked a radical departure from previous artillery and assault tactics. Not only were tactics of neutralization employed by the artillery, but Cambrai saw the first use of massed tank assaults in support of the infantry. The tank had been devised independently by British and French engineers during 1915 and 1916, as a solution to the trench deadlock. British tanks first saw action during the later stages of the Somme battles in September 1916. The French first used theirs in April 1917 during the disastrous Chemin des Dames offensive. Neither debut was a success, however, and their achievements, such as they were, were modest. From the outset, tanks were under-gunned, under-armoured, under-powered and mechanically unreliable, while they were quite unsuited to crossing the shell-cratered landscape of the Western Front as they easily stuck in craters and trenches, tended to throw a track on rough ground and sank in mud. Indeed, their unreliability was the biggest cause of operational losses; more tanks broke down or were ditched than were knocked out by enemy action. At Cambria, 378 tanks started out from the start line on the first day of the offensive and, although some tanks remained in continuous action for 16 hours, no fewer than 114 were lost through mechanical failure and ditching, while sixty-five were knocked out by enemy action.

Cambrai also saw the use of aircraft in an air-support role to suppress the enemy's ability to fight, an operational innovation pioneered by Lieutenant Colonel J.F.C. Fuller, one of the advocates of tank warfare. Moreover, there was an emphasis on air observation for communicating the fall of shot to the artillery batteries. The artillery did not fire registration shots before the battle so that complete surprise was possible. Instead, gunners used predicted fire for counter-battery work. Although predicted fire had been tried before, it was not until late 1917 that it could be relied upon as an effective means by which to hit enemy batteries. Predicted fire was a science, not an art, which combined the technical skills of several disciplines to ensure that the target was hit precisely. Not least among these was map-making. Without accurate maps, no amount of clever gunnery was ever going to result in the intended target being hit except by chance. To this end, thousands of aerial photographs were taken by reconnaissance aircraft flying over enemy-held territory, in support of which fighter aircraft flew escort patrols to prevent enemy aircraft shooting down the reconnaissance planes. From these photographs, accurate maps were prepared and regularly updated using new photographs by the map-making branch at GHQ.

Fundamental to accurate gunnery was an understanding of the science of ballistics. Aspects of this included the weight of the shell, muzzle velocity and the effect of barrel wear on range and accuracy. Such issues applied specifically, not

NUMBER OF GUNS and
AMMUNITION EXPENDITURE (BEF)

	LOOS (1915)	yd/gun rounds/yd	SOMME (1916)	yd/gun rounds/yd	MESSINES (1917)	yd/gun rounds/yd
FRONTAGE (yd)	11,200		25,000		17,000	
FIELD ARTILLERY						
13-pounder	4		0		0	
15-pounder	26		0		0	
18-pounder	304		808		1314	
4.5-inch howitzer	72		202		438	
TOTAL	406	27.45	1010	24.75	1752	9.70
HEAVY ARTILLERY						
4-inch	1		0		0	
4.7-inch	12		32		0	
60-pounder	24		128		198	
6-inch	5		20		24	
9.2-inch	2		1		1	
12-inch	0		1		1	
5-inch howitzer	8					
6-inch howitzer	36		104		348	
8-inch howitzer	16		64		108	
9.2-inch howitzer	10		60		116	
12-inch howitzer	0		11		20	
15-inch howitzer	3		6		3	
220m howitzer (French)	0		16		0	
75mm (French)	0		60		0	
120mm (French)	0		24		0	
TOTAL	117	95.72	527	47.44	819	20.76
TOTAL NUMBER OF GUNS	523	21.41	1537	16.27	2571	6.61
ROUNDS	255,883	22.85	1,732,872	69.31	3,258,000	191.65

to the artillery in general or to a battery, but to individual guns. Since 1915, gunners had become aware that the rifling in a barrel was worn down by each shot fired and that, as barrels became worn, so accuracy and range diminished. Indeed, shooting from very worn barrels could result in shells landing unpredictably on friendly troops. By the end of 1917, gunners were able to factor all this into their calculations, for each gun, along with the wind speed and direction as well as the air temperature to ensure that the first shot fired from each gun would have a very high probability of hitting the target. Thus, the need to fire registration shots became redundant and tactical and strategic surprise were once more realistic possibilities. Cambrai was the first opportunity for British gunners to put all this into practice. The object at Cambrai was not to destroy the Germans in a prolonged artillery bombardment, like those of the past, but to prevent the enemy from engaging the British artillery, tanks and infantry. In other words, the object was to neutralize the enemy's ability to fight. With this in mind, smoke and tear gas rounds were fired in addition to high explosive, while the tanks created corridors through the wire obstacles for the infantry and acted as mobile artillery to deal with pillboxes and strongpoints. There was no preliminary bombardment. When zero hour arrived, a creeping barrage from more than 1,000 guns led the way and the tanks and infantry moved forward, 300 yards behind the barrage.

The Germans were completely surprised and overwhelmed. The assault broke into the German line and penetrated to a depth of 5 miles on a 6-mile front in 10 hours, by which time tank crews and infantry were exhausted. Tanks outran their infantry, despite their slow speed. There were no tank reserves so that by the third day there were, in effect, no tanks in action. The initial success could not be exploited and when the Germans counter-attacked ten days after the start of the battle, the advantage had passed to them. The British lost most of the ground they had taken but more importantly they had been stopped from converting the break-in into breakthrough.

During the Cambrai counter-attack, the Germans applied infiltration techniques and used them again in their spring offensives of 1918. At the same time, they applied more flexible artillery tactics that, like the Allied artillery, now no longer focused on destruction, but on neutralization. The object was not so much suppression of the ability of the enemy's ability to fight, as destruction of their morale by subjecting them to a sudden and very intense bombardment of short duration, followed by an immediate infantry assault. Such artillery tactics were devised by an artillery commander, Lieutenant Colonel Bruchmüller, who tried them out on the Eastern Front before applying them to the Western Front. The Germans also used predicted fire without registration. The new artillery tactics were combined with infantry tactics which emphasized infiltration, as well as fire and movement, and both were integrated in a strategy which sought to apply a heavyweight punch on a short sector of front to achieve a breakthrough. Such tactics were named after General von Hutier who first applied them at Riga on the Eastern Front in September 1917. Part of this overall attack plan included so-called stormtroop tactics which were aggressively applied in the assault phase by elite units of stormtroopers, leaving more conventional troops to deal with pockets of resistance bypassed by the stormtroopers. This was how the spring offensives of 1918 were mounted.

Stormtroopers did not occupy trenches like ordinary infantry regiments but were moved into those sectors where and when they were required from behind the lines. They were highly trained for a specific purpose and the German high command could see no sense in allowing them to be whittled down by the day-to-day attrition of trench duty. Unfortunately, the rest of the infantry received more conventional training so that, in effect, there was a two-tier infantry system within the German Army, with the second tier lacking in skill, training and competence compared to the stormtroopers.

By 1918, both the Germans and the Allies had developed new offensive and defensive techniques based on a more flexible response to developing circumstances, which avoided the linear approach to battle that characterized the battles of 1915 and 1916. Moreover, there was a closer integration of all arms, including air power, within the overall strategy. The Allies were beginning to apply a zone principal to defence by the beginning of 1918, but the system was far from complete when the Germans struck on 21 March 1918 in the first of several offensives designed to break through the Allied lines and return to mobile warfare, whereby victory could be achieved. Although trench warfare was not to end for another four or five months, it was no longer of the form that typified the fighting of 1915 and 1916. Static permanent positions had become less useful and temporary positions began to assume greater importance, as the movement of battle lines could now be measured in miles rather than the yards that had typified the battles of the first two years of trench warfare.

The German Michael offensive of March 1918 employed neutralization tactics with infiltration and stormtroop tactics, aided by fog, to punch a hole in the line held the British Fifth Army. The Fifth Army was caught off-guard and lost men, material and ground at an alarming rate, although the Third Army faired better. By the time the Germans lost momentum at the beginning of April, they had driven a salient 40 miles deep into British-held territory. Their failure to produce a decisive breakthrough from this initial success was attributable to several factors, not least among them being the dogged resistance of those troops who were able to fight back. Indeed, where the island defences of the British were occupied by troops determined to resist, the Germans were held up and stopped. Nevertheless, the German failure was logistical, as well as being caused by a severe lack of mobile tactical support from the artillery which could not keep up with the pace of the initial advance. Logistically, the Germans had not planned how to carry ammunition, food and water across the devastated landscape over which the infantry advanced so rapidly. Moreover, for all their tactical fluidity at the start of the offensive, they lacked the mobility to exploit success.

These shortcomings were not solved in the succeeding offensives over the next few months, which became successively more desperate with an inevitable reversion to old-style tactics. This was in part due to the loss of trained stormtroop units who suffered very high casualties during these operations. The British, the French and, increasingly, the Americans, who were now actively involved in combat operations on the Western Front, succeeded in containing the Germans by employing greater tactical flexibility in defence than had been the case in previous years. British and French artillery fired in depth at the German reserves, ammunition supplies and headquarters, rather than on the leading waves of German troops who were engaged by the infantry, machine-guns and mortars. The Stokes mortar, in particular, proved quite capable of inflicting severe casualties on the German infantry.

By the time the Allies went on to the offensive in July 1918, the face of battle on the Western Front had changed completely from what it had been even nine months earlier, let alone during the battles of 1915 and 1916. While trench warfare persisted almost to the end of the war, the mobility of battles in the last few months was a far cry from the slogging matches of the earlier years. The manner in which the Allies employed artillery in defence and attack in 1918 was quite different from the past. The emphasis was on depth, engaging targets well beyond the reach of its infantry, and hitting them hard and simultaneously or in quick succession. Thus, instead of supporting the infantry by directly hitting targets which they were about to engage, the artillery struck targets which prevented the movement of enemy troops and artillery on the battlefield, thereby disrupting his ability to create effective counter-attacks. Areas where infantry might form up for a counter-attack, as well as defensive positions well behind the front line, were hit with sudden and intense predicted fire. Headquarters and gun batteries as well as road and rail links were all hit. Dead ground was targetted by Stokes mortars so that troops sheltering from the artillery were still hit. Air power also played a big role in operations, not only spotting for the artillery, but bombing troops behind the lines.

At Amiens in August 1918, tanks and aircraft worked cooperatively ahead of the infantry to deal with the wire, so that the artillery could focus on more distant targets. Tanks were employed to create gaps in the wire, ahead of the infantry, while aircraft flew ahead of the tanks to locate and engage anti-tank guns by bombing and machine-gunning them before the tanks arrived. Aircraft also flew interdiction sorties to hit roads and railways to disrupt reserves and cause mayhem. Nearly 2,000 Allied aircraft took part in the Amiens offensive as the German Army was severely mauled and forced into headlong retreat. There was no preliminary bombardment before the battle opened on 8 August with an unheralded hurricane bombardment which delivered a weight of fire that in 1917 would have been taken several days. The BEF employed 630 tanks on the first day, although the number of serviceable tanks fell off sharply over succeeding days. Their reliability and, indeed, workability was very poor. Tank crews could not tolerate more than a few hours of continuous action because the conditions inside the machines were too uncomfortable.

All these factors worked together in a new form of warfare, referred to as three-dimensional warfare. This year of the war saw the emergence of what was to become known as deep battle, whereby the artillery fired deep into enemy territory rather than focusing on the front line to be engaged in the infantry assault. These concepts were developed in direct response to the stalemate on the Western Front. They have remained at the heart of modern warfare ever since.

The emergence of these new forms of warfare, along with the ever-widening employment of tanks on the battlefield, led to the development of new types of weapon to, on the one hand, counter the tank, and on the other, provide close artillery support to the infantry who accompanied the tanks. The former led to the development of anti-tank guns, the anti-tank mine (extemporized from artillery shells buried in a hole), while the latter led to the self-propelled gun, an artillery piece on tracks which could keep up with the infantry. Warfare would never be quite the same again.

CHAPTER 11

Trench Warfare, 1939–53

The nature of warfare was changed by the First World War. The armies of 1918 were very different from those of 1914, technologically, tactically and strategically. The emergence of deep battle and three-dimensional warfare in response to the stalemate of the Western Front occurred very rapidly, although the immobility of the Western Front, along with the very high casualty lists in pursuit of what appeared to be little better than a few yards of smashed earth, led the post-war generations to consider the First World War to have been an aberration caused by failure and incompetence. In reality, the innovative approach to battle on both the small and large scales, pursued by British, French and German armies alike, brought about a conclusion to the war in a way that would not have been possible in the Russo-Japanese War. While trench warfare had been features of the fighting in Manchuria and in the American Civil War, mobility had been restored by conventional means without the need to develop new modes of warfare. In no other war but the First World War had a state of mutual siege pertained for almost the entire duration of the war so that most battles were about breaking the deadlock.

In the 1920s and 1930s, there was a universal dread of a recurrence of trench warfare and great efforts were made to reappraise how to fight a war. The advocates of the tank, such as Fuller and Liddell Hart, argued that mobile mechanized forces would always smash through defences, making trenches redundant. Equally, the advocates of air power, such as Mitchell and Douhet, argued that the bomber would render land armies redundant, while Stanley Baldwin, British Prime Minister in the 1920s and 1930s, stated that the bomber would always get through so that strategic bombing, as it was to become known, was the answer. Then there were the alternative strategic approaches, epitomized by the Liddell Hart school of the indirect approach. Yet the solution already existed and, indeed, the battles of the Second World War were fought on the principals of three-dimensional warfare and deep battle. The German Army of the 1930s did not devise a new form of warfare but adopted those principals by which its predecessor had been defeated on the battlefields of 1918. Through propaganda and a little help from the British press, this was transformed into *Blitzkrieg*. However, the British and the French had engaged in the same form of warfare in 1918. The only difference between so-called *Blitzkrieg* and the form of warfare pursued by the British and the French in 1918 was technological. Aircraft, tanks and mechanized transport of the 1930s and 1940s were much ahead of their predecessors of 1918, with greater range, greater firepower and much improved reliability.

One army which exemplified deep battle was the Soviet Red Army of the 1940s and, indeed, it continued to do so well into the 1980s. Between 1942 and 1945, the German armies on the Eastern Front were crushed by the overwhelming power of the Red Army, not merely in terms of numbers of men and machines but in tactical terms. The doctrine of destruction by itself was shown to be of very limited value by the battles of 1916 and 1917, but combine destruction with the principals of deep battle and the effect on the enemy is to destroy him and run over him.

Yet the idea that trench warfare could be eradicated from the battlefield if more mobile forces were employed was a false hope. While protracted trench warfare of the sort which dominated the Western Front was unlikely to occur again simply because the tactical and technological changes that had taken place during the First World War worked against the establishment of stalemate, nevertheless, immobility was still a factor in warfare. Indeed, trench warfare was no more made redundant by the more modern approaches to war than it had been avoidable in 1914. To suppose otherwise is to view trench warfare as a peculiarity of the Western Front of the First World War. However, while trenches remained of crucial importance to all forms of warfare after the First World War, the way in which they figured had changed. No longer were trenches in themselves seen as an obstacle to the enemy since the battles of 1918, in particular, had shown that even deep defences could be overcome. On the contrary, the value of trenches lay in the protection they afforded their occupants from incoming artillery fire and especially mortar fire. The strength of an entrenched position lay in the men who occupied the trenches and how they fought.

All of the wars fought between 1918 and 1939, irrespective of their location in the world, involved entrenchments. These were mostly temporary shelters rather than positions of strength that were intended to hold off an attacker. Even the trenches of the Spanish Civil War, fought between the Nationalists and the Republicans from 1936 to 1939, were more associated with siege of the form familiar down the centuries, albeit fought with aircraft, machine-guns, tanks and artillery. These trenches were more for protection than for anything else. Similarly, the trenches dug by the Japanese and Chinese in the fighting which could be construed as the start of the Second World War in 1937, were temporary shelters rather than defensive entrenchments intended to impede the progress of the enemy when he launched an assault. That is not to imply that trenches were no longer used in that capacity. Indeed, the use of permanent defensive networks of entrenchments and concrete bunkers did not end with the fall of the Hindenburg Line in 1918. The belief that strong fortifications still had a role in warfare, despite the effect of technologically sophisticated weapons in combination with modern tactical doctrines which played to the strengths of these weapons, persisted into the Second World War. While France built the ultimately impotent Maginot Line, constructed from 1930 to 1940 to keep the Germans out, which was successfully outflanked in

1940 by the German Army going through the supposedly impassable Ardennes, the Germans constructed first the West Wall along the border with France, Luxembourg, Belgium and Holland between 1936 and 1940, then the Atlantic Wall along the coast of occupied Europe from Norway to Spain between 1940 and 1944. The German defences were mirror images of the Hindenburg Line of 1917 in that they comprised strongpoints built around concrete bunkers and gun casemates sited to provide supportive crossfire, linked by trenches and protected by barbed wire, with the added refinement of anti-personnel mines. Similar defensive structures were built by Czechoslovakia along its border with Germany (1935–8) and by the Soviet Union (1930–9 and 1940–1), all in the belief that static defences were capable of stopping an invader, namely, Germany. Indeed, all the European nations built similar lines and forts for defence against Germany.

The reliance on static defences was an apparent contradiction of the military philosophy of attack being the best form of defence, at least, in the sense of the counter-attack being a better form of defence. However, that is not to say that deep defences could not stop an attacker. In the Battle of Kursk in 1943, the classic tank battle, the Russians prepared defensive lines in the manner of the Western Front of 1917 and 1918 but to a depth of 95 miles. The Soviets dug in the region of 3,000 miles of trenches in preparation for the battle, using thousands of civilians for the task. More than half a million anti-tank mines and nearly as many anti-personnel mines were laid at the same time. Tens of thousands of miles of barbed wire were laid, along with thousands of anti-tank obstacles. The difference, however, between the defence lines at Kursk and those on the Western Front was not merely scale but in tactical thinking behind their construction. Moreover, these trenches were not like those of the First World War, as they were temporary rather than permanent. There was no intention to hold the lines indefinitely but to break the German assault. Far from being a battle dominated by trenches, this was an example of the Red Army's ability to suck in the enemy to a carefully engineered killing zone, then destroy him in deep battle. Kursk illustrated that trench warfare of the sort conducted twenty years earlier had been laid to rest by the new doctrines of warfare that had emerged from the First World War.

Nevertheless, trench warfare had not been eradicated. Indeed, far from ending with the renewed mobility of the new military doctrines, it had merely been altered by them as well as by the new weapons which modern warfare made necessary. The ground-support role played by aircraft in the Second World War increased the importance of trenches for protection, as did the widespread use of tanks and self-propelled guns. The infantry was no less vulnerable to these modern weapons than it was to artillery and mortars. Moreover, the one-shot hand-held anti-tank weapon, exemplified by the *Panzerfaust*, was a serious threat to tanks and the machine-gun to accompanying infantry when they were sited in semi-permanent positions. There was no theatre of operations in the Second World War in which trenches did not figure. The difference between the two world wars was that in the Second World War the means to prevent stalemate existed in the form of weapons and tactics, whereas, at the start of the First World War, neither existed.

Whenever armies stopped, they dug in. On the Eastern Front, when the Red Army paused before it undertook its next offensive against the retreating Germans, both sides dug trenches, built temporary bunkers from logs and earth – much like the dugouts of 1914–18 – carried out patrols, sniped, mortared each other and, indeed, if the pause between offensives lasted weeks or months, undertook raids and small-scale operations in much the same way as the British, French and Germans had done in the First World War. And there was the added dimension of being attacked from the air by ground-attack aircraft. The Soviet Ilyushin Il-2 Stormovik, specifically designed for the ground-attack role, was a formidable aircraft and was much feared by German troops, whether they were out in the open or entrenched. The German Ju-87 Stuka, also designed for ground attack, was a far less effective aircraft as it was slower and therefore vulnerable to fighters and ground fire. The Germans also deployed the Henschel HS-129, which was faster than the Ju-87, but little more than a flying gun, more of a tank-buster than an anti-troop plane, and still too slow.

The depth of no-man's-land between the Russian and German trenches was anywhere between 500 and 900 yards. Major offensives often necessitated Soviet infantry making frontal assaults on German trenches in a manner that was not unlike the battles of 1916, that is, en masse and in waves. In this respect, there was little difference between the two world wars, except that the weapons were generally more advanced in the Second World War and the submachine-gun played a significant role in close-quarter fighting, whereas it had hardly figured at all in the First World War. It was a weapon of short-range and little accuracy but which produced a high volume of fire spread over a large area, making it ideal for fighting in enclosed spaces and against groups of enemy soldiers. The hand grenade retained its importance in trench fighting as did the rifle grenade as well as the knife and the sharpened spade. Whenever bunkers and pillboxes were encountered, the sort of tactics that had been employed on the Western Front in the First World War to deal with such defences were again the most effective, that is, team work to enable soldiers to toss grenades into the apertures.

> The firing trench stretches across bare country. It's narrow and fairly dry on the hills, but in the hollows it's flooded and you have to splash through the muddy water. The machine-gun posts jut forward like small bastions ... Short trenches lead to the latrines and refuse pits. A supply trench connects us to the rear. The only trouble is that because of the high water-level the dugouts are low. You have to crouch behind the parapet ... if you want to avoid ... a bullet.

This was Russia in September 1942, as recorded by Helmut Pabst, an NCO in an artillery unit, yet he could have been describing trenches in northern France in 1915. The trench fighting on the Eastern Front was often as brutal as any trench fighting in the First World War.

Where trench fighting was involved in north-west Europe following D-Day, it was every bit as savage as on the Eastern Front. However, the trenches of the Second World War were unlike those of the First in that they were shallower, narrower and less robustly constructed than those of 1915–18. Even those trenches that were part of permanent strongpoints, such as those along the Atlantic Wall, were not the deep, wide structures of the First World War. Those of 1914–18, apart from the earliest trenches of 1914, were built to allow head cover and to withstand all but direct hits from high-explosive shells. Trenches of the Second World War were far less permanent in form and, indeed, no occasion arose when permanence was a desirable feature. Ground-attack aircraft reduced the value of trenches, as did fast-moving armour, and made permanence a distinctly undesirable feature. Troops needed to be able to move quickly and dig in quickly rather than settle down into a semi-permanent position. Nevertheless, US commanders complained that British troops operating in north-west Europe in the final months of the Second World War had a tendency to advance cautiously until fired upon, then dug in and call for artillery support to deal with a few Germans in trenches the other side of a hedgerow.

There was a certain amount of truth in this but experience had taught the British that rushing headlong across a field when German troops were known to be entrenched on the other side was no way to deal with such a situation. Artillery or mortar fire was the surest way to drive the enemy out of their trenches and into the fire of the waiting British troops. However, the stop-go nature of advancing in this way made movement forwards slow and it gave the appearance of excessive caution. Such encounters were mainly purely infantry affairs and involved no aircraft, armour or even artillery. When the infantry had to deal with entrenched enemy troops who were concealed and waiting for them, there was no alternative but to reconnoitre before launching an assault in the form of a section attack. The No. 36 Mills grenade, which dated from 1918, was still the most effective weapon when used in conjunction with the point of a bayonet and supported by fire from a Bren gun. These small-unit tactics resembled those employed on the Western Front in 1918. In other words, clearing Germans from trenches was no easier in 1945 than it had been in 1944 or in 1918.

What tends to obscure the fact that trench warfare was a part of operational combat of the Second World War is that the trenches were not permanent, were dug quickly and abandoned quickly and, crucially, were referred to as slit trenches. These were not the joined-up trenches with bays and traverses that had been built in the First World War but, as the named suggests, short slits in the earth large enough to accommodate no more than two or three men. The alternative was the one-man foxhole. The small size of the slit trench and foxhole acted to protect the occupants in much the same way as traverses had done in the past. They minimised the effect of an artillery shell or a mortar bomb should one detonate among the dug-in troops. Moreover, slit trenches and foxholes were quicker to dig and less obtrusive than bigger, longer trenches, although these were dug by the Germans in fixed positions centred on concrete structures. These trenches tended to be a little deeper than slit trenches and followed a zigzag trace, which was typical of those in the strongpoints along the Atlantic Wall.

The campaign in Normandy following the landings on 6 June 1944 was a series of battles in which trenches figured prominently. Not the least reason for their importance to both sides was that the topography and landscape of Normandy made the region a defender's paradise and an attacker's nightmare. Not only did the thick impenetrable hedgerows act as barbed-wire entanglements or abattis, and the sunken lanes as tank traps and deadly funnels for infantry for the Allies, but the dominance of Allied air power made movement in daylight for German forces a distinctly risky business. As a consequence, the Germans dug lots of trenches following the invasion, in addition to those already dug in the area over the previous year for the defence of fixed gun batteries, headquarters, communications centres and many other sites that formed part of the Atlantic Wall. Indeed, it would have been hard for Allied troops to have crossed any part of the region without stumbling upon German trenches. Moreover, the roadside ditches could be also used as trenches when the need arose.

The fighting in Normandy was often an infantry only affair in which artillery, mortars, tanks and aircraft made guest appearances from time to time. Assaults by paratroops on the night of D-Day and on the following days were almost entirely infantry-infantry engagements in which the German defenders were in trenches. The paratroopers of the US 82nd and 101st Airborne Divisions had to make ad hoc assaults on the trenches of strongpoints and gun batteries inland of the landing beaches. The assault was often carried by sheer aggression by the paratroopers who were usually outnumbered. They tended not to make simple frontal assaults but endeavoured to use surprise and combine flanking attacks with a frontal assault, supported by machine-guns and BARs. Once again, grenades proved essential munitions for trench work. Because the paratroopers were armed only with infantry weapons, they had to employ tactics that would take away the defenders' advantage. Thus, stealth and surprise combined with aggression at the right moments could carry a position. The paratroopers were attacking above ground, so they could employ tactics similar to those used by the British in 1917 and 1918 to take trenches, although they had not been trained specifically in trench fighting. Fortunately, the lack of enemy artillery meant that they were usually only engaged by infantry weapons.

If the Allied troops needed any encouragement to dig in, the Germans often obliged by mortaring or shelling them. The siting of slit trenches was not random but arranged to provide a measure of all-round protection. The Germans, on the other hand, sometimes made unexpected use of their circumstances. Entering a graveyard in Normandy, Sidney Jary, a British subaltern in the Somerset Light Infantry, noticed a partly open grave. At one end the marble base had been prised up about two feet from the ground and from this aperture the muzzle of an MG 42 protruded ... Well stocked with ammunition for the machine gun and rows of stick grenades, the post was deserted.

This machine-gun in its improvised position, supported by German infantry armed with *Panzerfausts* along the hedgerow of the cemetery, had helped to hold up the British advance near Caen.

With the Allied advance eastwards along the Channel coast following the breakout from Normandy, a route assigned to the British and Canadians, Allied troops continually encountered the strongpoints and gun batteries of the Atlantic Wall, especially around towns such as Boulogne which had been turned into fortresses. In Brittany, the US forces found similar obstacles around the towns of the Atlantic coast, such as St Malo and Brest. While the effect of ground-attack aircraft firing semi-armour-piercing rockets and dropping napalm, combined with the effect of salvos of 6-inch and 14-inch shells fired by warships, on the concrete casemates and bunkers of these fortifications was spectacular, ferroconcrete withstood such onslaughts much better than the Allies were prepared to admit. To take these strongpoints and batteries from the Germans, it was necessary to resort to the kind of tactics that had been developed in the First World War when tackling the defences of Verdun or the Hindenburg Line. Despite the fact that the British, Canadians and Americans could all call on tremendous firepower from tanks, tank destroyers and artillery, as well as ground-attack aircraft, medium bombers and warships, none of this was ever enough to deal with the defenders inside the bunkers. Each bunker of each strongpoint had to be taken by artillery or tanks firing point blank into the apertures, while the infantry fought hand-to-hand with German troops in the support trenches, using grenades and bayonets. American infantry had to put grenades through bunker openings, fire rifle grenades to suppress German infantry and squirt flamethrowers into the bunkers. Sometimes, the bigger personnel and command bunkers had to be taken room by room. The troops of the US VIII Corps found that taking St Malo and Brest was very tough. This was trench warfare of the sort typical of the fighting at Verdun and against the Hindenburg Line.

British paratroopers at Arnhem made extensive use of trenches in their defence of the Ooserbeek perimeter. Here, the slit trenches dug by the paratroopers became their homes for six days. British mortars were often set up in pits, rather than in the open, positions that were very similar to the temporary emplacements dug for Stokes mortars in the First World War. Even in trenches, however, soldiers were vulnerable to incoming fire and to fragments from mortar bombs, in particular. Sniping was also a problem for the British as the Germans could get very close under cover of darkness and lie in wait in the undergrowth or in trees. The paratroopers mounted anti-sniper patrols and hunted them down, especially those who had infiltrated between the British trenches. The mortaring and grenading were typical of trench fighting and the value of the bayonet was shown time and again. Patrolling at night was typical but no one from either side embarked on a raid. Nevertheless, nearly all the fighting was close-quarters, although none of it actually took place in the trenches themselves for the simple reason that they were not large enough to fight in.

Yet, a slit trench had to be occupied with caution when enemy infantry were only a few hundred yards away. More than one Allied soldier was killed when he stood up in his slit trench and was hit by a sniper's bullet. Equally, caution needed to be exercised when digging trenches. A Panzergrenadier labouring to dig a trench near Elst in Holland in 1944, not 30 yards from British positions, became careless and was shot dead as he worked. Here, the British and Germans retained an uneasy stand-off, the troops entrenched opposite each other much like their fathers had been in the First World War. Patrols and raiders skirmished and a steady toll was taken of the troops on both sides. As a US soldier remarked when his unit arrived to take over from the British after two weeks of static warfare, 'Boy, is this place bloody!' Following the unsuccessful Market Garden operation, for about six weeks, the British found themselves engaged in static trench warfare in Holland, although patrolling was aggressively pursued by both sides. Some patrols were more in the nature of raids on enemy positions than they were about gathering information. This was about dominating no-man's-land. Such raids were conducted by stealthy infiltration rather than head-on frontal assaults. And there was a definite tit-for-tat philosophy. On one occasion, a six-man British raid penetrated nearly 200 yards into an enemy strongpoint that was still under construction by its company-sized garrison.

Mortaring was commonplace during this period of stalemate, which made slit trenches essential, while air bursts of mortar bombs and 88mm shells made head cover necessary for the slit trenches. Planks and house doors heaped with earth proved to be very effective defences against steel splinters. When not being mortared or shelled, living in slit trenches for any length of time presented practical problems of sanitation, especially when the trenches were within sight of the entrenched Germans. Cover of darkness and empty food cans were one solution, although in Normandy some tried wrapping up their excrement in old newspaper and chucking it out of the trench. In the heat of the summer sun, this turned out to be a bad idea and the smell became intolerable. Life in the trenches was dirty and generally unpleasant. The Germans tended to become lice infested, but the British had a good supply of clean clothing which helped prevent infestations. Swollen feet were not uncommon when circumstances prevented the removal of boots once a day. Although the temptation was to ease the laces and remove the boots, this was ill-advised as often the boots could not be pulled over swollen feet, and especially not in a hurry. However, wet feet in wet socks and left in wet boots led to trench foot as some US troops in the Hürtgen Forest discovered. As was well known in the trenches of the Western Front, looking after feet was a priority as bad feet turned the otherwise fit soldier into an evacuable casualty.

Perhaps the worst trench fighting in north-west Europe was that in the Hürtgen Forest in late 1944 and early 1945, after US troops ran up against the fortifications of the West Wall, or Siegfried Line, in September 1944. The West Wall consisted of two lines of fortifications, separated by several miles. The defences varied in depth as they wound through the forest in irregular curves and sweeps according to the local topography. In among the trees were concrete bunkers, gun casemates and pillboxes, as well as bunkers constructed from logs, which the US troops discovered were almost impossible to see until they were virtually on top of them. Barbed wire and minefields added to the problems faced by US infantry. The undergrowth was so thick and the trees so close together in places that armour and, indeed, any sort of vehicle, was restricted to the tracks that criss-crossed the slopes of the forest, although there were clearings the foresters kept open to act as firebreaks. The closeness of the trees and the thickness of the undergrowth sometimes made any sort of movement very difficult. German artillery fire intentionally hit the tops of the trees sending down lethal showers of pine splinters. American infantry discovered that their foxholes and slit trenches needed head cover in the form of logs and earth to make them proof against the splinters whenever German artillery shelled the American positions. Tanks moving along the forest tracks were especially vulnerable to enemy soldiers waiting in well-concealed trenches and foxholes, *Panzerfaust* or bazooka at the ready.

The conditions in the forest at that time of year were very difficult to tolerate for long. The ground was snow covered and frozen hard, although the tramping of boots turned it to muddy slush. Entrenched German and US soldiers alike were very cold and very wet for most of the time. Approximately 9,000 US troops succumbed to the bitter conditions and became 'weather casualties', suffering from exposure, frostbite and trench foot. And the nights were so dark in the forest that patrols got lost only a few yards from their own lines. It was all too easy for a man to lose himself in the forest, even in daylight. So no one ventured far on his own. The sanitary conditions were sometimes very bad because the fear of getting lost overrode everything else.

The Americans mounted several assaults towards the towns of Aachen, Schmidt and Düren, as well as towards the River Rur, which meant fighting in the forest and engaging the defences of the West Wall. Whereas the Atlantic Wall fortifications had been overcome along the Normandy coast in a matter of hours with relative ease due to the overwhelming firepower provided by air support and by warships, the same was not true of the West Wall, which proved a much tougher obstacle to overcome. The US forces could not call on warships or on airpower for the most part. Armour was of limited value and, whereas artillery played a significant role in the fighting, the US troops could not call on mortar fire for support because the trees prevented the bombs from hitting the targets. Hence, the combat in the forest was mostly infantry-infantry in nature with rifle, bayonet and grenade. The Americans came in for much criticism for the length of time it took them to break through the forest and the West Wall, since this was, perhaps, the least necessary battle of the war. Progress was slow and every yard had to be fought over as in the First World War. The notion of lines held by troops in the First World War sense was entirely erroneous, however, since the German and American positions tended to be intermingled in the thick forest.

The fighting in the forest lasted from mid-September 1944 to mid-February 1945 and was confined to a small area, about 50 square miles. The Germans fought hard to keep the Americans on the west side of the wall. This area was of strategic significance to the Germans, largely because of the build-up for the Ardennes offensive which was going to be launched at the end of the year just to the south of the Hürtgen area. Moreover, the dams on the River Rur, which flowed just to the east of the forest, were strategically important to the Americans since if the Germans opened the dams, US troops downstream would be caught in the flood. Whatever the justification for the Americans pushing through the forest instead of outflanking it, the fighting in the Hürtgen did not result in victory for the Americans, who failed to take the river and its dams, and at very high cost. The fighting was very reminiscent of the battles of 1917.

Following the German offensive in the Ardennes in December 1944, the American troops who were not initially overrun and captured fell back before the German armoured columns bypassing the town of Bastogne, which became an isolated bastion. Its outer defence perimeter was manned by paratroopers of the 101st Airborne Division who, along with the 82nd Airborne, had been rushed to the area by truck to halt the German advance. The paratroopers of the 101st put up an especially fierce defence of the town and helped prevent the Germans taking it. Again, this was more trench warfare than it was mobile battle. US troops entrenched to the west of St Vith held the advance of *Kampfgruppe* Peiper for a while, but could not halt its progress. Entrenched troops also met the *Kampfgruppe* as it approached the town of Stoumont. This time, however, Peiper was stopped by the US troops who were well prepared and his *Kampfgruppe* was forced to turn back, largely because his diminishing force was short of ammunition and fuel. The lack of fuel meant that many of the tanks and half-tracks had to be abandoned as he fell back.

Before the Germans began to retreat, much of the fighting in the Ardennes centred on entrenched American positions, especially in the defence of Bastogne, hastily dug in the frozen earth. These were not continuous lines but rather groupings of slit trenches and foxholes at strategic points, with machine-guns and, wherever possible, the guns of the 9th and 10th Armored Divisions in support, all intended to protect roads and road junctions as well as ridge lines and potential approaches through the woods and fields. Often, however, the ground was simply too hard for the light entrenching tools carried by the paratroopers to make much of impression on it and the troopers of the 101st sometimes had to resort to picks and heavy-duty spades.

The entrenchments were only temporarily occupied in the forward zone of the Bastogne perimeter but, closer to the town, the trenches were occupied as temporary homes. The paratroopers went out on regular fighting patrols to prevent the Germans from infiltrating through the perimeter and entering the town. Attacks on the perimeter were constant and often involved tanks and self-propelled guns, when the American trenches could be as much a grave, as well as a shelter, if the tank tracks ground over them causing them to collapse. Yet, to the tanks, the troopers in trenches armed with bazookas were a real threat. Anti-tank guns were at a premium and they were often sited in concealed positions from which the gun could be withdrawn when necessary.

The defence of Bastogne was not a static affair in which the US troops waited in their slit trenches and foxholes for the Germans to approach but was much more fluid. The paratroopers moved frequently from their present locations and dug new ones to prevent the Germans from getting a clear picture of how many troopers they faced or where they were located. Sometimes, in the course of a move, the paratroopers came upon foxholes previously dug by the enemy or by other US troops which saved them the trouble of digging new ones. Defence of any position was a case of carefully siting riflemen and machine-guns at tactically important points, then keeping a sharp lookout in all directions as it was unwise to make assumptions about the direction from which the enemy might approach. German and American patrols sometimes bumped into each other, or a US patrol would come upon entrenched Germans where there had been none the night before, all usually resulting in the development of furious firefights.

Entrenching in the snowy landscape presented not only problems of hard ground but the question of how to hide the spoil. The simplest way was to cover it with snow, as Don Burgett of the 101st discovered:

> We set about digging as quietly as possible … covered the dirt we dug and piled outside the front of the hole with snow; otherwise, when daylight came, the fresh dirt would stick out like a sore thumb, inviting anyone looking in our direction to take a shot at it … The Germans … could have been dug in on the other side of the same railroad bank just a few feet or yards away for all we knew … daylight would tell.

But spending even only a few hours in a slit trench at night when it was about ten degrees below freezing was almost intolerable. The hands and feet went numb, the arms and legs were only slightly less numb. The men shivered uncontrollably which gave them a headache because the muscles in the neck contracted so much. On occasion, it was possible to mitigate the cold by lining the hole with hay.

When time allowed, it was possible to dig more elaborate defences as the Germans did in some woods to the north-east of Bastogne. For two days, German Fallschirmjäger dug trenches and built bunkers, camouflaging them so that a company of patrolling paratroopers from the 101st were amongst the German positions before they knew it. Fighting under such circumstances was a mixture of intense running, shooting and cat-and-mouse with the Germans in their trenches, the paratroopers using trees as cover. Burgett described how firing erupted so intensely from both sides ... a deafening roar ... bullets lanced through trees and ricochets whined ... spinning in erratic directions ...We laid down a barrage of covering fire with our rifles while [the others] ... rushed forward ... we continued working our way forward in this manner, forcing the Germans to keep their heads down with our steady fire, until we reached their holes and began engaging them in hand-to-hand combat ... Many of the enemy were shot as they cowered in their holes by troopers firing down on them as they ran past.

This highlighted why it was unwise to remain in a foxhole once the enemy was close enough to charge through a position. Yet some played dead in the snow until disturbed. Then it was a question of who was faster on the draw as to who lived or died. The paratroopers did not remain in the forward German positions but quickly moved onwards again until they had cleared all the enemy from the whole site. Some of the fighting was very brutal when it became hand-to-hand and the paratroopers took no prisoners. Some of the German survivors bided their time, then made a dash for safety. Some made it. The wounded were left where they were since the paratroopers could not take them when they left. The freezing temperatures would finish them off during the night. When the men of the 101st had destroyed the enemy equipment, smashing rifles against trees, they moved out. This was the nature of trench fighting along the Bastogne perimeter. Such aggressive tactics by the American troops were essential if they were to defeat the Germans, who constantly pushed hard against the perimeter defences, trying to break through, but were always repulsed.

Towards the end of the war in Europe, after the Allies had crossed into Germany, semi-static warfare often developed in areas of relative unimportance to the drive into the heart of the Reich. Around the German town of Cleve just over the border with the Netherlands, for example, British troops found themselves in a vacuum. The countryside was empty of people and animals, which created an unnatural and menacing silence that was only occasionally broken by the sounds of skirmishing between British and German patrols. No-man's-land was not so much an area of contested land between fixed positions as a nebulous region in which neither side was in control. This was, perhaps, less dangerous than constantly taking on well-entrenched German troops who fought for a while, then melted away only to be confronted again further on in yet more trenches. Clearing the Germans out of their positions was neither quick nor risk free, so the work was stressful as it was obvious that the war was nearly over.

While the trench fighting during the Second World War was not of the sort experienced on the Western Front of the First World War, nevertheless, it was a crucial part of most operations, both large and small. The dramatic stalemate of the First World War did not arise, largely because of the tactical doctrines that had emerged from the war, employed most emphatically with more sophisticated weaponry than had been available twenty years earlier. In many respects, the far greater firepower of the armies of the Second World War made entrenchments even more important to the infantry and their support troops to provide protection from enemy fire. None of the trenches dug in any operation ever constituted a continuous and unbroken line of defences. Slit trenches and foxholes were invariably temporary, sometimes occupied by their diggers for less time than it took to excavate them, while others spent days and weeks in them. Mostly, these extemporized defence lines had no protective wire in front so that all-round defence had to be mounted to prevent infiltration by enemy infantry. These trenches were part of the tactics of mobility, rather than the tactics of static defence. While the trenches of the First World War had more than an element of siege associated with them, those of the Second World War had no such association. Thus, the role of entrenching was rather different in the Second World War compared to any preceding war. This was as much to do with how wars were now fought using the doctrines of deep battle and three-dimensional warfare as it was to do with more advanced technology.

Perhaps the only theatre of operations where this did not hold true was the Pacific theatre, especially in the island-hopping operations of the US Navy and Marines. The Japanese made some use of trenches and certainly built formidable log bunkers to hide field guns and machine-guns on some islands. Japanese troops were less reliant on earthworks than the Americans, however, who made extensive use of trenches to hold ground and as protection from Japanese artillery and machine-guns whenever the ground allowed men to dig, such as on Guadalcanal. The hard rocky surfaces of the coral islands such as Tinian and Saipan did not lend themselves to digging in. On Iwo Jima, in particular, the Japanese garrison constructed a formidable network of bunkers and trenches linked by underground passageways, all with multiple entrances that were well camouflaged. The only way to deal with the Japanese defenders was to conduct trench warfare operations using artillery, tanks and flamethrowers, with the added support of considerable air power. The fighting was especially intense because the Japanese were disinclined to surrender even when they faced overwhelming odds.

There is no question, however, that trench warfare was an unavoidable element of warfare irrespective of the combatants and the theatre of operations, so deeply ingrained was the practice of digging in and so valuable were entrenchments to defenders. However, whereas digging in had tended to immobilize the troops of the American Civil War, and had led to mutual siege on the Western Front in the First World War, the notion of protection rather than obstacle prevented static warfare from taking hold. Even under conditions of siege, heavy firepower delivered by aircraft and armour helped to overcome stubborn defenders, although at a high cost in casualties suffered by the attackers, as demonstrated at St Malo and Brest in 1944. The Red Army, which never shied away from heavy casualties, had the same experience when it launched offensives against cities such as Memel and Berlin. Defending German troops often had to be cleared trench by trench and they inflicted heavy casualties on the Red Army. The Soviet Union's lack of concern for the number of casualties suffered in the Great Patriotic War meant that, ultimately, the German defenders were always overcome by the sheer firepower and weight of numbers of the Red Army.

Similar conditions arose again in 1950 during the Korean War, first in the fighting on the Pusan perimeter from August to September, then, following the Chinese intervention in November, during the bitter fighting of the Battle of the River Imjin in April 1951. Finally, stalemate developed in May 1951 when the UN forces ceased offensive operations just north of the 38th Parallel. Trench warfare subsequently became an unexpected mode of fighting for the next two years. The Chinese mounted several offensives against the UN forces during this period. Battles such as Heartbreak Ridge, which lasted a month from 13 September to 15 October 1951, and Pork Chop Hill, which went on for four times as long from 23 March to 16 July 1953, were not about seizing territory or about defeating UN forces militarily were strategic operations with a political component, designed to influence the negotiations to end the fighting and resolve the question of who controlled Korea. These talks began in July 1951 and continued until 27 July 1953 when a ceasefire came into force. The war has never ended although the ceasefire has been upheld.

After the Communist invasion of the south, the final line of defence was the enforced perimeter around the city of Pusan on the south-eastern corner of the Korean peninsular. Here, the battle for Korea would be won or lost. Everyone, including civilians, was pressed into digging slit trenches and anti-tank obstacles. Whenever the North Koreans came up against the perimeter, which they tended to do piecemeal rather than in a coherent assault, the defenders fought them off in a series of bloody encounters in which the latter were little more than a disparate and ad hoc collection of survivors of the retreat down Korea. Ammunition was short and men tended to drift away from their posts on the defence line, knowing the North Koreans were close. The perimeter was not a continuous line of dug-in troops and armour but rather a series of outposts at strategic points such as road junctions, some little more than a machine-gun and a section of infantry. The key to survival and to defeating the invaders was not allowing these defence islands to dissolve into a general withdrawal when the enemy infiltrated past them, but for the outposts to stand their ground and wait for a counter-attack to deal with the incursion. This was the same principal that had been employed by the Germans on the Western Front from about 1916 onwards and especially in 1917 during the Allied assaults on the Hindenburg Line. The difference in Korea was the heavy presence of reliable and effective tanks on both sides and the considerable air power at the disposal of the UN forces. While the fluid use of reserves to plug gaps, acting as a fire brigade to deal with emergencies, was undoubtedly crucial to the successful defence of the Pusan perimeter, nevertheless, the defence was very much in the spirit of large-scale trench warfare in that it employed similar tactics.

The Battle of the Imjin in April 1951 occurred after the UN forces had mounted an amphibious assault at Inchon and pushed the North Koreans all the way to the border with China. The Chinese intervened and pushed the UN forces back again. During one of the last Chinese offensives before the start of ceasefire talks, the Chinese People's Liberation Army (PLA) struck hard and without warning at the UN forces north of the 38th Parallel. Some UN troops, such as the British 29th Brigade on the Imjin, became surrounded. A similar situation developed around the Princess Patricia's Canadian Light Infantry, to the east of the British, who had to be supplied by air drop, a contingency that was first employed in the First World War in 1918. The 29th Brigade, who held the hills through which the River Imjin flowed, were dispersed in strongpoints on hilltops, each separated by a few miles and thus independent of each other but supported by the 25-pounders of 45 Field Regiment, Royal Artillery. Each regimental unit in the Brigade, all of them infantry, held its own hill, the defensive line covering some 7.5 miles. This was a questionable tactical defence, given the fact that the battalion strongpoints could not support each other because they were too far apart. Each position comprised a series of well-dug trenches, foxholes and bunkers, with mortar pits and machine-gun positions sited to give maximum fire support, and arranged by company. While each strongpoint was set out to provide supportive crossfire, the defensive perimeters were open towards the rear and thus vulnerable to encirclement. No barbed wire or anti-personnel mines were available so vigilance was essential and, with that in mind, once contact had been made with PLA soldiers on 22 April, the British had 50 per cent of the Brigade on stand-to during the hours of darkness.

The three divisions of the 63rd Army of the PLA infiltrated across the Imjin and cut between the isolated British strongpoints to attack simultaneously the Northumberland Fusiliers, the Gloucesters and the Belgian infantry battalion that was part of the 29th Brigade during the following night. Initially, the Chinese probed forward with mortar fire but this was merely a preliminary to the infantry assault. Some Chinese even managed to infiltrate among the British trenches in the darkness. Under cover of long-range machine-gun fire, the waves of PLA soldiers crawled to within 10 yards of the British trenches, then threw themselves forward firing submachine-guns and throwing grenades. Wave after wave continued the assault after it became light. Captain Anthony Farrar-Hockley described the fight:

> Someone is throwing grenades, and they are throwing them at us. Here comes another one: a small, dark object against the background of blue sky, its wooden handle turning over and over as it begins the descent on to our positions. It falls near Master's slit-trench; he ducks for a moment as it explodes … Another grenade rises suddenly into the air.

Some Chinese had stayed behind after the last assault on the Gloucesters and concealed themselves behind some felled trees some 15 yards in front of the Gloucesters' trenches.

> Three of us draw the pins from our Mills grenades, three arms draw back for the throw, three arms come up and over. We take cover as the grenades drop to the ground beyond the tree trunk where we suspect the enemy lies.

This exchange of grenades in which one PLA soldier was killed by the grenades and another shot as he tried to break cover took no more than a few minutes. Grenade fighting, bombing as it would have been termed in the First World War, was typical of trench warfare. This also illustrated the relative lethalities of the Chinese and British grenades. The British No. 36 was one of the most lethal grenades ever devised.

While they suffered heavy casualties, the PLA also caused a significant number of losses among the British troops. Eventually, the British were forced back to new positions which, the following night, were attacked in the same way. In the end, the survivors had no choice but to withdraw. Many of the Gloucesters became prisoners because the 1st Battalion had been cut off.

While this battle, one of the best-known engagements of the war, is usually described in terms of a last stand, it was a trench warfare battle in that the Chinese attacked entrenched static positions. The Chinese tactics and their lack of artillery and air support made this an infantry battle. Had the deployment of the four battalions of the 29th Brigade been such that the strongpoints could have provided supportive fire to each other, the Chinese, who were estimated to have lost 10,000 men in the fighting, would have been faced with a much more formidable obstacle. Given the lack of UN air support and heavy artillery available to the 29th Brigade on the Imjin, it would have made sense to have taken more notice of the principals of defence in depth employed on the Western Front in the First World War. As it was, the 29th Brigade was dispersed in a piecemeal fashion, fought hard and lost.

The Battle of Pork Chop Hill, fought two years later under very different circumstances, was a battle in the trench warfare mould. In many respects, it was little different from the smaller offensives that focused on strongpoints on the Western Front in the First World War. There were, in fact, two battles for Pork Chop Hill, fought a few months apart. Pork Chop Hill was an outpost in the Iron Triangle astride the 38th Parallel and part of the defensive line held by UN forces following the cessation of mobile warfare in Korea. Other than the fact that it was an outpost, the US position on Pork Chop Hill had little military significance. Nevertheless, the US troops who seized and occupied the Hill in October 1951 dug trenches and built bunkers on it to turn the position into a strongpoint, purely for defensive reasons. Nothing much happened for the next two years. Then, in March 1953, the Chinese attacked and took the nearby outpost of Old Baldy, which left the US forces on Pork Chop Hill exposed on three sides. Although PLA patrols tested the defences and the resolve of the defenders of Pork Chop Hill each night for the next three weeks, the Chinese did not mount an attack until 16 April when a short but intense artillery bombardment preceded an infantry assault which pushed the Americans off the hill. Some US troops fought on in isolated bunkers but the hill was now in Chinese hands.

With the loss of Pork Chop Hill, the Americans launched an unsuccessful counter-attack on 17 April, followed by a second, this time successful, counter-attack the next day, supported by US artillery and mortars which fired approximately 20,000 shells on to the hill. Over the course of two days, US artillery fired 77,000 rounds. The PLA fired a similar number of shells so that Pork Chop Hill was pounded very heavily during the fighting. When the Chinese were dislodged, they mounted counter-attacks to take back what they had lost but failed to push the Americans off this time. The fighting was very much of the type seen on the Western Front in 1917 and 1918, with heavy preparatory bombardments, followed by infiltration into the enemy-held positions. Much of the fighting was hand-to-hand. The occupants of bunkers had to be attacked using techniques similar to those devised during the First World War, modified only insofar as to take into account the greater use of automatic weapons in 1953 compared to 1918. The hand grenade was still one of the essential tools. The US troops had access to what the British had termed SOS fire in the First World War, that is, pre-registered artillery fire to hit their own positions in the event of a break-in, but which had been discontinued by 1918. It had been found to be more likely to cause friendly casualties and waste ammunition than to dislodge the enemy from the position. This was especially true of the fighting on Pork Chop Hill, which was very confused.

The conclusion of this fighting left the US troops in possession and, during May and June, they set about rebuilding and reinforcing the defences. Then, on 6 July, the PLA launched yet another major assault on Pork Chop Hill. Again, the fighting was hand-to-hand trench warfare of the sort typical of the Western Front thirty-five years earlier. To make matters worse, it was the monsoon season and for three days the fighting was in torrential rain. This was a replay of the battle a few months earlier, this time with five battalions of the US 7th Division, instead of a few companies, against two PLA divisions instead one battalion. While the second battle was more intense than the first, it followed a similar pattern to its predecessor, with both sides constantly counter-attacking each other, both sides pounding the hill with artillery and mortar fire, until the commander of the US I Corps decided that enough was enough and withdrew the US companies from Pork Chop Hill, which they left under fire.

If any two battles in any war could be described as pointless, these must surely qualify since Pork Chop Hill had no strategic or tactical significance. However, the ferocity of the fighting and the fact that the UN had not abandoned Pork Chop Hill at the outset, convinced the Chinese that the war and the fighting would continue if a ceasefire was not agreed upon at the talks that were underway at the time of the assaults on Pork Chop Hill. Moreover, a Chinese tactical victory at this stage was politically unacceptable as it would have given the Communists greater bargaining power. In this sense, the battles were far from pointless. Indeed, a ceasefire was agreed within two weeks of the US troops leaving Pork Chop Hill. As was often the case in battles with the Chinese, the casualties were disproportionate. While 243 of the 7th Division were killed in action and another 916 were wounded, the Chinese lost 5,500 men of whom 1,500 were killed in action. The US casualties in April had been about one-third of those in July but the July fighting had gone on for longer and involved many more troops.

Perhaps, the clearest example of trench warfare in Korea was the fighting at the Hook in October and November 1952 and in May 1953. This curving ridge above the River Samichon near the west coast of Korea was part of the static defensive line held by the UN forces since the end of offensive operations in 1951. Like the other posts along this line, the Hook was fortified with trenches and bunkers. It was first occupied by the US 7th Marines who fought off a Chinese assault on 26 October 1952. The Hook was then occupied by the 1st Black Watch of the Commonwealth Division, who reinforced the defences. Barely a month after the first assault, the Chinese launched a second one on 18 November. Again the defenders successfully fought off the Chinese. By the time of the third assault in May 1953, by far the largest battle of the three, the defences had been reinforced further so that the position closely resembled a strongpoint on the Western Front.

A network of trenches followed the contours of the slopes of the ridge, with bunkers, weapon pits and observation posts dotted along their trace, the whole site being arranged for all-round defence. And like many trenches of the First World War, those in the Hook were infested with rats. Underground passageways, like those constructed by the Japanese on Iwo Jima towards the end of the Second World War, connected the trenches below ground, acting in the same capacity as the communication trenches of the First World War. The bunkers were reinforced with concrete lintels, courtesy of the Royal Engineers, to make them bomb-proof. The position was heavily wired and, when the Chinese eventually attacked, many of them were caught in the entanglements, much as soldiers had been caught in the barbed wire in the First World War. Indeed, for the Chinese to reach the British trenches, now manned by 1st Battalion the Duke of Wellington's Regiment which consisted mostly of National Service conscripts, they had first to cut the wire entanglements. Yet, there was much dead ground below the ridge line due to the many gullies that lay between the spurs of the ridge. It was up these gullies that the Chinese attacked in May 1953.

An important aspect of the defence of the Hook was the defensive fire plan whereby UN artillery would pound the slopes in the event of an attack. At the same time, machine-guns were sited to sweep the slopes with interlocking fire zones, although these could not engage the dead ground. Without artillery support, the Hook would not have been defendable. The effect of artillery and machine-guns on the waves of Chinese was predictable and they suffered very high casualties.

Like so many battles, the third battle of the Hook opened with an intense artillery bombardment by the Chinese which lasted until well into the night. Indeed, so intense was the shelling that many of the forward positions of the Hook were obliterated. The UN guns responded with counter-battery fire and the result was a prolonged and sustained artillery duel. A little before 8.00 pm, the Chinese launched their assault up the gullies and into the first line of trenches, of which little now remained. The whole topography of the landscape was altered by the weight of 10,000 Chinese shells. The survivors of the 1st Battalion fought back but were overwhelmed. The Chinese threw satchel charges into the tunnels and bunkers. Much of the fighting was again hand-to-hand. British reinforcements arrived to hold the Chinese before another wave of assaults was launched.

This time, the Chinese were met with concentrated small-arms and machine-gun fire, as well as mortar fire. UN artillery destroyed a Chinese battalion forming up below the Hook to make another assault. Nevertheless, a third Chinese assault was made from another direction around midnight. This was met with withering fire and, although Chinese troops managed to get in among the British trenches, the Dukes progressed systematically along their trenches bombing the Chinese out. Not since the First World War had bombing been undertaken from trench to trench as it was in the Hook. And once again, the lethal effectiveness of the Mills No. 36 was shown to be superior to the concussive blast grenades favoured by the Chinese. There were instances of Chinese grenades exploding very close to British troops and wounding them, whereas the No. 36 killed under such circumstances because of the large number of lethal fragments it produced on detonation.

What is perhaps surprising is the low level of British casualties given the intensity of the Chinese bombardment and their persistent assaults on the Dukes. While estimates of the number of the Chinese killed and wounded in the course of the third battle suggest that between 1,500 and 2,000 may have died, most of them to the defensive artillery fire of the UN forces, the Dukes and supporting units suffered only twenty-four fatalities, while 105 men were wounded and another twenty were unaccounted for, probably becoming prisoners. Although well-entrenched troops can inflict such casualties on an attacker, the level of Chinese casualties suggests that, apart from a lack of concern for how many men they lost, their tactics were unsuited to assaults on well-defended positions. Indeed, it is tempting to suggest that had they taken the trouble to study the First World War, the evolution of frontal assaults and the role of artillery bombardments, the Chinese would have devised much more effective tactics in Korea. As it was, they neither learned from the past nor from their own experience and continued to make the same mistakes. While their massed-wave tactics could overwhelm less robust troops, and especially troops who had no cover, to apply such tactics in trench warfare was a recipe for failure. And, indeed, none of the Chinese assaults on the UN positions along the defence line across Korea succeeded. Moreover, their own trenches on the other side of no-man's-land were too shallow and too weak to serve as more than jumping-off points for assaults.

The period of stalemate that lasted from mid-1951 to mid-1953 was marked by Chinese assaults across no-man's-land on UN positions. The techniques of trench warfare which might have been applied in this phase of the war were not considered by the UN forces, although their defensive strongpoints often reflected the lessons of the First World War. However, tactics of trench fighting at the small-unit level had to be reinvented as they had not been taught for several decades. It is significant, however, that when the Dukes came to fight down their trenches to remove the Chinese from the Hook, they used similar tactics to those taught in 1917. That this was possible shows that the techniques of fighting in the 1950s, while not specifically related to trench warfare, were much more flexible to the specific demands of the situation than had been the tactics of 1914. That the infantry of the 1920s and afterwards were trained in the use of all infantry weapons, from rifle and bayonet to grenade and machine-gun, was down to the experience of the First World War. These factors enabled most UN troops to adapt to the demands of trench fighting, while the Chinese seem to have ignored them and relied solely on firepower and weight of numbers to achieve their aims. When it came to trench warfare, they were not successful.

CHAPTER 12

The End of Trench Warfare?

There is a temptation to regard the trench warfare that characterized the Western Front during the First World War as an aberration of warfare, brought about by bad tactics, bad generalship or bad circumstances, rather than as an element in that so very complex process which we call war. While no war before or since has been fought along a relatively narrow strip of land that stretched for hundreds of miles, trench warfare was neither a product of the First World War nor the sole focus of that war. Indeed, the war was also fought in the East. Here, trench warfare also arose but the vast openness of the country precluded a continuous line of trenches and, hence, any period of static warfare was only a pause before mobile operations were resumed. Herein lies a clue to apparent stasis on the Western Front: geography. The huge armies that tried to out-manoeuvre each other in the autumn of 1914 were as much constrained by geography as they were by their enemies. Moreover, France and Belgium are both crossed by major roads and railways which connect the towns and cities, whereas in the East this was not the case. Thus, in the West there was far less room to manoeuvre than in the East. While armies had remained relatively small and moved under the power of their own feet rather than by motor vehicle and, in particular, by railway, which allowed rapid movement of large bodies of men, the topography was much less of a constraint on how armies manoeuvred and fought. With the increase in firepower that made the battle zone very much larger during the nineteenth century than hitherto, the room for manoeuvre had been very much reduced by the turn of the century. These factors contributed greatly to the establishment of the ribbon-like combat zone across northern France in late 1914.

Trench warfare did not arise because of the First World War. Indeed, as a mode of warfare, it had been around for a good fifty years and it remained a part of the complexity of war fifty years after the First World War. In Korea, between mid-1951 and mid-1953, trench warfare was conducted along a ribbon of land that cut the peninsular in half. While this immobility was voluntary rather than enforced by circumstances, so that a mutual stand-off was established rather than mutual siege, nevertheless, the mode of warfare in Korea at that time was little different from the fighting on the Western Front fifty years earlier. The fact that in Korea more sophisticated military technology was available to the combatants does not alter the fact that the same principals pertained in both wars. There was, however, a major difference between the Western Front of the First World War and Korea. The enforced immobility of the Western Front was an obstacle which the combatants struggled to overcome and from the outset sought ways to break the deadlock. In Korea, the opposite was the case: the idea was to maintain immobility and prevent a return to open warfare. This was a political choice rather than a military necessity, whereas the stalemate on the Western Front was a consequence of military doctrines, neither a failure of generalship nor an avoidable mistake.

To suggest that trench warfare on the Western Front was the result of military failure is to misread the development of warfare, not only during the nineteenth and early twentieth centuries but during the previous 200 years. Trenches had been a feature of warfare long before the introduction of gunpowder to the battlefield. Siege work always required the use of trenches and, with the advent of cannon, constructing parallels and gun emplacements became an established practice. Even on open battlefields, field guns were placed in earthworks to protect the gunners. Although the birth of trench warfare in the modern sense is usually put at the siege of Sebastopol in the Crimean War, the entrenchments and the fighting in them were merely parts of an evolutionary process. With the advent of rifled small arms and artillery, along with all the other technological developments which exponentially increased the firepower of weapons during the second half of the nineteenth century, entrenching became the only reasonable solution to the increasing size of the lethal area of the battlefield.

Tactics and technology did not change each other during the nineteenth century. Indeed, neither had much impact on the other for much of the time, although increasing firepower forced some changes on armies, largely in order to use the advantage it gave one army over another not similarly equipped. This had an effect on trench warfare which gradually evolved over the same period. By the time of the Russo-Japanese War, trench warfare had developed to the point where it was on the verge of changing the nature of warfare as a whole. This did not happen because the battles could be resolved, albeit at a high price in casualties, without changing substantially their tactics. Moreover, no significant technological change occurred during the war to increase firepower yet further. With some degree of hindsight, it is evident that the Russo-Japanese War served as a warning to the European powers that their approach to battle might well lead to stalemate if a war was not finished quickly, that is, within a matter of months. This was exactly how Germany perceived its next war against France and Russia. It planned for a quick war.

The First World War was a watershed, during which warfare was changed fundamentally. The armies of 1918 were very different from the armies of 1914. They were armed differently and they followed an entirely different tactical doctrine which evolved during the war on the Western Front. The drive to overcome the stalemate of trench warfare conducted along this narrow, yet very long, ribbon of territory brought about huge changes. Deep battle and three-dimensional warfare evolved to overcome the increasing depth of the defences on the Western Front. And from this emerged modern warfare. The battles of the Second World War and those of the two Gulf Wars in 1990–1 and 2001 were mostly fought by these principals.

Two crucial elements in the evolution of trench warfare, which contributed to the emergence of these new doctrines, were the invention and development of automatically lit hand grenades and the rapid-fire infantry mortar. These novel weapons were products of the First World War, more specifically, of trench warfare. Although the hand grenade had existed for hundreds of years before the First World War, it had played an insignificant role in warfare. The automatically lit hand grenade, which was capable of mass production, was an innovation that changed trench warfare. Tens of millions of hand grenades were used on the Western Front. Hitherto, the numbers of grenades used in an entire war had numbered only a few tens of thousands. On the Western Front, that many could be expended by a single division in one day of fighting. The huge increase in the availability of reliable hand grenades led to the development of systemized tactics for their use. From this emerged the specialist bomber who, over the course of a couple of years, was absorbed into the rest of the infantry so that by 1918 the specialist had gone and every infantryman was trained as a bomber. At the same time, the widespread use of light machine-guns began to transform infantry into an all-arms entity, capable of a flexible response to a given situation. This was a direct consequence of trench warfare.

Artillery tactics changed in direct response to the demands of trench warfare. Similarly, the rise of air support and the invention of the tank were direct consequences of trench warfare. The deadlock on the Western Front was not broken by chance or by a sudden rush of blood to the brains of the generals. Rather, it was broken by the development of new ways of waging war. In this process of evolution, trench warfare was not eliminated as a mode of warfare but was itself changed. Thus, in the Second World War and in Korea, trench warfare was still very much part of how the fighting was conducted. The difference between the Western Front and other theatres of war, in other times and places, lay in the duration of the immobility, enforced or voluntary, and the physical extent of the immobile part of the battlefield. Merely because trench warfare in subsequent wars did not resemble the Western Front does not mean that trench warfare had been banished from the battlefield. Indeed, nothing could be further from the truth. Trench warfare is today as much a feature of the battlefield as it ever was but widespread use of tactical air support and armour gives the illusion that trench warfare is a thing of the past and that it was a military aberration.

This, of course, comes down to the presumption that trench warfare is something to be avoided at all costs. Indeed, following the end of the First World War, military thinkers were determined that the Western Front would never again happen in warfare. Advocates of the tank, such as Fuller and Liddell Hart, believed that armour was the answer to avoiding a repetition of the Western Front, while the advocates of aerial warfare believed that the bomber was the answer. Only in the Soviet Union did the notion of casualty avoidance have no power to influence tactical thinking. While no Western government then or now would countenance the employment of any tactics which would inevitably lead to high casualties, nevertheless, the idea that in battle, if the right approach is taken, casualties can be either avoided altogether or, at least, kept to a comfortably low number is rather fanciful. Its origins lay in the huge casualty lists of the First World War when thousands died in what are still perceived today as having been pointless battles.

The casualty rates during the Normandy campaign of June, July and August 1944 were every bit as high as on the Western Front in the First World War. The Red Army's casualty rates were often even higher. The idea that trench warfare should be avoided so that high casualties will, therefore, also be avoided has led to many technological advances in military hardware over the years, all aimed at removing the soldier from harm's way. The pilotless drone and the heavily armoured tank, as well as the fast jet and body armour, are all responses to the urge to prevent soldiers becoming bogged down in stalemate by giving them the means to move quickly and safely across the battlefield irrespective of the firepower of the enemy. He, of course, devises means to overcome these innovations and keep his weapons effective. It is a constant cycle of threat response.

There is no question that there have been times in wars when remaining static and keeping the enemy at bay has been the right tactic. Sometimes, the only way to successfully defend a place is to entrench and fortify the positions. Often, however, such a tactic has been presented as an action of last resort. Disastrous defences of static positions, such as occurred during the Battle of Bien Dien Phu in 1954, lends credence to the notion of failure that is associated with static warfare. The apparent static nature of the Western Front is always held up as the epitome of fruitlessness when, in fact, nothing could be further from the truth. The siege of Khe Sanh in 1967 and 1968, on the other hand, while another example of trench warfare, was unsuccessful from the perspective of the People's Liberation Army of Vietnam (PLAV) who laid siege to the US Marines in the fortified hilltop position but failed to capture it from the Americans. Strategically, the fighting at Khe Sanh was irrelevant to the war in Vietnam as a whole and only served to reinforce the ideas that the USA should withdraw and that static warfare was pointless and bloody. The fighting at the outposts in Korea are often portrayed in the same way, but the successful defence of such features as Pork Chop Hill and the Hook served a political purpose. To have not stood and fought would have had serious repercussions for UN operations in Korea and may well have prolonged the war. Similarly, the German defence of fortified Boulogne in 1944 was a far-from-pointless act since, although the German garrison was trapped, retaining control of the port seriously hindered the Allies in their push into Germany. But perhaps the epitome of successful static defence was at the siege of Bastogne during the Ardennes offensive of late 1944. Far from being worthless, trench warfare has proved to be effective in achieving political and military goals.

Rather than being a sign of military failure, trench warfare is an essential element of military operations. Indeed, success in battle depends on the employment of tactics appropriate to the threat. That threat sometimes requires the use of trenches in order to deal with it effectively. It was true 150 years ago. It is still true today.

Bibliography

Cheshire and Chester Archives.
DHB/55, the papers of Colonel Hugh Robert Hibbert (1828–1895).

Department of Special Collections and Western Manuscripts, Bodleian Library.
Addison papers D2/5, Department of Trench Warfare, and gas Warfare, 1915–17, (ff. 251–348), MS Addison dep. c. 74.

Liddell Hart Centre, Imperial College London.
Robertson: 8/5/80, 30 November 1916.

Robertson: 8/5/81, 1 December 1916.

National Archives, Kew.
BT 31/22958/141366, Pall Mall Grenades.

MUN 4/2557, grenades.

MUN 4/2604, grenades.

MUN 4/2615, Trench Mortar & Ammunition Requirements.

MUN 4/2638, 6" Newton Trench Mortar.

MUN 4/3076, Reports of Munitions Inventions Department.

MUN 4/3589, Intelligence Service reports, 16 June–21 November 1917.

MUN 4/3590, Intelligence Service reports, 20 December 1917–30 May 1918.

MUN 4/6870, History of the Trench Warfare Supply Department, provisional notes by Sir Alexander Roger.

MUN 4/6878, Trench Warfare Committee papers.

MUN 5/117/700/4, Munitions Inventions Department, Report of the Departmental Committee on Reconstruction, July 1917.

MUN 5/120/810/6, *Annual Report of the President, Ordnance Board for the year 1915*, London, 1917.

MUN 5/196/1610/3, List of Changes in War Matériel and of Patterns of Military Stores relating to trench mortars and ammunition, covering approximately January 1915 to November 1916.

MUN 5/196/1611/4, Minutes on defects in Stokes time fuze for 3" HE shell.

MUN 5/196/1610/12, Extracts from Lieutenant F.A. Sutton's diary relating to the early history of the Stokes gun, 12 June 1915–31 October 1915.

MUN 5/196/1610/17, Instruction to pay royalties to Société de Construction de Batignolles in respect of the 9.45-inch mortar.

MUN 5/196/1610/18, Memorandum on diversity of types of trench howitzers.

MUN 5/196/1610/21, Memorandum on French Trench Howitzers.

MUN 5/197/1640/5, Production of grenades.

MUN 5/197/1640/7, Newton Pippin rifle grenade.

MUN 5/197/1640/9, Ordnance Board Minute on use of grenades.

MUN 5/321A, *History of the Ministry of Munitions*, 12 vols, 1918–22.

MUN 5/382/1600/6, History of Trench Warfare Supply, Part I, Departmental Organisation for the Production of Trench Warfare Stores, first draft.

MUN 5/382/1600/7, Trench Warfare Supply Department, June 1915 –September 1917.

MUN 5/382/1600/8, Notes on the History of Trench Warfare Research, Aug 1914–May 1915.

MUN 5/382/1600/10, History of the Production of Trench Warfare Stores by the Trade, July 1915–December 1916.

MUN 5/382/1600/11, Record of History and Work, Ministry of Munitions, Trench Warfare Supply Department, OEB.

MUN 5/383/1600/14, The Development of Weapons Used in Trench Warfare.

MUN 5/384/1610/2, Trench Warfare Supply History, TW3(B), Medium Trench Mortars and their Ammunition.

MUN 5/384/1610/4, Notes on the early history of the Stokes gun, 8 January 1915–30 October 1915.

MUN 5/384/1610/9, Personal Notes on the Work and History of TW3 by A.P. Stockings.

MUN 5/384/1610/16, Record of History and Work, Ministry of Munitions, Trench Warfare Supply Department, TW3(D), Trench Howitzers and Ammunition by Mr W.A. Tanner.

MUN 5/384/1630/2, Record of History and Work, Ministry of Munitions, Trench Warfare Supply Department, TW3(F).

MUN 5/385/1640/1, History of the Grenade Section, Trench Warfare Supply Department.

MUN 5/385/1650/1, Work of Trench Warfare Section 5 on flame projectors, sprayers, etc. from June 1915 to March 1916.

MUN 5/385/1650/6, History of the Supply of Flame Projectors, June 1915–March 1918.

SUPP 6/184, Ordnance Board proceedings.

SUPP 6/185, Ordnance Board proceedings.

SUPP 6/186, Ordnance Board proceedings

SUPP 6/187, Ordnance Board proceedings.

SUPP 6/509, Report of Proceedings of Ordnance Committee, Trench Warfare Section, 11 December 1915 to 23 April 1917.

SUPP 28/40, grenades.

WO 32/5152, Shortage of artillery ammunition in the field, 1914–1915.

WO 32/18989, Hale Rifle Grenade.

WO 33/14, Lieutenant Colonel T.L. Gallwey and Captain H.J. Anderson, 'Report upon the Military Affairs of the United States of America', 1864.

WO 33/337, A Report by Major J.M. Home, 2nd PWO Gurkhas, lately attached to the Russian Army in Manchuria, 1905.

WO 33/934, Handbook on Bombs and Grenades.

WO 33/1520, The Russo-Japanese War, Selection of Reports from Officers attached to the Japanese Forces, vol. 2, London, 1906.

WO 33/1524, The Russo-Japanese War, Selection of Reports from Officers attached to the Japanese Forces, vol. 4, London, 1906.

WO 33/1526, The Russo-Japanese War, Reports from Officers Attached to the Japanese Forces in the Field, vol. 5 London, 1906.

WO 44/631, Ordnance Board papers.

WO 44/634, Ordnance Board papers.

WO 106/432, mortars.

WO 108/5551, 'Journal of the Principal Events connected with the Russo-Japanese War', February 1905.

WO 140/13, Reports on trials, School of Musketry.

WO 140/14, Reports on trials, School of Musketry.

WO 140/15, Reports on trials, School of Musketry.

WO 142/206, Proceedings of the Trench Warfare Department.

WO 142/207, Proceedings of the Trench Warfare Department.

WO 142/208, Proceedings of the Trench Warfare Department.

WO 142/337, Report on the Activity of the Special Brigade during the War.

OFFICIAL PUBLICATIONS

CDS50, Tactical Notes, July 1915.

CDS66, Notes on British, French and German Grenades, September 1915.

CDS74, The Training and Employment of Grenadiers, October 1915.

CDS383, Extract from 'Notes on Minor Tactics of Trench Warfare' by 'A Casualty', June 1915 and reprinted December 1915.

Description and Use of Ring Charges in 3-inch Stokes Trench Howitzers, issued by the Ministry of Munitions, nd.

Field Service Regulations, Part I, Operations, 1909.

Grenade Training Manual, US War Department, January 1918.

Handbook for the Stokes Trench Mortar, 3″, Mark I, April 1916.

Handbook of the ML 2-inch Trench Mortar, Mark I, Land Service, 1917.

Handbook of the ML 9.45-inch Trench Mortars, Marks I, II and III, 1918.

Handbook of the ML Stokes 3-inch Trench Mortar Equipments, Land Service, 1919, 1920.

List of Changes in War Matériel and of Patterns of Military Stores.

Manual for Hand Bombers and Rifle Grenadiers, GHQ AEF, February 1918.

Manual for Trench Artillery, United States Army, Part III, The Newton 6-inch Trench Mortar, July 1918.

Manual of Patent Practice, fifth edition, 31 May 2004.

Memorandum on the Training and Employment of Grenadiers in Notes from the Front, Part IV, May 1915.

Musketry Regulations, Part I, 1909.

Notes from the Front, Part I, 1914.

Notes from the Front, Part II, 1914.

Notes from the Front, Part II, and Further Notes on Field Defences, February 1915.

Notes from the Front, Part III, and Further Notes on Field Defences, February 1915.

Notes from the Front, Part IV, and Further Notes on Field Defences, May 1915.

Notes on Field Defences, 1914.

Range Table of 3-inch Stokes Mortar, July 1917.

Range Table for 3-inch Stokes Mortar (Provisional), September 1917.

Small Arms Training, vol. 1, Pamphlet No. 9, Mortar (3-inch), 1939, reprinted March 1940.

SS98/5, Artillery Notes No. 5 – Wire Cutting by Artillery.

SS98/6, Artillery Notes No. 6 – Trench Mortars, March 1916.

SS107, Notes on Minor Enterprises, March 1916.

SS110, Medium Trench Mortar Gun Drill, 2″ Trench Mortars, May 1916.

SS110, Medium Trench Mortar Gun Drill, 2″ Trench Mortars, May 1916, revised March 1917.

SS119, Preliminary Notes on the Tactical Lessons of the Recent Operations, July 1916.

SS126, The Training and Employment of Bombers, September 1916.

SS135, Instructions for the Training of Divisions for Offensive Action, December 1916.

SS135, Instructions for the Training of Divisions for Offensive Action, December 1916, amendments August 1917.

SS135, The Training and Employment of Divisions, January 1918.

SS139/6, Artillery Notes No. 6 – Trench Mortars, March 1917.

SS143, Instructions for the Training of Platoons for Offensive Action, February 1917.

SS143, Instructions for the Training of Platoons for Offensive Action, 1917, June printing.

SS143, Amendments, November 1917.

SS147, 9.45in Trench Mortar Drill, March 1917.

SS152, Instructions for the Training of the British Armies in France, January 1918.

SS155, Notes on Dealing with Hostile Machine Guns in an Advance, April 1917.

SS169, Employment of 3-in Stokes Mortars in Recent Fighting, June 1917.

SS181, (revised edition) Trench Mortar Drill 6-in (Newton) Trench Mortar, March 1918.

SS182, Instructions on Bombing, Part I, British and German Bombs, December 1917.

SS182, Instructions on Bombing, Part II, Training and Employment of Bombers, November 1917.

SS182, "Instructions on Bombing", Part I, Amendment, March 1918.

SS182, "Instructions on Bombing", Part II, Amendment, November 1918.

SS183, Light (Stokes) Mortar Drill, September 1917.

SS189, Light Mortar Training, June 1918.

SS190, Rifle Grenade Discharger, No. 1, Mark I, Description and Instructions for Use, October 1917.

SS197, Notes on Minor Enterprises, March 1916.

SS398, The Training and Employment of Bombers, March 1916 (author's collection).

Trench Warfare, Articles Manufactured by RE Workshops in France, E-in-C, GHQ, nd.

PUBLISHED BOOKS

Addison, Colonel G.H. (ed.), *The Work of the Royal Engineers in the Late European War, 1914–19, Miscellaneous*, Chatham, 1927.

Anon, *Abridgements of the Patent Specifications Relating to Firearms & Other Weapons, Ammunition & Accoutrements from 1588–1858*, London, 1960.

Anon, *Battles and Leaders of the Civil War*, Edison, nd.

Anon, *British Trench Warfare 1917–1918*, London, 1997.

Anon, *Handbook of Artillery*, Washington, 1925.

Anon, *Textbook of Small Arms*, London, 1929.

Ashworth, Tony, *Trench Warfare, 1914–1918, The Live and Let Live System*, London, 2000.

Bailey, Maj. Gen. J.B.A., *Field Artillery and Firepower*, 2nd ed., Annapolis, 2004.

Barbier, M.K., *Kursk: The Greatest Tank Battle, 1943*, Hersham, 2002.

Becket, Ian F.W., *The First World War: The Essential Guide to Sources in the UK National Archives*, London, 2002.

Beevor, Antony, *Stalingrad*, London, 1998.

——, *Berlin: The Downfall 1945*, London, 2002.

Bidwell, Shelford & Graham, Dominick, *Fire-Power, British Army Weapons and Theories of War, 1904–45*, London, 1982.

Binding, Rudolf, *A Fatalist at War*, London, 1929.

Bond, Brian (ed.), *Look to Your Front*, Staplehurst, 1999.

Brose, Eric Dorn, *The Kaiser's Army: The Politics of Technology in Germany during the Machine Age, 1870–1918*, New York, 2001.

Burgett, Donald R., *Seven Roads to Hell: A Screaming Eagle at Bastogne*, Novato, 1999.

Carver, Field Marshal Lord, *British Army in the 20th Century*, London, 1998.

Chandler, David, *The Art of Warfare in the Age of Marlborough*, Staplehurst, 1990.

Chapman, Guy, *A Passionate Prodigality*, London, 1953.

Coates jr, Colonel James Boyd (ed.), *Wound Ballistics, Medical Department United States Army in World War II*, 1962, 2nd ed.

Coggins, Jack, *Arms and Equipment of the Civil War*, Mineola, 2004.

Connelly, Mark, *Steady the Buffs! A Regiment, a Region, & the Great War*, Oxford, 2006.

Coppard, George, *With a Machine Gun to Cambrai*, London, 1968.

Crowell, Benedict, *America's Munitions, 1917–1918*, Washington, 1919.

Dean, Bashford, *Helmets and Body Armor in Modern Warfare*, New Haven, 1920.

Dennis, Peter & Grey, Jeffrey (eds), *1918, Defining Victory*, Canberra, 1999.

Dewar, George, *The Great Munitions Feat, 1914–1918*, London, 1921.

Dunn, Captain J.C. (ed.), *The War the Infantry Knew, 1914–1919: A Chronicle of Service in France and Belgium*, London, 1987.

Edmonds, J.E., *History of the Great War: Military Operations, France and Belgium, 1914*, 2 vols, London, 1925.

——,*History of the Great War: Military Operations, France and Belgium, 1915, 2 vols*, London, 1927.

——, *History of the Great War: Military Operations France and Belgium, 1916, 2 vols*, London, 1932.

——, *History of the Great War: Military Operations France and Belgium, 1917, 2 vols*, London, 1948.

——, *History of the Great War: Military Operations France and Belgium, 1918, 2 vols*, London, 1935.

Ellis, John, *Eye-Deep in Hell: The Western Front 1914–18*, London, 2002.

Ellis, Major L.F., *Victory in the West: The Battle of Normandy*, London 1962.

——, *Victory in the West: The Defeat of Germany*, London, 1968.

Farrar-Hockley, Anthony, *The Edge of the Sword*, London, 1954.

Featherstone, Donald, *Weapons and Equipment of the Victorian Soldier*, Poole, 1978.

Field, Ron, *American Civil War Fortifications (2): Land and Field Fortifications*, Botley, 2005.

Fleischer, Wolfgang, *German Trench Mortars and Infantry Mortars, 1914–1945*, Atglen, 1996.

Forrest, R., *Illustrated Handbook of Military Engineering and the Implements of War*, London, 1858.

Foulkes, Major General C.H., *"Gas!" The Story of the Special Brigade*, Edinburgh & London, 1934.

Fuller, J.F.C., *Tanks in the Great War 1914–1918*, London, 1920.

George, David Lloyd, *War Memoirs*, 6 vols, London, 1933.

Gowing, Timothy, *A Soldier's Experience or A Voice from the Ranks*, Nottingham, 1885.

Grave, L.W. de, *The War History of the Fifth Battalion The Sherwood Foresters, Notts and Derby Regiment, 1914–1918*, London, 1930.

Griffith, Paddy, *Rally Once Again*, Marlborough, 1987.

——, *Battle Tactics of the Western Front: The British Army's Art of Attack 1916–18*, London, 1994.

——, *Fortifications of the Western Front 1914–18*, Botley, 2004.

Haber, L.F., *Poisonous Cloud: Chemical Warfare in the First World War*, Oxford, 1986.

Hart, Peter, *The Somme*, London, 2005.

216

Hastings, Max, *The Korean War*, London, 1987.

——, *Armageddon: The Battle for Germany 1944–5*, London, 2004.

Hesketh-Pritchard, Major H., *Sniping in France*, London, 1994.

Hess, Earl J., *Trench Warfare under Grant & Lee: Field Fortifications in the Overland Campaign*, Chapel Hill, 2007.

Hicks, Major James E., *Notes on German Ordnance 1841–1918*, New York, 1937.

Hitchcock, F.C., *"Stand To": A Diary of the Trenches 1915–1918*, London, 1988.

Hogg, I.V. & Thurston, L.F., *British Artillery Weapons and Ammunition 1914–1918*, London, 1972.

Holmes, Richard, *Firing Line*, London, 1985.

——, *Tommy: The British Soldier on the Western Front 1914–1918*, London, 2004.

Horne, Alistair, *The Price of Glory, Verdun 1916*, London, 1962.

Hughes, Major General B.P., *Firepower: Weapons Effectiveness on the Battlefield, 1630–1850*, London, 1974.

Jary, Sidney, *18 Platoon*, Carshalton, 1987.

Jünger, Ernst, *The Storm of Steel*, London, 1929.

Keegan, John, *Six Armies in Normandy*, London, 1982.

Kemp, Anthony, *Weapons and Equipment of the Marlborough Wars*, Poole, 1980.

Knightley, Philip, *The First Casualty*, London, 1987.

Knox, MacGregor & Williamson, Murray (eds), *The Dynamics of Military Revolution, 1300–2050*, Cambridge, 2001.

Kuhn, Major Joseph E., *Reports of Military Observers attached to the Armies in Manchuria during the Russo-Japanese War*, Part III, Washington, 1906.

Landers, Rick, *'Grenade': British and Commonwealth Hand and Rifle Grenades*, Dural, 2001.

Liddell Hart, Basil, *The Strategy of the Indirect Approach*, London, 1941.

Luvaas, Jay, *The Military Legacy of the Civil War*, Lawrence, 1988.

MacDonald, Charles, *The Battle of the Huertgen Forest*, New York, 1963.

McKee, Alexander, *Caen: Anvil of Victory*, London, 1964.

McNeill, William H., *The Pursuit of Power*, Chicago, 1984.

Middlebrook, Martin, *Arnhem 1944*, London, 1994.

Moore, William, *Gas Attack: Chemical Warfare 1915 to the Present Day*, London, 1987.

Neillands, Robin, *The Conquest of the Reich*, London, 1995.

Oldham, Peter, *Pill Boxes on the Western Front*, London, 1995.

Pabst, Helmut, *The Outermost Frontier: A German Soldier in the Russian Campaign*, London, 1957.

Penhallow, Dunlap Pearce, *Military Surgery*, London, 1916.

Pollard, Captain A.O., *Fire-Eater: The Memoirs of a VC*, London, 1932.

Ramsey, Winston G., *D-Day, Then and Now*, 2 vols, London, 1995.

Rawling, Bill, *Surviving Trench Warfare: Technology and the Canadian Corps, 1914–1918*, Toronto, 1992.

Reid, William, *The Lore of Arms*, Abingdon, 1976.

Richards, Frank, *Old Soldiers Never Die*, London, 1933.

Richter, Donald, *Chemical Soldiers: British Gas Warfare in World War One*, London, 1994.

Ross, Steven T., *From Flintlock to Rifle*, London, 1996.

Russell, John, *No Triumphant Procession: The Forgotten Battles of April 1945*, London, 1994.

Saunders, Anthony, *Weapons of the Trench War, 1914–1918*, Stroud, 1999.

——, *Dominating the Enemy*, Stroud, 2000.

——, *Hitler's Atlantic Wall*, Stroud, 2001.

Scott, J.D., *Vickers: A History*, London, 1963.

Sheffield, Gary, *Forgotten Victory, The First World War: Myths and Realities*, London, 2001.

Sheffield, Gary & Todman, Dan (eds), *Command and Control on the Western Front: The British Army's Experience 1914–18*, Staplehurst, 2004.

Simpson, Andy, *Directing Operations: British Corps Command on the Western Front 1914–18*, Staplehurst, 2006.

Stern, Sir Albert, *Tanks 1914–1918: The Log-Book of a Pioneer*, London, 1919.

Sweetman, John, *The Crimean War*, Botley, 2001.

Tarassuk, Leonid & Blair, Claude (eds), *The Complete Encyclopaedia of Arms & Weapons*, London, 1982.

Terraine, John (ed.), *General Jack's Diary 1914–1918*, London, 1964.

——, *The Smoke and the Fire*, London, 1980.

——, *White Heat: The New Warfare 1914–18*, London, 1982.

Travers, Tim, *The Killing Ground: The British Army, The Western Front and the Emergence of Modern Warfare, 1900–1918*, London, 1990.

——, *How the War was Won*, London, 1992.

Walter, John, *Modern Military Rifles*, London, 2001.

Whinyates, R. (ed.), *Artillery & Trench Mortar Memories*, London, 1932.

PAPERS AND PHD & MPHIL THESES

Reid, Major (Retired) R.J., MBE, 'The Development of Artillery Ammunition'. Paper presented at the Winter Meeting of the Royal Artillery Historical Society, 19 January 2005, at Larkhill.

Saunders, Anthony, 'A Muse of Fire – British Trench Warfare Munitions, their Invention, Manufacture and Tactical Employment on the Western Front, 1914–18', PhD thesis, Exeter, September 2008.

Snowden, Kathryn, 'British 21st Infantry Division on the Western Front, 1914–1918. A Case Study in Tactical Evolution', MPhil thesis, Birmingham, 2001.

Wilkes, J., 'Fragmentation Data for Eight Grenades', RARDE report TR1/12/72, October 1972.

Williams, Robert, 'A Social and Military History of the 1/8th Battalion, The Royal Warwickshire Regiment, in the Great War', MPhil thesis, Birmingham, 1999.

MAGAZINE & JOURNAL ARTICLES

Anon, 'The Work of the Royal Engineers in the European War, 1914–19', *The Royal Engineers Journal*, September 1924.

Anon, 'The Work of the Royal Engineers in the European War', *The Royal Engineers Journal*, vol. XXXIX, No. 1, March 1925.

Haydon, F. Stansbury, 'Grant's Wooden Mortars and some Incidents of the Siege of Vicksburg', *The Journal of the American Military Institute*, vol. 4, No. 1, (spring 1940), pp. 30–8.

Martel, Captain, 'The Use of Inventions in War', *The Royal Engineers Journal*, December 1924.

McClintock, Major R.L., 'An Extemporised Hand Grenade', *The Royal Engineers Journal*, April 1913, pp. 193–200.

McClintock, Major R.L., 'An Extemporised Rifle Grenade, The Bangalore "Universal" Grenade', *The Royal Engineers Journal*, November 1914, pp. 281–94.

Scott, Peter T., 'Mr Stokes and his Educated Drainpipe', *The Great War*, vol. 2, No. 3, May 1990.

Whitmarsh, Andrew, 'The Development of Infantry Tactics in the British 12th (Eastern) Division, 1915–1918, *Stand To!*, January 1997, No. 48.

WEBSITES

www-cgsc.army.mil/carl/resources/csi/gabel5/gabel5.asp (Report of Captain Andrew Hickenlooper, Chief Engineer XVIIth Army Corps, and the Reports of Colonel O.P. Lyles, 23rd Arkansas Infantry at Fort Hudson), accessed June 2008.

http://ehistory.osu.edu/uscw/features/Articles_New/display.cfm?NationId=62 (Civil War Newsletter issue of 19 June 2002), accessed June 2008.

www.civilwar.si.edu/weapons_grenades.html (Smithsonian Institution, Ketchum grenades), accessed June 2008.

www.infernal-machines.com/_sgg/m1m4_1.htm (grenades), accessed May 2008.

www.sdchamber.co.uk (History of the Derby and Derbyshire Chamber of Commerce and Industry 1864–1995), accessed May 2005.

www.pals.org.uk/lais_e.htm (Lais, Otto, Experiences of Baden Soldiers at the Front, vol. 1, Machine-guns in the Iron Regiment (8th Baden Infantry Regiment No.169), Karlsruhe, 1935), accessed June 2008.

www.millsgrenades.co.uk (grenades), accessed June 2008.

http://members.shaw.ca/dwlynn/tgrm.htm (grenades), accessed June 2008.

www.inert-ord.net/brit (grenades), accessed June 2008.

www.greenhowards.org.uk/servicejournals.php (The Service Journal of Sergeant
Charles Usherwood, Part 1, who served with the 1st Battalion 19th Regiment
of Foot in the Crimea), accessed June 2009.

http://www.nationalarchives.gov.uk/a2a/records.aspx?cat=017-dhb&cid=3-1-3#-
1-3 (Letters and papers of Colonel Hugh Robert Hibbert (1828–1895) mainly
relating to service in the Crimean War, 1854–1855)

Index